Eight Mile Island
n Connecticut River

Eight Mile River   Rock   Connecticut River

A Ledge of Rocks
in-Sah-chook

amp

Natchamudus

ap of Stones
Natchamudus East Bounds
sed of Owenico 1702 lying
s from Wattumsk.

ester

A

...ems
...try,

Platted Aug: 1st 1705.

By John Chandler, Surveyor.

Ash-o-Wog
the Crotch of a River

Ung-guun-Suck-Cook

Hock-kan-nun-path
Arrama-met

Thomas Edward..

Wa-frioug   A high Hill

Wi-ash-qua-gwan-Suck

Woodstock to Hartford

Moshe Nup Suck

Uncas

Uncas
First of the Mohegans

MICHAEL LEROY OBERG

CORNELL UNIVERSITY PRESS

ITHACA AND LONDON

First published 2003 by Cornell University Press

Printed in the United States of America

Library of Congress Cataloging-in-Publication Data
Oberg, Michael Leroy.
   Uncas : first of the Mohegans / Michael Leroy Oberg.
      p. cm.
Includes bibliographical references and index.
ISBN 0-8014-3877-2 (cloth : alk. paper)
   1. Uncas, Chief of the Mohegans, d. 1684.
2. Mohegan Indians—Biography.   3. Mohegan
Indians—History.   4. Connecticut—History—
Colonial period, ca. 1600–1775.   I. Title: First of the
Mohegans.   II. Title.
   E99.M83 U536 2003
   974.6′02′092—dc21

                                        2002015646

Cornell University Press strives to use environmentally responsible suppliers and materials to the fullest extent possible in the publishing of its books. Such materials include vegetable-based, low-VOC inks and acid-free papers that are recycled, totally chlorine-free, or partly composed of nonwood fibers. For further information, visit our website at www.cornellpress.cornell.edu.

Cloth printing   10 9 8 7 6 5 4 3 2 1

Contents

Preface

Uncas, the Mohegan Indian sachem who flourished in seventeenth-century Connecticut, led his people through the tremendous changes produced by the coming of the Europeans and forged a regional power in colonial New England. Employing diplomacy, rumor, the threat of violance, and war, Uncas was tremendously successful in dealing with a great variety of Native New Englanders and English colonists. By examining his life and the world in which he lived, this book aims to broaden our understanding of Native American history, American colonial history, and the many ties that bind these important stories together.

Writing the biography of an American Indian leader is fundamentally a difficult task, especially when that leader was born over four hundred years ago. The evidence is ambiguous and, at times, difficult to decipher. Almost all of it is second-hand, in that Uncas's words and deeds come to us translated by English observers who did not always understand the language and culture of their native neighbors. Even with attention to archaeological research and oral tradition, important ethnohistorical sources, one still must rely on evidence that raises all sorts of interpretive challenges: the problems of bias, perception, and incompleteness that historians and ethnohistorians have long confronted in their attempts to reconstruct the early American past. That Uncas is a historical figure about whom generations of New Englanders have had strong feelings, and whose life has taken on mythic proportions, makes writing his life history all the more challenging. What observers of his life knew, and what they wanted to believe, often are difficult to distinguish. My goal has been to tell a good story based upon the extant sources. In places, gaps in the evidence have forced me to make certain interpretive leaps of faith, and as a result not everyone will agree with the interpretation of Uncas's life and career that appears in these pages. I am comfortable with that. But I hope that all who read this book will share my appreciation of the significant role Uncas and other Native American leaders played in the history of colonial North America.

I did not confront the challenges of this project alone. A great many friends and colleagues have generously given support and assistance. In the department of history at SUNY–Geneseo, Tzi-ki Hon read the entire manuscript, taking time from his own research to give me advice. David Tamarin and my fellow American historians in the department, Carol Faulkner and Kathy Mapes, read and commented upon portions of the manuscript. Jim Williams has been a supportive department chair. I have been talking with Stephen Saunders Webb about this project for over eight years now, and I am grateful to him for taking the time to read the manuscript, and for allowing me to try out early versions of several chapters with the students in his graduate seminar in early American history at Syracuse University. The members of the Rochester U.S. Historians' Group strengthened the second chapter with their criticism, and I thank audiences at SUNY–Geneseo and SUNY–Brockport for commenting on early versions of the introduction. Peter Mancall, Alden T. Vaughan, and Pat Cleary all read the manuscript. Wendy St. Jean was always willing to share with me her own research on the Mohegans, and Francis Bremer of Millersville University and the Winthrop Papers project helped track down crucial citations at the last moment. At Cornell University Press, Sheri Englund, Karen Laun, and Kay Scheuer have done a wonderful job of seeing the manuscript through to publication.

Harriet Sleggs runs an outstanding interlibrary loan department in Milne Library at SUNY–Geneseo. Librarians and archivists at the Connecticut State Library, the Huntington Library, and at the Massachusetts State Archives all helped in the search for source material. I am grateful as well to the staff at the Huntington for granting me a Michael J. Connell Foundation Fellowship in the summer of 1999, which allowed me to complete much of the research. Additional support for travel to archives and libraries in southern New England was provided by a Geneseo Presidential Summer Fellowship and smaller grants from the Geneseo Foundation.

Finally, I thank my family. Leticia Ontiveros willingly allowed me to skulk off to the University of Rochester Library to work on "the Uncas thing." My two younger children, Adam and Eliana, could not care less about Indian leaders in seventeenth-century New England, but they have made my life much richer by their presence. And last, I need to thank my oldest son, Nathan, who listened to all I had to say about Uncas and who wants to write his own books someday.

Uncas

INTRODUCTION

Uncas in Myth and Memory

Historians long have struggled to make sense of the life and times of Uncas, the Mohegan Indian sachem, or leader, who played so fundamental a role in the history of the Puritan colonies in New England. A signal example is Charles Frederick Chapin. In 1903, addressing the Society of Colonial Wars in the State of Connecticut, Chapin recounted the assistance Uncas had tendered the fledgling colony of Connecticut during its brief but violent struggle against the Pequots in 1636 and 1637. He also described the hatred-filled conflict between Uncas and the Narragansett sachem Miantonomi, which resulted in the execution of Miantonomi by Uncas in 1643 and decades of retaliatory warfare between the Mohegans and Narragansetts. As he chronicled the sachem's career, Chapin's tone was one of ambivalence. He described Uncas as a character of "courage, enterprise and strong individuality," but only until "ease and safety taught him to rely on the English." Uncas "built up a tribe out of nothing, and left it at his death the chief native body in Connecticut, with greater possessions than any other . . . an Indian, unique among his kind, who formed a consistent theory of conduct and pursued it through life . . . [and] an ally of our fathers whose faithfulness mingled with their enterprise and piety in the enduring foundations of our commonwealth." Yet nonetheless, despite his many accomplishments, Uncas shared in "the inevitable degeneracy of his race under the influence of civilization."[1] Chapin knew his audience well enough to recognize that Uncas was a controversial figure, about whom many of his readers likely held strong feelings. He thus attempted the difficult task of providing them with a balanced answer to a question that rests at the heart of this book, written a century later: "Who then, and what was Uncas?"[2]

For James Fenimore Cooper, who first published his novel *The Last of the Mohicans* in 1826, Uncas represented the tragic decline and ultimate disappearance of Indians from the American landscape, the epitome of the doomed and noble savage. Uncas reflected, for Cooper, the best of a way of life that had vanished. After the death of Cooper's Uncas at the hands of the black-hearted Huron Magua, the aged Delaware shaman Tamenund sadly noted that now "the pale-faces are masters of the earth." Reflecting with sorrow upon his own too long life, Tamenund lamented, "In the morning I saw the sons of the Unamis happy and strong; and yet, before the night has come, have I lived to see the last warrior of the wise race of Mohicans."[3]

To a friendly reviewer of Cooper's work, Uncas seemed "an Indian Apollo, a living personification of one of those active and graceful forms, which an Indian's fancy might dream of, as bounding over the hunting grounds of his Elysium, lighter than the air he seemed to tread, with eye, and limb, and thought alike untiring." To others, however, Cooper's Uncas seemed entirely implausible, too civilized and altogether too romantic to be convincing as an Indian. As Lewis Cass wrote in April 1828, just before he became one of the principal architects of Andrew Jackson's policy of Indian removal, Cooper's Indian characters "have no living prototype in our forests." They were figments of the author's imagination, he wrote, "and not the fierce and crafty warriors and hunters, that roam through our forests."[4]

Cooper, despite his novel's shortcomings, created in Uncas a powerful and influential figure who came to represent for many all that was good in the Indian character, the quintessential "noble savage" and "vanishing American." So potent were Cooper's images of Indian nobility that the Mohegans, who still revere Uncas, and who have devoted a considerable amount of time, money, and energy to preserving his memory, have allowed Cooper's fictional account to color, in part, their own understanding of their great leader.[5] Yet Cooper's work was fiction, and his Uncas a product of the author's imagination. The historical Uncas bore little resemblance to Cooper's highly romanticized and tragic character.

The real Uncas flourished in the colony of Connecticut in the middle decades of the seventeenth century, not in frontier New York a century later. He was a Mohegan, not a "Mohican," a significant difference that still confuses many historians. He dealt confidently and competently with Puritan magistrates and traveled frequently to the provincial capitals to defend his people's interests—a far cry from the loyal sidekick of Hawkeye, who wandered with him the margins of Cooper's battle-scarred world. His people spent much of the year in settled agricultural villages; they did not "roam" through the "wilds." Uncas was not the "Last of the Mohicans," and his people did not vanish. Today they still dwell in the territory Uncas won for them.

In Cooper's defense, he made no attempt to pattern his character upon the historical Uncas, and his Indian characters were far more complex than most of his readers have recognized.[6] Cooper merely chose for his "Mohican" the name of the best known of the Mohegans, conflating the history of the two tribes. Still, Cooper's powerful images of Indian nobility and inevitable extinction bled into popular understandings of the historical Uncas. As a result, the symbolic grave of Uncas in Norwich, Connecticut, became a site for reflection, the object of numerous pilgrimages and paeans to the myth of the vanishing American.

In 1833, for example, the citizens of Norwich began planning to erect a memorial to Uncas in the "Royal Mohegan Burying Ground" just off the town green. That summer, only three years after he had signed the Indian removal bill into law, President Jackson and much of his cabinet visited the site during their tour of New England. "At the burial place of the royal family of the Mohegans," the *Norwich Courier* reported, Jackson, with the assistance of Secretary of War Lewis Cass, "laid the foundation of a Monument to be erected to the memory of the Great Uncas, 'the friend of the whites,' than whom, no monarch was more faithful to his allies, and none so well deserved to be remembered by the descendants of those whom he befriended in the 'hour of need.'" Cass, who had been less than impressed by Cooper's Uncas, observed of the ceremony "that the earth afforded but few more striking spectacles than that of one hero doing homage to another."[7] For Cass and Jackson, it seems, Uncas was the perfect Indian: he helped English colonists settle the land, fought against his, and their, native enemies, and then, with the rest of his people, conveniently disappeared, making room for the inevitable progress of white Anglo-Saxon civilization.[8]

Building the actual monument posed all sorts of challenges. The sponsors asked Charles L. Lincoln, the warden of the Massachusetts

State Prison, to acquire the stone for the obelisk they would erect in Uncas's honor. The first block of granite that Lincoln's "quarrymen" cut out was found, upon examination, "to be stained and therefore unsuitable." They tried again. The next block the prisoners quarried was an inch-and-a-half too short on one side. Lincoln did not think that anyone would notice so small an error, but George L. Perkins, a leader in Norwich's efforts, apparently disagreed. Beyond the unexpectedly complicated problem of quarrying a stone of suitable size and quality, the Norwich planners had to decide what to put on the base of the monument. That, too, was not as simple as it first had seemed. Perkins noted that Uncas's name was spelled a number of different ways in the historical records. No one version prevailed, and Perkins was not certain whether Uncas, Unkas, or Onkas should be engraved at the base. He asked Noah Webster for his "opinion to the best spelling of the name of this ancient Sachem and firm friend of the white man." After mulling it over for some time, and finally acquiring a properly sized stone, Perkins and his fellow planners apparently decided to follow Cooper's lead: the name "Uncas" would grace the base of the monument.[9]

Only with all these problems resolved could the "Ladies of Norwich" at long last celebrate the completion of the Uncas Monument on the Fourth of July, 1842, nine years after Jackson's visit. The women took inspiration from the reform activity then coursing through New England and, in the souvenir pamphlet they published to commemorate the event, touted the success of temperance groups like the Cold Water Army and the Washingtonians in reducing the amount of drinking in Norwich. Their celebration of Uncas, certainly, was to be no alcohol-soaked debauch. The women also looked hopefully to the newly "repaired, enlarged, and entirely remodeled" Mohegan Church, finished just two weeks earlier, which would aid in the "progress of the Gospel" among their Indian neighbors. Their gathering, apparently, would be pious as well. But aside from reprinting a number of old Mohegan deeds as curiosities, the "Ladies" had nothing to say about Uncas. That they left to the historian William Leete Stone, who traveled from New York City to "say what will be appropriate for the occasion."[10]

Uncas, Stone told his audience, "was the white man's friend, at a period when the friendship even of savage royalty was most wel-

FIG. 1   Uncas Monument in Norwich, Connecticut. Photograph by the author.

come." He consistently befriended the English "from the day when the Pilgrim fathers planted their feet on the soil of Connecticut . . . until the day of his death." His qualities, Stone continued, marked Uncas for greatness. "In a different hemisphere, and belonging to another race, he might have been at least a Turenne, a Marlborough, or a Wellington, if not a Gustavas, a Kosciusko or a Washington." Uncas,

5

however, "was only a red man; and the great powers of mind and noble qualities of heart with which his Maker had endowed him, limited in their action by the narrow boundaries of savage life, found room and occasion for such exercise alone as was afforded by the petty but ferocious warfare of tribe against tribe, and for such cultivation only as might be serviceable in the rudest condition of society, where strength, and craft, and courage, are the most available, and therefore the most admired qualities." Though his audience might "shudder at his ferocity, or pity at his limited range of understanding and knowledge," Stone encouraged his listeners to hold Uncas "in greater honor for those exhibitions of generosity, of forbearance and magnanimity, which, as we have seen, were by no means wanting in his career."[11]

Stone, alas, showed no awareness that the neighboring Mohegans even existed. For him, and for so many others, the Mohegans were extinct, actors in a colorful story from a distant past. One might pause for reflection, and draw moral lessons, but one did not need real Indians to do that. Indeed, at the conclusion of his long address, Stone himself imagined what Uncas felt as he watched from his heavenly perch the proceedings held in his honor.

> The spirit of the red man had beheld with anguish the gradual extinction of his race,—the occupation of his forests and his broad hunting-grounds by the dwellings of the pale-faces—the triumph of that civilization which he abhorred, over the wide domain which once owned him for its lord: but the spirit of the hero would rejoice in knowing that his greatness was recognized and honored, and in seeing his renown perpetuated, even by the hated and dreaded white man, in whose advance was written the destiny of the Indian to perish.

For other Indians watching from above, Stone imagined that

> the scowl of hatred is on their dusky brows; the fire of revenge is gleaming in their fixed and angry eyes; the sense of injury and wrong is burning in their vindictive hearts; but, mingled with these dark passions there is grim delight in the honors paid to a great man of their race, and as they gaze upon the stone that bears the name of Uncas, they feel as if they could almost forgive the detested pale-

faces, who so well know how to appreciate and exalt the noble qualities of their brother.

Only Miantonomi, Uncas's implacable enemy, stood aloof from this heavenly gallery, forever scowling upon the English and their descendants.[12]

Long after the Ladies of Norwich dedicated the monument, Uncas would continue to inspire similar honorifics and lamentations celebrating both the assistance he gave to the English and the tragic passing of the red man. When, for instance, John Uncas, the last male descendant of Uncas, died five months after the dedication ceremony, the *Newark (N.J.) Daily Advertiser* declared the "Last of the Mohegans Gone." John Uncas was buried next to the Uncas Monument (the editor never said by whom, though presumably by "extinct" Mohegans), inspiring melancholy reflections on Indian extinction. "The passing away of a whole tribe of men, once the free, dauntless lords of the soil, is certainly well-calculated to awaken sensibility; and the contemplation of the oppression and wrongs under which they have dwindled away, and finally perished, naturally excites painful emotions." Weeping, however, was pointless. The passing of the Indians, the *Daily Advertiser* continued, "is the natural, inevitable result of the progress of society." Barbarism, the editor wrote, must recede in the face of civilization. As a result, "we are not necessarily responsible . . . for the extinction of the Indian race, though we may well blush at the remembrance of the wrong and outrage they have suffered at our hands."[13]

Musicians got into the act as well. George H. Martin, in a plodding musical number published in 1850, urged his listeners to pay their respects to Uncas, the "last chief of his race."[14] Antiquarians, too, contributed their mite. Daniel Coit Gilman, during the massive "Jubilee" celebrating Norwich's bicentennial in 1859, interrupted his painfully long "historical discourse" to address the twenty or so Mohegans who attended the festivities, and who were seated at the foot of the stage. The joy he felt on so glorious an occasion, Gilman confessed, "is not without its sorrow when we see that you have lost what we have gained, that your numbers are few, and your sachems gone." One wonders what comfort the assembled Indians took from Gilman's solemn assurance "that it is the Great Spirit himself who has ordered that every race, like every man, should act his part and die." At least the Mohegans could rest content that "gratefull remembrance shall live, and until yonder memorial shaft of granite shall have crumbled to the dust, until our race shall be no more, succeeding generations shall be taught that Uncas," noble to the end, "was the white man's friend."[15]

Fifty years after Gilman's address, William F. "Buffalo Bill" Cody brought his touring Wild West Show to Norwich, rolling into town early in July 1907. On the rainy morning of July 2, Cody and some of the 127 Indians who traveled with him made a pilgrimage to the Royal Mohegan Burying Ground to pay their respects to Uncas. Accompanied by Chief Rocky Bear, "the oldest member of the Sioux tribe and Chief Iron Tail," Cody laid a wreath at the foot of the Uncas Monument. That Cody should remember the "last of the Mohicans" was, according to the *Norwich Bulletin*, "very pleasing to the redmen."[16]

Buffalo Bill's Wild West Show, of course, with its pageantry and elaborately staged reenactments of the Plains wars, commemorated the passing of the American frontier, which the United States Bureau of the Census had declared closed in 1890. Nothing appealed to the citizens of Norwich so much as the Plains Indians who accompanied Cody. They were, the *Bulletin* reported, "the center of attention," the crowd appreciating the "touch of realism" in their Plains costume. Yet these were historicized Indians, prisoners of time, defined by recent memories of the Plains Wars and admired by an overwhelmingly white audience for what they imagined those Indians once had been. Uncas's Mohegan descendants, living mostly in the vicinity of the neighboring town of Montville, remained invisible to those who attended Cody's extravaganza. In laying a wreath at the Uncas Monument, accompanied by a phalanx of Plains Indians in "traditional" dress, Cody incorporated the Mohegan sachem into his mythic construction of American frontier history. Uncas was good, noble, and just, but he, his people, and his way of life were gone.[17]

Indians for the people of Norwich, and elsewhere around the country, were a source of nostalgia and entertainment early in the twentieth century. The evening after Buffalo Bill visited the Uncas Monument, for instance, another ceremony was held in town. "The chiefs of Tecumseh tribe, No. 43, Red Men," a white fraternal organization, "were raised to their stumps" according to the *Bulletin*. The "deputy grand sachem" of the organization performed the ceremony, assisted by the group's "great prophet" and "great sannap." They appointed gentlemen from the town to positions such as "prophet," "sachem," "junior sagamore," "senior sagamore," first and second "warriors," first, second, and fourth "braves," and "guard of the wigwam."[18] This was role-playing, acting, with white men dressing as Indians in a backward-looking and custodial attempt to preserve traditional "American" values as they imagined them to have been embodied in the lost virtues of a vanished race. Such play-acting more closely reflected the concerns and insecurities of white men during a period of social change than it did the historical place of Indians in New England and the world in which Uncas lived.[19]

In such a cultural environment Uncas, "proud sagamore, up to life's end / The white man's faithful and unswerving friend, / Indian blood-brother, through those years of stress / To settlers building in the wilderness," could be considered significant only for the role he played in the dramatic unfolding of the settlement of America. The "Ladies of Norwich," after all, had celebrated the completion of the Uncas Monument on the Fourth of July. Uncas was now part of the American saga. He had become a symbol, a mythical figure, incorporated into a story that inspired great pride among white Americans. Abstracted from historical reality, Uncas joined that gallery of images that helped explain to Americans their own past—to give it significance and meaning. His story served to explain and justify both the colonization of America and the carrying of law, civility, and Christianity into what was widely considered a virgin and savage wilderness.[20]

But myths have a flip side, and symbols their anti-image. For each writer, poet, or public figure who romanticized the story of Uncas, another hated the Mohegan sachem for what was considered his disloyalty to Indian peoples and his crass opportunism. For those inclined to view English colonization and the westward expansion of white settlement less as the unfolding of God's providence than as a blood-drenched invasion and conquest, Uncas looked much more like an unprincipled and treacherous collaborator than a trustworthy and admirable friend.

The Tory historian Samuel Peters, for example, argued in his *Gen-*

eral History of Connecticut (1781) that the Puritan founders of New England demonstrated a level of rapacity and violence equaling the brutality of the Spanish conquest of Central and South America. Uncas helped the Saints carry out their bloody and genocidal deeds. "Upwards of 180,000 Indians, at least," he wrote, "have been slaughtered in Massachusetts Bay and Connecticut, to make way for the Protestant religion." Peters felt he had first-hand experience with the cruelty of Puritan New Englanders: they had driven him into exile for choosing the wrong side in the American Revolution and, later, ordered his book publicly burned. Still, his view of Uncas was common, then and later. The Mohegan sachem, who gave lands to the Connecticut settlers that "he had no right or title to," and who offered his assistance to the conquerors, in Peters's eyes had collaborated in a heinous crime against his own people.[21]

John W. De Forest, who published his *History of the Indians of Connecticut* in 1851, thought Uncas "entirely devoted to his own interest." Uncas, who "had lived to see the time when a new people ... was spreading over the land, and when the tribes of the forest were fading away before it, as the light of the stars grows dim at the rising of the sun," pursued his goals by fawning on the colonists, pretending great affection toward them. He was faithful to the English, De Forest observed, "just as the jackal is faithful to the lion, not because it loves the lion, but because it gains something by remaining in his company."[22] Echoing De Forest's bleak assessment of Uncas's character early in the twentieth century was Herbert Milton Sylvester, a crude racist who believed "that, like the leopard's spots, the instinct of savagery in the Indian was ineradicable." Sylvester noted that the Mohegan sachem "possessed ... many bad traits, [and] he had no great ones." Uncas served the English as a means to an end, "the consummation of his own personal animosities." Lest any reader miss the point in the body of his three-volume work, Sylvester's index included the entry "Uncas, pliant tool of the English."[23]

And so it went. Alvin Weeks, the "Past Great Sachem of the Improved Order of Red Men of Massachusetts and President of the Massasoit Memorial Association" and, apparently, a confident judge of Indian virtues and vices, complained that Uncas spent much of his time "truckling to the English, and running to them with complaints." Weeks compared Uncas unfavorably to Miantonomi and the

Wampanoag sachems Massasoit and Metacom, also known as King Philip. Reflecting on the poverty of the Mohegans early in the twentieth century, Weeks believed that they had received their just desserts for following the "ambitious, unscrupulous, lying and treacherous Uncas, who sought by subterfuge and treachery to grasp the sceptre of Empire from all the New England Indians, and died, as he lived, despised by the men for whose favor he sold his birthright and betrayed his countrymen." If Indian "character" was to be judged by the likes of Uncas, Weeks continued, "we would have no difficulty in agreeing with the appraisals usually made of it, but, fortunately for the memory of the race, it has produced not only an Uncas, but a Massasoit, a Miantonimo and a Pometacom, whose heroic deeds save it from oblivion, or disgrace."[24]

Time did not improve Uncas's reputation. John Sainsbury, in a 1971 essay strongly sympathetic to the Narragansett sachem Miantonomi, described Uncas as a "devious" schemer whose "sycophancy won him favor" with colonial magistrates. The support of the Puritan leadership allowed him to prosper as he pursued "a career of extortion and petty crime which drew only moderate condemnation from his Puritan associates." The historian Francis Jennings simply argued that "Uncas understood his dependence and willingly played his role." The English, Jennings believed, could count on the "dependably subservient" Mohegans and their leader. More recently, an amateur historian of colonial Connecticut described Uncas as "a Judas in Red," who with his "exultant bloodhounds," delighted in the murder of innocent Pequot women and children.[25]

The Pequots, for their part, whose ancestors unquestionably suffered at the hands of the Mohegans, continue to despise Uncas. In the 1970s, the anthropologist Jack Campisi asked a Pequot woman about the nearby Mohegans and recorded her reply "that she had not much contact 'ever since what they did to us,'" referring specifically to Mohegan participation in the massacre and subjugation of the tribe during the Pequot War.[26]

Was Uncas an ally or a villain, a hero or an antihero? Was he a generous and benevolent "friend to the English," or an amoral and unprincipled manipulator who advanced his personal interests while aiding in the subjugation of his own people? Neither picture is particularly helpful for understanding the historical Uncas. In both cases, Uncas serves as an explanatory tool. In the former he helps account for the civilizing of a "savage" America; in the latter he helps to explain the devastating and violent consequences of the "Invasion of America." Both stories end the same way: Indians are replaced on the land by Europeans and subjected to English dominion. Only assessments of the main character's qualities change.[27]

•

There can be no question that Uncas's life has given rise to starkly polarized interpretations. Faced with partial accounts, frequently sparse documentation, and an ambiguous historical record, his biographers rushed to fill in the considerable gaps with speculation and opinion informed by their understanding of New England's past.

Uncas, of course, was seldom allowed to speak for himself. His words, where they appear in the historical record, always are transmitted to us through an interpreter or messenger. What we have, in consequence, is hearsay, information once removed. Despite his frequent appearances in the records of the various colonial governments, the writings of leading colonial figures, and the vital records of Connecticut towns, Uncas is remote from us and his life distinctly difficult to recover.

His remoteness, however, is not solely a product of incomplete and ambiguous sources or the challenge of finding an authentic Indian voice in the historical records. Flawed and overly simplistic understandings of his life have resulted also from what the historian Calvin Luther Martin described as the "metaphysical" problems of writing Native American history. Indians brought to their encounter with Europeans a way of looking at the world very different from non-Indians. This thought-world, this cultural cosmos, Martin argues, has eluded historians. "The Indian," Martin said, "simply does not make sense when measured against our cognitive yardstick."[28]

The early chroniclers of Uncas's career, pouring him into a mold formed by their own preconceptions of American colonial history, Indian character, and the ultimate fate of America's native peoples, cast his story in static and one-dimensional terms. Uncas was worthy of friendship, or too treacherous to be relied upon. He was a selfless friend, or a driven manipulator who would stop at nothing to advance his own interests. He was a good Indian, or a drunken heathen. He could be trusted as an ally of the English, or should be hated as an enemy of his own people. The reality is that such categories obscure vastly more than they explain. History seldom is so simple. Certainly Uncas worked closely with English colonial officials, and his relationship with the English constituted an important and defining part of his life. No Native American leader could afford to ignore the English, and much of the status Uncas achieved he owed to his skillful interaction with this utterly alien culture. He learned quickly how colonial society functioned—no small accomplishment, given the societal norms, structures, and beliefs that fueled English society in America. These hidden mechanisms, taken for granted by an English colonist, Uncas had to watch and learn as an outsider.

The stakes were enormous. Throughout the colonial period metropolitan magistrates and governors tried to prevent the land-hungry frontier population from pressing upon Indian lands, threatening native subsistence systems, and driving Indians to armed resistance.[29] Connecticut enjoyed more success in this respect than its Puritan neighbors; after 1637, Indians in the colony did not directly face the wrath of English warfare. Uncas deserves much of the credit for the two generations of Anglo-Indian peace that followed the Pequot War, for he dealt effectively not only with English officials in the provincial capitals, but also with frontier settlers on the margins of Puritan New England.

Yet Uncas was more than the sum of his appearances before colonial magistrates and English settlers. Like so many Native American leaders, he has too often been characterized primarily by the nature and quality of his relationships with neighboring whites. Uncas was a Mohegan, a simple but important point. He spent the vast majority of his time interacting with native peoples in southern New England. At the height of his power, he controlled several multiethnic village communities along the Thames River in Connecticut, and he collected tribute from villages throughout the region. When Uncas broke with the Pequots in 1636, however, he had few followers, less than fifty men in all according to some sources. Under his direction, the Mohegans built a regional power on the ruin of the Pequots. Uncas held the resulting multiethnic communities together as he confronted a complex Native American political scene within the

"maelstrom of change" produced by English colonization.[30] In so doing, he played a critical role in the intercultural politics that shaped
New England's development and as significant a part in the region's
history as that of any other individual. His was an American life of
tremendous importance.

Who then, and what was Uncas? This book is an attempt to answer
Charles Frederick Chapin's question and to restore to the life of
Uncas the considerable historical significance of which mythical
retellings have robbed it.

CHAPTER 1

World in Balance

The story of Uncas begins with the land. Land rested at the heart of all things.

The first English voyagers to these shores, this New England as they soon would call it, wondered at the seemingly limitless natural bounty of the new world they had discovered. On Cape Cod, Gabriel Archer found in 1602 the land "full of wood, vines, Gooseberie bushes, Hurtberies, Raspices, Eglentine, &c." Three decades later Francis Higginson marveled at the great "store of pumpions, cowcumbers, and other things of that nature which I know not" along the Massachusetts coast. Many "excellent pot-herbs grow abundantly among the grass," he continued, "as strawberry leaves in all places of the country, and plenty of strawberries in their time, and penny-royal, winter savory, sorrel, brooklime, liverwort, carvel, and watercresses; Also leeks and onions are ordinary, and divers physical herbs." Rivers teeming with fish; forests filled "with excellent good timber"; flocks of birds—passenger pigeons—so thick, at times, one observer wrote, "that I could see no sun"; and plentifull game—bears and "severall sorts of Deere," Higginson wrote, "also Wolves, Foxes, Beavers, Otters, Martins, great wilde Cats," and moose, a "great beast . . . as bigge as an Oxe"—all gave to this region in English eyes an appearance of great natural abundance. Thomas Morton thought this new world "a paradice: for in mine eie t'was Natures Masterpeece." Like many of his countrymen, Morton concluded that "if this Land be not rich, then is the whole world poore."[1]

Of course Europeans had not "discovered" this land, if by discovery they meant they were the first to set eyes upon a virgin wilderness. This "New England" had been home for thousands of years to somewhere between 150,000 and 200,000 Native Americans living in small communities scattered along the region's many river drainages. The Indians here went by different names, but Roger Williams, who first settled the English colony at Rhode Island and Providence Plantations, and who knew better than most of his contemporaries what he was talking about, found that they called themselves "Ninnuock, Ninnimissinuwock, Eniskeetompauwog, which signifies Men, folke, or People." They were, in their own eyes, the *real* people, the only human beings. Over many centuries they had developed lifeways that allowed them to provide for their needs with a great deal of security and comfort, and to live in harmony with all the forces in their cosmos. Theirs was indeed a world in balance.[2]

At the southern margins of this region, in what is today the state of Connecticut, Uncas was born, sometime very near the end of what Europeans counted as the sixteenth century. For many years, archaeologists and historians had assumed that Uncas's people, the Mohegans, had migrated with the Pequots into Connecticut from New York during the late prehistoric period. This assumption rested on little more than a superficial similarity between the tribal names "Mohegan" and "Mahican," the latter an important Hudson River Valley tribe. Neither linguistic nor archaeological data, however, support any other conclusion than that the Mohegans and Pequots had resided in Connecticut for several centuries prior to their first contact with Europeans.[3]

Mohegan settlement at the time of Uncas's birth centered upon the western side of the Thames River, roughly between present-day New London and Norwich, Connecticut. This was the vital heart of the Mohegan country. Settlement extended as far north as the Quinebaug and Yantic Rivers and, at times, west to the Connecticut River. Arriving at reliable population estimates for the pre-contact Mohegans is difficult owing both to a lack of sources and to their close intertwining through marriage, kinship, and alliance with the Pequots and other regional native communities. The largest Mohegan settlement site, at Shantok, built upon a triangular promontory on the west bank of the Thames well before the Mohegans had developed close contact with Europeans, could easily have housed a population of several hundred people. Other Mohegans lived in settlements at Fort Hill, at Massapeag, at Pomechaug, and along the southwestern bank of the Yantic near its junction with Hammer

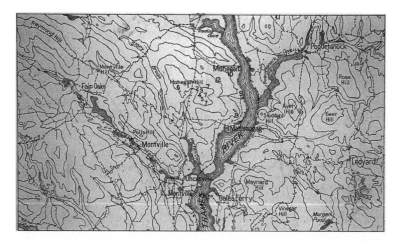

FIG. 2   Part of the United States Geological Survey chart (Norwich sheet), showing the location of the Mohegan settlement with legendary places indicated by numbers. From plate 31, *43rd Annual Report of the Bureau of American Ethnology, 1925–1926* (Washington, D.C., 1928), courtesy of the Smithsonian Institution.

The Mohegan homeland lay along the western bank of the Thames River in eastern Connecticut, between the present-day towns of Norwich to the north and New London to the south. The numbers on the map correspond to the following locations: 1: Uncas's fortification on Fort Hill where, Frank Speck learned early in the twentieth century from his Mohegan informants, "persons passing by this place on the roadway after dark are likely to perceive stones being thrown at them. Some even have felt themselves struck by the missiles. . . . Somewhere, also, in the vicinity a murdered Indian is said to have been buried. The sound of digging has been fancied to come from the place, even within the last few years." 2: The Mohegan Church, erected in 1831. 3: The "Devil's Footprint," a large granite boulder upon which, according to Fidelia Fielding, the devil left his footprint when he jumped out of southern New England. 4, 5, and 6: Indian springs. 7: The extensive remains of Indian corn hills. 8: Papoose Rock, a ledge above the Thames near Massapeag, from which an embittered Mohegan woman, according to tribal tradition, threw her young child to his death. 9: Fort Shantok. For more information about these sites see Speck, "Native Tribes and Dialects of Connecticut: A Mohegan-Pequot Diary," *43rd Annual Report of the Bureau of American Ethnology, 1925–1926*, 253–258.

Brook. Here, in this land of hardwoods and hills, ponds, marshes, and rivers, Uncas grew up and learned values and beliefs that had sustained his people for centuries.[4]

Uncas's family clearly was of high status, and this would have made his life markedly different from that of commoners in his community. Southern New England Algonquian societies were highly stratified, and Uncas would have signaled his status through attire and ornamentation. He, and Mohegans of his sort, would have the opportunity to marry multiple wives, and he would not have shared in the labor of his followers. If his experience was like that of the Narragansetts whom Roger Williams observed, he would have enjoyed an indulgent childhood. Algonquian parents, by English colonial standards, were remarkably affectionate and reluctant to use physical punishment in their relationships with their children. According to the genealogy he dictated late in life, Uncas had descended lineally from principal sachems, or leaders, of the Pequots, Mohegans, Rhode Island Narragansetts, and some of the Algonquian bands on eastern Long Island. His paternal great-grandfather, Woipequund, had been the principal sachem of the Pequots. Woipequund married Mukunnup, the daughter of a principal sachem of the Narragansetts. Owaneco, Uncas's father, descended from Woipequund and, on his mother's side, from Tamaquawshad, "chief sachem of the Moheags." Owaneco long presided over a site known in the records as "Montonesuck."[5]

Despite these close connections, Mohegan and Pequot lands were distinct, and the two groups, before European contact, apparently were never a single entity. Though they spoke almost identical variants of the Eastern Algonquin language, they lived in separate communities long enough to develop distinctive ceramic styles.[6] Pequot settlement centered upon the Mystic River Valley and adjacent parts of the coast of Long Island Sound, and extended eastward to the Pawcatuck River and westward to the Thames. The northern limit of Pequot settlement probably did not extend much past the present site of Griswold, Connecticut. It was not until after the arrival of Europeans in the seventeenth century that the Pequots began to spread their often unwanted influence over Algonquian communities along the Connecticut River and on eastern Long Island. Perhaps 13,000 people lived in the Mohegan and Pequot territories.[7]

West of Uncas's homeland, dozens of small native communities dotted the banks of the Connecticut River. In loosely organized villages, scattered farmsteads, and a variety of task-specific and seasonal camps, nearly 40,000 people lived.[8] Near where the towns of Deerfield and Springfield later grew up in western Massachusetts lived the Pocumtucks. East of the present site of Hartford lived the Podunks, governed by the sachems Wahginnacut and Arramament when first they encountered the English. The Podunks maintained close ties with the Sequins, whose territories on the western side of the Connecticut River included the village of Pyquag, soon to become Wethersfield. Ten miles or so farther west, the Tunxis lived along the Farmington River. They appear to have paid tribute to the Sequins from a very early period. Moving south down the Connecticut River toward Long Island Sound, Wangunk, Hammonosett, and Western Niantic communities could be found. The territory of the Quinnipiacs stretched from the mouth of the Connecticut westward, with most of the population concentrated around the present site of New Haven.[9]

The Narragansetts and their Eastern Niantic allies occupied the region east of the Mohegan and Pequot territories. Narragansett land, Connecticut's John Mason later wrote, stretched in the early seventeenth century from Narragansett Bay in the east "to Pawcatuck River, now the Boundary between the Governments of Rhode Island and Connecticut," in the west. At times, the Narragansetts exerted control over the Shawomet, Coweset, and Patuxent communities to their north, interacting with them so closely and so routinely as to create the impression, in the eyes of more than one observer, that together they constituted a single tribe. The Narragansetts on occasion also exercised authority over the native inhabitants of Block, Conanicut, and Prudence Islands, the Montauks on eastern Long Island, the Nipmucks to the north, and the Wampanoags on the eastern side of Narragansett Bay. Their control was never perfect, but at the time Europeans began settling southern New England, the Narragansetts possessed a great deal of power. A native population of between 21,000 and 40,000 likely resided in the Narragansett Bay region on the eve of European settlement.[10]

The Mohegans and their neighbors, all speakers of closely related Algonquin languages, culturally had much in common. Indians in southern New England held their lands in ways that colonial Englishmen found difficult to comprehend. Though Roger Williams could write that "the Natives are very exact and punctuall in the bounds of their lands, belonging to this or that Prince or People," southern New England Indians did not "own" land in the European sense. Native communities claimed not the land, but the things that were upon it. Individual families might farm a piece of land, hunt there, fish, and gather firewood, but when they finished, others in the community could use it as they saw fit.[11]

To trace in such broad outline the lands held by the Mohegans and their neighbors is a relatively simple matter. Most European observers, anxious to acquire title to the lands they hoped to colonize, made some effort to delineate the holdings of the various tribes they encountered. As a result, we have a fairly good, though far from perfect, understanding of the general location of certain native communities. To reconstruct Mohegan culture, however, and the world from which Uncas emerged, poses a much more complicated challenge. Though the accounts of European voyagers along the New England coast offer an abundance of details on New England Algonquian culture, none of these works dealt specifically with the Mohegans. Conclusions might be drawn about the Mohegans by looking at accounts describing their neighbors, but this, as the anthropologist Kathleen J. Bragdon has pointed out, may create "a false impression of homogeneity and stasis among the Native people of southern New England" through "the interchangeable use of sources derived from different regions and peoples." Bragdon's warning is worth keeping in mind; one must use caution when generalizing about New England Indians.[12] Still, the extant ethnohistorical and archaeological records indicate that Mohegan culture corresponded closely with that of other Algonquian groups in southern New England. Though the famous early twentieth-century anthropologist Frank Speck may have overstated things when he argued that "the material and mental life of the Mohegan should be regarded as something of a blend of the minor ethnological types represented among the peoples inhabiting the immediate region," Uncas's genealogy clearly shows the close connections between the Mohegans and their much better documented neighbors.[13]

The Mohegans and their neighbors were a "tall and strong-limbed people," Francis Higginson wrote. William Wood described the Indians he encountered in Massachusetts as "between five or six foot high, straight bodied, strongly composed, smooth skinned, merry countenanced, of complexion something more swarthy than Spaniards, black-haired, high foreheaded, black eyed, out-nosed, broad shouldered, brawny armed, long and slender handed, out breasted, small waisted, lank bellied, well thighed, flat kneed, handsome grown legs and small feet." For clothing, Wood continued, New England natives needed to wear little, "saving for a pair of Indian breeches to cover that which modesty commands to be hid, which is but a piece of cloth a yard and a half long, put between their groinings, tied with a snake's skin about their middles." When the weather grew cold, "the more aged of them wear leather drawers, in form of Irish trousers, fastened under their girdle with buttons." They also wore shoes, "likewise of their own making, to cut of a moose's hide." Many wore "skins about them, in form of an Irish mantle, and of these some be bear's skins, moose's skins, and beaver skins sewed together, otter skins, and raccoon skins, most of them in winter having his deep-furred cat skin, like a long large muff, which he shifts to that arm which lieth most exposed to the wind." Thus clad, Wood stated admiringly, "he bustles better through a world of cold in a frost-paned wilderness than the furred citizen in his warmer stove."[14] Many also wore "pendants in their ears, as forms of birds, beasts and fishes, carved out of bone, shells and stone." These, and the tattoos, painting, and scarring that "many of the better sort" wore (consisting of "certain portraitures of beasts, as bears, deers, mooses, wolves, etc; some of fowls, as of eagles, hawks, etc.") represented contact with powerful spiritual figures and denoted social status in the community.[15]

If curiosity and a need to describe the unfamiliar drove English observers to provide colorful accounts of what Indians in the region looked like, they had much more difficulty making sense of the organization and structure of the communities in which these Indians lived. When the early chroniclers did comment on native social structure, they often did so by drawing misleading analogies to European forms of social organization and governance, so the complexity of how Native American communities organized their lives was obscured. To describe these communities as "tribes" is useful only part of the time. The center of community life for southern New England Algonquians was the village, a collection of kin relations governed by a sachem. Such a community enjoyed a degree of autonomy in managing its affairs that English observers found difficult to comprehend. Villages did act together, and did so increasingly in the years after Europeans arrived in America. To meet the European invasion, and in response to the changes it produced, villages drew together into hierarchical chiefdoms dominated by powerful sachems. These "tribes," however, remained episodic and highly fluid in their composition, with members able to shift allegiance from one community to another with little difficulty.[16]

English observers, faced with the unfamiliar political practices of the natives, quickly drew analogies between the powers of the sachem and the powers of their own king. A sachem, William Wood wrote, has "no kingly robes to make him glorious in the view of his subjects, nor daily guards to secure his person, or court-like attendance, nor sumptuous palaces," but his followers "yield all submissive subjection to him, accounting him their sovereign, going at his command and coming at his beck."[17]

Sachems, in theory, inherited their titles, with the office passing usually from father to son. Among native communities in southern New England like the Mohegans, patrilineality seems to have been the rule. In practice, ties to the mother's line clearly played an important additional role in establishing the sachem's status in the community. As we shall see with Uncas, ties to both matrilineal and patrilineal kin linked sachems to the homelands they presided over and the people they led.[18]

English observers, making the easy comparison to their king, consistently overstated the powers of the sachem. Sachems like Uncas could not rule without the consent of their followers, an important limit on their supposedly sovereign powers. As a result, Roger Williams reported, sachems "will not conclude of ought that concerns all, either Lawes, or Subsides, or warres, unto which the people are averse, and by gentle perswasion cannot be brought." A sachem seldom acted on "any waighty matter without the consent of his great men" and spiritual advisers. "Harsh dealing" on the part of the sachem, Daniel Gookin noted, might force villagers to "go live under other sachems that can protect them." Thus sachems tried "to carry it obligingly and lovingly unto their people, lest they should desert them, and thereby their strength, power, and tribute would be diminished."[19]

As sachem of the Mohegans, Uncas would have looked inward and outward, maintaining order and balance within his community as well as in its relations with the outside world. He balanced the unity of the "tribe" and the interests of the community with the autonomy of villages and individuals.[20]

Sachems, for instance, oversaw the economic life of their community. They allocated land to their followers and determined how it would be used. They directed the community's trading activities as well, both in local exchange and in long-distance trading networks.[21] They also collected tribute from their followers, often in corn or in wampum, small purple or white shell beads manufactured by Indians along the coast of Long Island Sound. According to the Pilgrim founder Edward Winslow, once a year the sachem's closest advisers "provoke the people to bestow much corn on the sachim. To that end, they appoint a certain time and place, near the sachim's dwelling, where the people bring many baskets of corn, and make a great stack thereof."[22]

The wealth they collected allowed sachems to enjoy a unique social status and to live in great comfort. Yet much of this wealth was redistributed, flowing downward from the sachem to other members of the community. In this sense, a network of duty and obligation always balanced the powers of the sachem. The sachem's right to collect tribute from his followers balanced the interests of commoners who expected sachems to demonstrate generosity and provide certain benefits. Individuals paid tribute to acquire the sachem's assistance in personal and spiritual matters. Subject groups expected from the sachem military protection. The sachem's wealth allowed him to gain the respect of his followers through strategic gifts and deliver to them certain high-status items. The important point is that the tributary relationship appears to have been conditional: subjects paid tribute not out of unquestioning subservience but in expectation of receiving from the sachem certain advantages. Sachems who failed to deliver could lose their following. Sachems and commoners thus engaged in a reciprocal and balanced relationship. The sachem expected support so long as he served the needs of the community and the individuals within it.[23]

Generosity and reciprocity, indeed, constituted cardinal social values among southern New England Algonquians, a fact underscored in the Mohegan tale of the Makiawisug, or "little people," recorded early in the twentieth century. According to Frank Speck's Mohegan informant Fidelia Fielding, "the 'little men' would come to your house, so they used to say, asking for something to eat. You must always give them what they wanted, for if you didn't they would point at you, then, while you couldn't see them, they would take what they wanted. That is what the old people told the children about the 'little men.'"[24] Such socially sanctioned expectations of generosity, Kathleen Bragdon has concluded, ensured that "no one in a Native community was allowed to go hungry or unclothed, no request for goods or service was to be denied, and ungenerous acts were counted among the most heinous of anti-social acts."[25]

In addition to their economic and tributary responsibilities, sachems worked to preserve order. They served as judges, hearing disputes and dispensing justice among their followers. By administering punishment for offenses committed in the community, sachems insulated their followers from the vengeance and blood feud that could tear villages apart. They worked to satisfy the aggrieved member's kin, restoring peace between the parties involved.[26]

Sachems oversaw their community's relations with the outside world as well. They entertained guests who visited the community, conducted diplomacy, and led in the ritualized exchange of gifts this involved. Sachems also led the community's warriors into battle to avenge wrongs suffered at the hands of another community, to acquire captives, to demonstrate valor, or to exert the authority of the sachem over a tributary village. Sachems, in short, oversaw those matters that concerned the community as a whole—its economic life, justice among the members, and warfare and diplomacy. They worked to maintain balance within their community and in their community's relations with its neighbors.[27]

Uncas would have learned that balance provided the bedrock value in the social organization of the Mohegans and their neighbors. He would have known, as well, that balance provided an appropriate and workable metaphor governing Mohegan relations with the natural and supernatural worlds. Experience had taught New England Algonquians how best to survive on the land and exploit the resources available to them in their seasonally shifting environment. Mohegans knew to begin setting their precious seed corn when the dogwood leaves grew to the size of a squirrel's ear. The appearance of dogwood blossoms foretold the arrival of anadromous fish such as shad.[28] The Mohegans might, as well, have looked to the Pleiades, like other Eastern Woodlands peoples, to determine when best to plant their crops. If they could see this bright cluster of stars in the early evening sky, a danger of frost damaging the tender plants existed. Heaven, in this case, existed in balance with earth.[29] Mohegans believed that thunder in winter meant that spring would soon arrive; the sound of snapping ice announced a thaw. The song of crickets, or cobwebs on the grass, heralded the imminent arrival of a hot spell, while they expected the first frost six weeks after the locusts began their song. The Mohegans listened closely to nature, and trusted deeply what they heard.[30]

Yet Indians like the Mohegans did not live in a pristine, edenic paradise, the hyperbole of English colonial promoters aside. They altered and shaped the environment in ways designed to best meet their needs. Staying alive required work, and Indians lived in a certain tension with their environment. They were both a part of, and apart from, nature, conservers and destroyers of parts of the world around them.[31] How long they lived this way, and how they preserved this balance, has been debated by historians, anthropologists, and archaeologists.

During the Late Woodland Period, which lasted from approximately 1000 to 1500 A.D., three distinct land use and settlement systems developed in southern New England. Maize, the fabled Indian corn of which the English settlers so commonly spoke, entered the region perhaps one thousand years ago, but native peoples occupying coastal and estuarine areas did not adopt its cultivation until much later.[32] The archaeologist Lynn Ceci has argued that the adoption of maize agriculture and a resulting "sedentary" lifestyle occurred after, and as a result of, the arrival of Europeans. Drawn into powerful colonial economic systems, coastal and estuarine Indians began to occupy fortified agricultural settlements, reliant upon maize cultivation, for progressively longer periods of the year. In these large settlement sites, Indians could harvest the shellfish necessary to manufacture wampum beads, critical to the conduct of the fur trade and vital for acquiring the European trade goods upon which they increasingly relied. As Indian communities spent longer portions of the year at these large fortified sites, moreover, Ceci found evidence that they developed increasingly centralized and hierarchical social structures.[33]

Not everyone has accepted Ceci's findings, however, arguing instead that ecological and population pressures upon coastal and estuarine resources, rather than the arrival of Europeans, dictated the move toward large, sedentary agricultural settlements. In short, increasingly centralized coastal villages resulted from indigenous causes. Though agriculture remained well into the contact period only one of a number of subsistence strategies employed by coastal peoples, and though the arrival of Europeans unquestionably accelerated trends toward larger, year-round village sites, the move toward increasingly concentrated settlement patterns began, in this view, well before the arrival of Europeans.[34]

Little evidence of agriculture exists in the upland regions of southern New England. Settlement in this area has been less studied, and the relationship between upland settlements and those in the coastal and riverine regions is not at all clear. Some archaeologists believe that upland settlement sites reflect seasonal exploitation by coastal and riverine peoples. Others argue that a distinct settlement pattern developed in the uplands, different from that in lower-lying areas, and considerably less reliant upon agriculture.[35]

Indians in riverine regions of southern New England most rapidly adopted an agriculture based on maize. By 1300 A.D., native peoples living along the banks of the many rivers had committed themselves fully to agriculture, growing corn along with beans, squash, and sunflowers. In these regions archaeologists most commonly find evidence of large, grass-lined pits ideal for the storage of an agricultural surplus.[36]

The adoption of maize agriculture was important. In the riverine regions as well as in coastal and estuarine areas, the productivity of maize provided the economic base for growing, nucleated settlements occupying specific sites for ever-longer portions of the year.

Corn became the staff of life for the Mohegans and their neighbors, as central to them as the bison would become to the Plains tribes. Maize produced a settlement pattern of "tethered mobility" as southern New England Algonquians, including the Mohegans, tied themselves to their villages and corn fields for significant parts of the year.[37]

Preparation for the planting of corn and other crops began in March, as parties of men and women cleared the land. They girdled the trees, burned the trunks and branches, and planted the crops among the stumps. Women planted the corn, according to William Pynchon, in small hills during the first month of the Indian year, "Squanikesos: part of Aprill and pt. of May, when they set Indian corne." Beans, squash, pumpkins, artichokes, tobacco, cucumbers, strawberries, and watermelons grew around the corn in a fashion that to Europeans appeared most haphazard.[38]

The corn crop required constant attention. Mohegan women would have worked through the early spring and into July to keep the fields clear of weeds. According to Roger Williams, the neighboring Narragansetts also built "little watch-houses in the middle of their fields, in which they, or their biggest children lodge, and earely in the morning prevent the birds" from preying upon the crop.[39] A significant portion of the community remained close to the fields throughout the planting season, tending the corn crop and, in time, harvesting beans and squash. Others dispersed to a variety of seasonal and task-specific sites.[40]

While women tended crops, for example, Mohegan men would have constructed fishing weirs and in other ways prepared for the spring spawning runs of anadromous fish that climbed the Thames and its tributaries each year. Clearly fishing was important to the Mohegans. Their name for the site that ultimately became New London, "Nameag," meant "the fishing place." Wochsquamugguck Brook, near Norwich, was the "place of taking salmon." Alewives, shad, eels, and salmon might be had along the Thames and other waterways as Indians gathered at falls and narrows. At these gatherings, Thomas Morton wrote, Indians enjoyed "themselves in gaminge, and playing of juglinge trickes, and all manner of revelles, which they are delighted in, that it is admirable to behold, what pastime they use, of several kindes, every one striving to surpasse each other, after this manner they spend their time." With supplies from the previous harvest nearing exhaustion, and the first corn crop several months away, fish provided southern New England Algonquians with a vital source of food.[41]

Mohegans also could gather shellfish in the Thames and along the coast of Long Island Sound. Roger Williams wrote that "all the Indians generally over the Country, Winter and summer delight in" clams. Large shell middens, indeed, have been found at Shantok. Women, in addition to harvesting shellfish, gathered wild plants in marshes and in other areas for a variety of purposes. Nuts and berries could be gathered as well, dried, and preserved for use over the winter.[42]

By the end of summer, the community reunited in the village to prepare for the harvest. Women gathered "all the corne, and Fruites of the field," producing directly through their labor perhaps three-fourths of the food their families consumed. The surplus was stored in what Thomas Morton called "Barnes" dug into the earth, lined with reeds, "that will hold a Hogshead of corne a peece in them," clear evidence of a planned agricultural economy. The well-watered lands around Shantok could have easily produced a bountiful corn harvest.[43]

Southern New England Algonquians held their largest festivals and celebrations near the time of the harvest. Corn, beans, and squash, along with gathered acorns, chestnuts, groundnuts, and other wild plants provided sufficient bounty to support large gatherings in the village. Indians gambled, ate, danced, and exchanged gifts, establishing reciprocal relationships of obligation during this comfortable time of the year.[44]

By late October, with the harvest and celebrations concluded—and with animals like deer and bear at their fattest—villagers prepared for the winter hunt. Occasionally, large communal hunts involving two-to-three hundred warriors at a time may have taken place. Much more often, hunting seemed a small-scale affair. The elderly and very young remained behind while small groups of hunters or single families spread out across a familiar countryside in search of the game that was so important a part of the Mohegans' way of life. Faunal remains excavated at Shantok reveal that the surrounding woods of oak, hickory, and beech supported a large population of deer and

bear, and smaller animals like raccoons, woodchucks, skunks, bob-
cats, and foxes. Deer were by far the favorite quarry. The men established lodges, "hunting houses" William Wood called them, "in such
places where they know the deer usually doth frequent." From here
they stalked deer or caught them in traps or snares, staying in the
field for extended periods of time. Women, meanwhile, hauled dead
game back to camp for processing, which involved preparing and
dressing the hides and smoking the meat for use later in the winter.
During this time of the year many families remained rather isolated
until December when, according to Roger Williams, "they will travel
home, men, women and children, thorow the snow, thirtie, yea fiftie
or sixtie miles."[45]

From the close of the hunt through the early spring thaw, southern
New England Algonquians once again concentrated in their villages.
They relied upon the foods they had gathered and prepared over the
preceding months. Individuals may have continued to hunt for whatever game was available in the vicinity. Others may have tried ice
fishing to add variety to their diet. Scarcity was not uncommon, but
overall, Indians such as the Mohegans were able through these subsistence strategies to meet their dietary needs. In these winter villages, Algonquians waited for the snow to disappear and for the
seasonal round to begin once again.[46]

This yearly round of subsistence activities at least in part contributed to a marked sexual division of labor in southern New England Algonquian communities. Men engaged in activities that took
place for the most part away from the village community, and often
out of the sight of judgmental English observers. Women's work centered on the village and its surrounding fields. The amount of work
performed by Algonquian women led many English writers to con-
demn their "lazy" and "gormandizing" husbands who, they thought,
forced their wives to lead "a most slavish life."[47] These observers may
have failed to appreciate the onerous duties their own wives and
daughters performed. Certainly they failed to recognize the extent to
which the Algonquian division of labor arose from certain founda-
tional beliefs about the balanced and complementary roles of men
and women in village communities. Men and women occupied distinct yet interdependent spheres in the Eastern Woodlands.[48]

The role of men in hunting and fighting shaped their relationship with other beings in the native cosmos. Their job was to kill, albeit in the name of sustaining and protecting life. Men killed. Women created. They were growers and nurturers, and cultural practices among New England Algonquians reflected a widespread belief in the elemental power of women to create life. They raised the crops, bore the children, and tended the fire. They preserved intact the community's oral tradition. Childbirth took place away from men, perhaps to protect them from the powerful forces present when women gave birth. Menstruating women remained apart from the rest of the community, Edward Winslow wrote, living "certain days in a house alone; after which, she washeth herself and all that she hath touched or used, and is again received to her husband's bed or family." According to Roger Williams, this "custome in all parts of the Countrey they strictly observe, and no male may come into that house." Men as life-sustaining killers, women as creators of life, a power represented in menstrual blood: the sexual division of labor in New England Algonquian communities and the attendant cultural practices underscored the Mohegans' belief that theirs was a world of balance, in which each being had its place.[49]

Yet men and women could not maintain and sustain their communities without the assistance of powerful spiritual forces in the native cosmos. European observers described native religious life in tones of incomprehension, condescension, and contempt. They never understood that Indian religions met the spiritual needs of native peoples, allowing them to explain, predict, and control their universe in ways that made sense intellectually and emotionally.

The Mohegans and their neighbors lived in a crowded cosmos. Human beings interacted frequently with a great variety of spirits and sacred beings, and the line between human and other-than-human beings always remained fluid. Roger Williams learned from the Narragansetts, for example, the "names of thirty seven" gods, "all which in their solemne worships they invocate."[50] The Mohegans, certainly, believed in the existence of Makiawisug, or "little people," who punished the selfish and miserly and rewarded the good as they walked the borderlands between the earth and the spirit world. Mohegans believed as well in two spirits who appeared at night, one benign and the other a haunting "stone-cutter" who frightened nocturnal travelers.[51]

Mohegans believed in "witches" as well. The Mohegan Indian Chahnameed, according to one legend, married a beautiful woman and carried her away to the island upon which he lived. Chahnameed neglected his wife, and spent much of his time away from the island. Chahnameed's wife missed her family, and so she resolved to leave her husband. She used magic to do so. He pursued her as she tried to escape, so she pulled a hair from her head, ran it through her fingers, and it became a spear. She threw the spear, hitting Chahnameed in the forehead, killing him. The woman was, according to Frank Speck, a witch, or *moigu*, who had acquired special powers from dark forces in the native cosmos. Dwarves, spirits, witches—together these stories reflect the extraordinarily active and vibrant spiritual world with which the Mohegans interacted.[52]

Like those of other New England Algonquians, the Mohegans' cosmos was dominated by two powerful figures. "They do worship," wrote Francis Higginson, "two Gods, a good God and an evil God." The benevolent god went by several names: along the coast of Massachusetts he was Tantum, or Kiehtan. The Narragansetts and those to their west called him Cautantouwwit.[53]

Cautantouwwit created the world and sent a crow to carry corn and beans to southern New England Algonquians, a belief reflected in the Indians' unwillingness to harm the birds "although they doe the corne also some hurt." The crow brought the corn from the southwest where, according to Roger Williams, "they say . . . is the Court of their great God Cautantouwwit." Toward the southwest, furthermore, were "their Fore fathers soules: to the South-west they goe themselves when they die." Graves in a Narragansett cemetery dating to the mid-seventeenth century pointed to the southwest, toward Cautantouwwit's house.[54]

Cautantouwwit was a benevolent provider, a distant creator. He required little in terms of ritualized attendance. Southern New England Algonquians devoted the bulk of their religious activity to deflecting the wrath and gaining the favor of a more ambivalent figure known variously as Chepi, Hobbomok, or Abbomocho. Abbomocho, according to John Josselyn, "many times smites them with incurable diseases" and "scares them with his apparitions and pannick Terrours." Edward Winslow wrote that "Hobbamock . . . as far as we can conceive, is the devil." It was he whom they called "upon to cure their wounds and diseases." It was he who sent these misfortunes "for some conceived anger against them."[55]

To appease Abbomocho and to gain his assistance, southern New England Algonquians participated in a tremendous variety of ritual. According to Roger Williams, the Narragansetts held a "Nickommo, a feast or dance," during times of sickness, drought, war, or famine. They held a Nickommo also "when they enjoy a caulme of Peace, Health, Plenty, Prosperity." Misfortune could not be a random incident, they believed, and such disasters could occur only in a world out of balance. Ritual provided an instrument to set things right.[56]

Religious leaders called powwows directed the ritual life of the community. These visionaries inspired both fear and contempt among English observers, who denounced the "diabolical art" and "rude ceremonies" they used to cure the sick, while dancing "in an Antick manner" and "beating their naked breasts with a strong hand, and making hideous faces, sometimes calling upon the Devil for his help, mingling their prayers with horrid and barbarous charms."[57] Summoned by Abbomocho, who appeared to them in dreams, or in the form of a snake, a bird, or some other sacred being, powwows had access to enormous power. Early English voyagers to the region learned of powwows who made ice appear in summer, water burn, rocks move, and trees dance. Powwows cured disease by using their powers to draw sickness from the body. With the assistance of guardian spirits like eagles and snakes, powwows predicted the future. Sachems seldom made important decisions without first consulting their powwows, who served as vital intermediaries, maintaining a crucial balance between Abbomocho and the sachem's followers, between the world of humans and other-than-humans.[58]

Mohegans and their neighbors engaged in ritual to secure the power necessary to preserve this balance. The concept of power rested at the heart of Mohegan assumptions about how the cosmos functioned. Those with spiritual power enjoyed abundant harvests, successful hunts, and victory in battle. Power—*manit* or *manitou* to New England Algonquians—meant survival. Ritual provided the means for its acquisition.[59] Roger Williams found that the Narragansetts believed "that God is" and "that hee is a rewarder of all them that diligently seek him." Williams understood the Algonquian concept of *manitou* in terms analogous to the English *god*, when in reality *manitou* meant an immediate and pervasive power beyond and greater than that of humans. Those who sought out this spiritual power, Williams suggested, would, with proper attention to ritual, enjoy its many benefits.

Power manifested itself in a variety of ways in animals, plants, objects, and people. Williams observed among the Narragansetts "a generall Custome" "at the apprehension of any Excellency in Men, Women, Birds, Beasts, Fish, &c. to cry out Manitoc, that is, it is a God, as thus if they see one man excell others in wisdome, valour, strength, activity, &c. they cry out Manitoo, A God." Certain types of animals possessed manitou, giving them great or special powers. Crows, as the messengers of Cautantouwwit, were not harmed, despite the damage they could do in corn fields. Black foxes, which the Narragansetts had seen but never managed to catch, "they say are Manittooes, that is, Gods, Spirits, or Divine Powers, as they say of every thing that they cannot comprehend." Hunters were "very tender of their Traps, where they lie, and what comes at them; for they say, the Deere (whom they conceive have a Divine Power in them) will soone smell and be gone." Successful hunting required the performance of certain rituals. Hunters thus made a request, and not a demand, of the animals they stalked. Without proper attention to ritual, and without the proper demonstration of respect, deer would never allow themselves to be taken by Algonquian hunters.[60]

Uncas would have engaged in ritual and ceremony to appease the spiritual forces that controlled the growth of crops and the supply of game. With proper attention to ritual, his people need not fear a bad harvest or a poor hunt. Disregard for ceremony, however, risked provoking forces in the spirit world that could rain misery and destruction upon Mohegan villages. Through ritual and ceremony, the Mohegans maintained a delicate balance with spiritual forces in their world that allowed them to survive.

At the beginning of his life, Uncas lived in a world in balance. Over centuries the Mohegans and their neighbors had devised means to preserve a vital balance with their neighbors, among themselves, and with the spiritual forces that ordered the cosmos. The arrival of Europeans would upset this balance, forcing Native American leaders like Uncas to confront a new world of unprecedented and rending change.

CHAPTER 2

The Mohegans' New World

The Mohegans still preserve the memory of their first contact with Europeans. Uncas would have been a child at the time. One day early in the seventeenth century, according to tribal tradition, an old sachem looked "out across the Great Water." On the horizon he "saw a Great White Bird coming toward him." The chief hurried back to his village and informed his followers of the extraordinary sight he had seen. Together, the villagers and their leader ran back to the shore. As the Great White Bird came closer, "they could see the figures of strange looking men in its beak and wings. The chief was fearful for his people." Many changes, he predicted, "would take place after the coming of the White Man in his strange canoe."[1]

This old Mohegan story has much in common with other "first contact" narratives. It raises questions, more, perhaps, than it answers: it is not clear from the tale which Europeans the Mohegans encountered, where they encountered them, and why this initial contact should at that time have inspired such gloomy predictions for the future. Still, the story shows the Mohegans struggling to make sense of the newcomers who began to settle in their world beginning early in the seventeenth century and brought unprecedented changes to American shores. Uncas, who became the Mohegans' greatest sachem, would prove himself a master in leading his people through the "new world" that Dutch and English colonization produced.[2]

•

Initial contacts with Europeans in southern New England were for the most part peaceful, as Indians cautiously approached the newcomers and, in time, sought opportunities to engage in trade with them. Southern New England Algonquians, including the Mohegans, extended the concept of *manit* to things European, allowing them from a very early period to adopt and incorporate into their own way of living elements of this foreign material culture. The technology and trade goods that the Europeans carried with them suggested to Indians that the newcomers were a powerful people, perhaps even otherworldly or magical. Many New England Algonquians sought to acquire elements of English material culture because they seemed to possess such great manitou.[3]

The early English explorer James Rosier, for example, sailing off the coast of New England early in the seventeenth century, took part in a demonstration of English power for the native peoples he encountered. "Our Captaine," Rosier wrote, "showed them a strange thing which they wondered at. His sword and mine having beene touched with the Loadstone, tooke up a knife, and held it fast when they plucked it away, made the knife turne, being laid on a blocke, and touching it with his sword, made that take up a needle, whereat they much marvelled." The sailors' understanding of magnetism, Rosier concluded, caused the Indians "to imagine some great power in us, and for that to love and fear us." William Wood, similarly, wrote three decades later of how the Massachusetts Indians "much extol and wonder at the English for their strange inventions."[4]

Yet if English technology impressed the Indians, convincing them that the newcomers possessed powerful items permeated with *manit*, European diseases—virgin soil epidemics against which Indians found themselves immunologically defenseless—raised a much more horrifying prospect. Indians died while Englishmen did not. Between 1616 and 1619 an epidemic tore through New England Algonquian villages, leaving thousands dead. Thomas Morton, who traveled through the region shortly afterward, encountered "a new found Golgotha," as Indians "died on heapes as they lay in their houses."[5] This epidemic shattered native communities in eastern New England. By killing Indians along the Massachusetts coast, it allowed the Pilgrims, who arrived in 1620, to build Plymouth Plantation on the ruins of an abandoned native village. The epidemic, however, did not travel west of Narragansett Bay and, as a result, the Mohegans and their immediate neighbors managed to avoid at this time some of the most disruptive and devastating elements of European colonization in America.

Isolated from the nascent English settlements to their east, Uncas and the Mohegans had only occasional contact with Europeans. In 1614, when Uncas would have been in his teens, the Dutch navigator Adriaen Block explored the waters feeding into Long Island Sound. He entered what later would become the Thames River, encountering the "Pequatoos" and their enemies, the "Wapanoos." Just west of the river's mouth, Block traded "with the natives, who are called Morhicans." He then sailed a short distance westward before ascending the Connecticut and encountering other Indian communities there.[6]

Block led the first Europeans into the Connecticut region, but other Dutch traders soon followed. Jacques Elekes, in 1622, imprisoned the chief of the "Sickenanes" and "obliged him to pay a heavy ransom, or else he would cut off his head." The damage to Dutch-Indian relations, apparently, was short-lived, and the mutual desire for trade

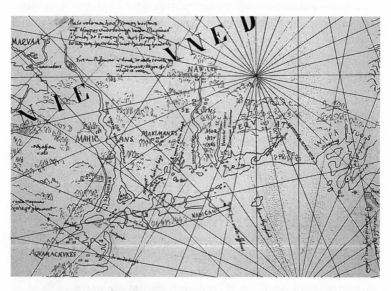

FIG. 3 Dutch map of about 1614, the earliest source showing the location of the Mohegan and neighboring tribes, along the Thames River in eastern Connecticut. From plate 15, *43rd Annual Report of the Bureau of American Ethnology, 1925–1926* (Washington, D.C., 1928), courtesy of the Smithsonian Institution.

great. By 1626 the multilingual Pieter Barentz, who could "understand all the tribes thereabout," was regularly visiting the Sequins, Wampanoags, Mohegans, and Long Island Shinnecocks.[7]

These Dutch traders sought fur. Connecticut, one of the state's earliest historians wrote, "abounded with beaver." Though there is little evidence about Dutch activity in the region, it seems likely that West India Company traders visited the waters emptying into Long Island Sound frequently. Between 1614 and 1624 according to some estimates, the fur trade along the banks of the Connecticut alone may have reached the impressive total of 10,000 beaver skins annually.[8]

Trade with the newcomers immediately transformed the native villages of Connecticut. Dutch traders learned quickly that the use of wampum could facilitate the growth and expansion of the fur trade. Small tubular white and purple beads made from the shell of the quahog, or hard-shell clam, and a variety of conch or whelk shells, wampum long had been employed by southern New England Algonquians for purposes of ornamentation and for the payment of ransom, compensation, and tribute. Dutch traders acquired wampum from the Pequots and Narragansetts in exchange for European trade goods. The Dutch then carried this wampum to Indians in the interior, exchanging it for furs. The Pequots and Narragansetts, too, exchanged their surplus trade goods with interior natives for additional furs, which they then delivered to the Dutch.[9]

The effects of this "wampum revolution" were dramatic. The Narragansetts, who already had earned a reputation for power among their native rivals by avoiding the plague of 1616–1619, began to consolidate their control over the production of wampum along the coast of Long Island Sound. They also moved to monopolize all European trade in the region. The Pequots, meanwhile, followed suit and had by 1626 extended their control over the Sequins and a number of small bands to their west along the Connecticut River. Control of wampum production, Plymouth's William Bradford noted, allowed the Pequots and Narragansetts to grow "rich and powerful and also proud thereby, and fills them with pieces, powder and shot."[10]

Bradford noted how "strange it was to see the great alteration" wampum "made in a few years among the Indians." Indians replaced skin clothing, Bradford wrote, with European cloth. Trade increased. Settlements were consolidated and fortified. Indians spent more time harvesting the shellfish necessary for wampum production, and these coastal sites were easily accessible to European traders. As different native groups tried to break into the trade, competition and rivalry over control of wampum production produced unprecedented levels of intertribal warfare. Warfare provided a further impulse toward sedentarism: many villagers chose to reside in secure and permanent fortified sites housing relatively dense populations. The Pequots had forts on the Mystic River and at Weinshauks, across the Thames from present-day New London. The Mohegans constructed palisades around their settlement at Shantok.[11]

Certainly the Mohegans traded with Europeans at Shantok. They were able to provide the newcomers with venison, fish, corn, and furs. They also manufactured both purple and white wampum. With these items, the Mohegans acquired from European traders a tremendous variety of goods. Archaeologists have excavated axes, knives, drills, and nails at the Shantok site. The Mohegans cut up European brassware to produce metal arrowheads. Glass beads and gunflints also have been found, leading the archaeologist Lorraine Williams to conclude that "the Mohegans had acquired at least some guns and iron" by the early 1630s.[12]

Uncas's father, the Mohegan sachem Owaneco, worked to secure for his followers a share of the growing volume of European trade. Uncas had an older brother. In 1626 Owaneco proposed to the great Pequot sachem Tatobem that this elder son marry Tatobem's daughter. According to the genealogy Uncas dictated late in life, Tatobem "did readily imbrace" an alliance, secured by marriage, with the Mohegans. Uncas's brother, however, died before the marriage could take place. Owaneco and Tatobem then decided, after consulting their advisers, "that Uncas the next brother to the deceased should proceed in the said Match, which thing Uncas accepted." Southern New England Algonquians commonly used marriages to secure alliances between native communities.[13] The evidence, however, sheds little light on the nature of this alliance and how it initially functioned. Owaneco died shortly after Uncas married the daughter of Tatobem. Uncas, who grew to become "a man of large frame and great physical strength," nonetheless was forced to subject himself to Tatobem's authority in the wake of his father's death. Disease had by then ravaged the Mohegans, reducing Uncas's ability to resist the

Pequots. Only by humbling himself before Tatobem, several of his rivals later recalled, could Uncas and the Mohegans secure access to European traders, and only then could Uncas "have liberty to live in his own Countrey" along the Thames River.[14]

By monopolizing access to European traders, Daniel Gookin wrote, the Pequots became "the stoutest, proudest, and most successful in their wars of all the Indians." They held "dominion over divers petty sagamores; as over part of Long Island, over the Mohegans, and over the sagamores of Quinnapeake, yea over all the people that dealt upon Connecticut River, and some of the most southerly inhabitants of the Nipmuck Country, about Quinebaug." Native communities in Connecticut that wanted access to European trade goods could obtain it only through the payment of tribute, in wampum, to the Pequots, who served as both middlemen and overlords.[15]

Uncas chafed under Tatobem's control. So, too, did others of the Pequots' tributaries. So long as the Dutch were the only source of European trade goods in the region, however, they could do little if they wanted to trade with the newcomers. Access to the European items that seemed to manifest such great manitou and power could be gained only through the Pequots, and only if one were willing to pay for the privilege. When English settlers arrived in America, planting their first outposts along the Massachusetts coast, some Indians at last saw an opportunity to break free from Pequot hegemony.[16]

In the spring of 1631, Governors William Bradford of Plymouth Plantation and John Winthrop of the Massachusetts Bay Colony received appeals from Wahginnacut, a sachem "upon the River Quonehtacut," to "have some Englishmen to come plant in his Country." Wahginnacut offered his would-be protectors and suppliers corn and a yearly tribute of eighty beaver skins. He assured the English governors that they would find his lands "very fruitful."[17]

More than a desire for English friendship motivated Wahginnacut. He sought a supply of trade goods independent of Dutch and Pequot control. Described by Bradford, moreover, as the leader of "a company of banished Indians . . . that were driven out" of the Connecticut "by the potency of the Pequots," and by Winthrop as "a very treacherous man, and at war with the Pekoath (a far greater sagamore)," he hoped as well for English protection, and was willing to pay for it. Finally, that Wahginnacut traveled to Boston with John Sagamore, a Massachusetts Indian and close ally of the Narragansetts, suggests that the Narragansetts, too, were willing to undermine the growing power of the Pequots. Indeed in April and May 1632, a year after Wahginnacut's visit to Boston, Governor Winthrop received word of warfare between the Pequots and Narragansetts.[18]

For a short time the Pequots' control of the Connecticut River placed them in a position to dominate both the production of wampum along the seacoast and the fur trade flowing down the river. They monopolized access to European trade goods and grew "rich and potent." In doing so, however, they alienated their tributaries, Uncas among them, and created an exceptionally unstable system of control. In the coming months and years, the Pequots would collapse entirely, a result of both native resistance and the intervention of European settlers and magistrates who sought to control the region and its many resources. The Pequot hegemony would prove a remarkably short-lived affair.

•

The English settlements to the east of the Mohegan homelands grew at a remarkable rate. The Separatist Pilgrims, who settled Plymouth in 1620, and the Puritans, who planted their outpost in Massachusetts Bay in 1630, thrived after struggling through their first winters. These colonists saw in Old England's religious turmoil, rising social and economic tension, unemployment, landlessness, famine, and plague clear signs of God's disfavor. If the English church refused to reform and cleanse itself of the lingering taint of popery, they believed, the Lord would pour his wrath upon England. Their native land no longer looked to them an elect nation, and these vexed and troubled English men and women feared that if they remained at home, they could no longer claim the mantle of God's chosen people. In America, they thought, things might be different. There, John Winthrop wrote, the Puritans could establish a Bible-based commonwealth, making the Massachusetts Bay Colony "a citty upon a hill," and a model for Old England's regeneration.[19]

Yet secular concerns always existed side by side with the Puritans' spiritual imperatives. They hoped to establish stable, secure, and productive settlements on the margins of England's Atlantic world. They also hoped to profit from their endeavor, and to do so they had to trade with their Indian neighbors. Exchange, they believed, could provide the colonies with capital that would free them from debt, finance the construction of forts and churches, and secure their self-sufficiency. Establishing this trade, however, proved difficult. Especially problematic, the Puritan magistrates could provide European trade goods in neither the quantity nor the quality of those offered by the Dutch.

Traders, mostly from Plymouth, initially directed their attention to the north, along the Kennebec and Penobscot rivers in what now is Maine. There Abenakis, who already had altered their subsistence routines to meet the demands of French fur traders, needed food, which the New Englanders could provide in quantity.[20] Only in 1627 did the Plymouth men learn of wampum, when the Dutch trader Isaac De Rasieres introduced them to it. Rasieres, apparently, feared competition for control of the region's limited supply of furs, and hoped the English, if provided with a valuable medium of exchange, might occupy themselves in the north, leaving Dutch interests along the Connecticut and on Long Island alone.[21] He was wrong. With the Bay region largely worthless for furs, and competition with French traders limiting prospects to the north, Englishmen in Plymouth and Massachusetts Bay cast covetous eyes toward the Connecticut. In 1632, in response to Wahginnacut's appeal, Edward Winslow of Plymouth led an expedition to explore the river's valley.[22]

Viewing with great apprehension the English settlers' growing interest in the region, the Dutch worked to solidify their control. In 1632 Hans Ercluys, an officer of the Dutch West India Company, purchased a point of land from the Indians at the river's mouth, known as Kievet's Hook. Jacob Van Curler, in June 1633, purchased twenty acres at the present site of Hartford from a Pequot sachem named Nepuquash. There the Dutch erected a trading post that they called the House of Good Hope.[23]

The Plymouth men never respected Dutch claims to the river. Accompanied by Natawante, another River Indian who had appealed for English assistance against the Pequots, William Holmes of Plymouth sailed up the Connecticut River shortly after the Dutch had finished constructing their post. Holmes carried in the hold of his ship a prefabricated fort, and he planned to occupy a tract of land along the river just north of the Dutch. Despite Dutch threats, Holmes and his crew proceeded. When they arrived at a site near present-day Windsor, "they clapped up their house quickly and landed their provisions and left the company appointed, and sent the bark home, and after palisadoed their house and fortified themselves better."[24]

According to Plymouth governor William Bradford, the English fortified their post because "they were to encounter with a double danger in this attempt, both the Dutch and the Indians." The Pequots, Bradford believed, "were much offended" that the English "brought home and restored" to power Natawante, "the right sachem of the place." Indeed, though the Pequots eagerly desired European trade, they did not want their native rivals acquiring independent access to European traders. In the fall, a group of Pequot warriors ambushed and killed several Narragansetts, or Narragansett tributaries, along the path leading to the House of Good Hope. The Pequots could not allow a rival to undermine their hold upon the Connecticut.[25]

Killing the Narragansetts was a serious mistake. The Dutch considered this attack a violation of their agreement with the Pequots. When they had negotiated with Nepuquash the purchase of the site for their trading house, the Dutch believed that the Pequots would allow other Indians to visit the post. The Dutch reacted to this perceived breach swiftly and violently. They seized the Pequots' great principal sachem, Tatobem, as a hostage. Eager for the release of the skillful and charismatic leader who had orchestrated and overseen the Pequots' dramatic rise to power, his followers paid the Dutch a huge ransom. They received Tatobem's murdered corpse in return.[26]

The Pequots were in trouble. Tatobem's immediate successor, whose name we do not know, sought to avenge the slain leader. The Englishman John Stone sailed into this arena in the winter of 1634 and unwittingly made himself available for that purpose. Certainly Stone was no angel. He had been banished from the Massachusetts Bay Colony for his relentless drinking, his insubordination, an attempt at piracy, and being caught in bed with another man's wife. Rumors that he had engaged in cannibalism while on a voyage to the West Indies circulated throughout the colony. Before setting off for his new home in Virginia, where the Puritans believed such behavior was tolerated, Stone detoured into the Connecticut River.

On his way upstream, Stone and his men may have roughed up

some of the Indians they encountered. Without question, they failed to stand guard. Instead Stone and his men, nine in all, drank themselves into a state of unconsciousness. The Pequots who attacked and killed them found little resistance and would have escaped without casualties had Stone's ship not caught fire and exploded.[27]

These Pequots thought Stone and his men were Dutch. They killed them in retaliation for the murder of their sachem. In this sense the death of Stone and his crew was a mistake. The Pequots had enemies enough. The Narragansetts harassed them from the east. Their war with the Dutch was going badly. Shortly after Stone's death, in fact, Tatobem's successor was killed by the Dutch in an ambush gone awry, cut to ribbons by a blast of cannon fire. Trying desperately to repair the damage that had been done, Sassacus, the Pequots' new chief sachem, sent a delegation to Massachusetts Bay seeking friendship. His ambassadors offered the English a gift of seventy beaver and otter skins along with four hundred fathoms of wampum. This, Sassacus hoped, would justly and adequately compensate the English for the death of Stone's crew and serve as the foundation for an alliance in which the English would take the place of the Dutch, providing them with European trade goods and protection from their enemies. Sassacus promised the English, in return, "all their right at Connecticut," according to Governor Winthrop, "and to further us what they could, if we would settle a plantation there."[28]

The Pequots' offer certainly interested the Bay Colony magistrates, but only if certain conditions first were met. The Puritans demanded that Sassacus hand over "those men who killed Captain Stone." The Pequot ambassadors explained that some of those guilty of Stone's murder had died when his ship caught fire. Smallpox had killed the others. The Bay Colony magistrates were not satisfied. They would "send a pinnace with cloath to trade with them" only after they had received the wampum, the furs, title to the Connecticut, and the heads of those who killed Stone and his men. Governor Winthrop, furthermore, told the Pequot ambassadors that any alliance would be limited strictly to trade, and "not to defend them." Winthrop believed that he had a deal, but these were terms that the Pequots simply could not accept.[29]

The murder of John Stone and his crew and the Pequots' subsequent efforts to make peace with the English reveal much about the tumultuous intercultural situation in Connecticut. Sassacus might easily have destroyed the Dutch post in retaliation for the slaying of Tatobem. He did not. Neither did he or the Pequots do anything more than threaten Plymouth's small post. Despite the claims of one nineteenth-century historian that Sassacus "resolved to extirpate the English by means the most diabolical and inhuman that Indian sagacity could contrive," the Pequots needed the English. They sought peace, protection, and an opportunity to trade for the European goods upon which their power rested. Friendship and alliance with the English offered the possibility of escaping from the Dutch and Narragansett vise.[30]

The Pequot ambassadors who traveled to Boston came as hunted men. "Two to three hundred of the Narragansetts," Winthrop reported, lined the Indian trails west of the Bay waiting for a chance "to kill the Pekod Ambassadors." Winthrop managed to negotiate a safe passage with the Narragansetts for Sassacus's lieutenants. Still, the Pequots, at war with the Dutch and besieged by the Narragansetts, had, in William Bradford's words, "overmany enemies at once."[31] Disease rendered the Pequots' situation even more critical. In 1633 smallpox broke out in the Massachusetts Bay Colony. There followed "a great mortality among the Indians." By the following spring John Winthrop observed that the Indians "are neere all dead of the smal Poxe, so as the Lord hathe cleared our title to what we possess." The epidemic moved swiftly. As of January 1634, seven hundred Narragansetts had died. The disease then moved through Connecticut. Indians there "fell sick of the small pox and died most miserably." Plymouth's governor William Bradford, in perhaps one of the most riveting statements on the human consequences of European settlement in America, described the horrors of smallpox for Indians:

> A sorer disease cannot befall them, they fear it more than the plague. For usually they that have this disease have them in abundance, and for want of bedding and linen and other helps they fall into a lamentable condition as they lie on their hard mats, the pox breaking and mattering and running one into another, their skin cleaving by reason thereof to the mats they lie on. When they turn them, a whole side will flay off at once as it were, and they will be all of a gore blood most fearful to behold. And then being what with cold and other distempers, they die like rotten sheep.[32]

According to some estimates, the Narragansetts and Massachusetts Indians lost 86 percent of their population. The Pocumtucks, in western Massachusetts, may have lost 81 percent. Uncas likely watched more than eight out of every ten Mohegans die from the disease while the Pequots, too, lost more than 80 percent of their numbers.[33]

Beyond its dreadful demographic consequences, the smallpox epidemic shattered a world in balance. Disease weakened traditional religion in the village communities as powwows found their healing powers useless. Villages that lost their sachems and 80 percent of their population no longer had the critical mass necessary to survive. The few survivors relocated to new villages, with new political alignments and balances of power. A massive reshuffling of peoples must have resulted as Indians sought safer quarters. An epidemic that reduced an Indian population of well over 100,000 to nearly 12,000 in less than a year, moreover, opened leadership positions that could not be filled through traditional means. Ambitious people rushed to fill the resulting void. Finally, so precipitous a drop in population seriously weakened the last meaningful obstacle to English settlement in the Connecticut River Valley.[34]

•

The English population of New England exploded against this backdrop of epidemic disease, adding an urgency to the struggle between Pequots and Puritans, and Narragansetts and the Dutch, for control of the Connecticut River Valley and its resources. As 21,000 newcomers arrived from England during the 1630s, Puritan farmers felt the pressure of increasing numbers. Seeking pasture and meadowland, residents of Newtown, Watertown, Roxbury, and Dorchester in Massachusetts looked westward to the Connecticut. According to Newtown's minister, Thomas Hooker, his flock found "the fruitfulness and commodiousness of Connecticut" immensely attractive.[35]

The leaders of Massachusetts Bay and Plymouth, however, feared the consequences of a rapid movement of population outward from their core settlement areas. Since arriving in America, Puritan leaders had worked to maintain an orderly frontier by regulating those instances when Indians and English settlers came into contact. The careless expansion of settlement, they believed, could create tensions along the frontier that might easily flare into expensive warfare with enemies both Native American and European.[36]

Winthrop and Bradford denounced colonists who broke away "under one pretence or other, thinking that their owne conceived necessitie, and the examples of others, a warrante sufficiente for them," but they could not stem the tide of emigration. In May 1635 the Bay Colony magistrates reluctantly granted the planters at Roxbury and Watertown the right to emigrate to the Connecticut River Valley, "provided that they continue still under this government." The emigrants ignored the restriction, and the flood of settlers westward continued. Since they could not prevent the growth of the new settlements, the Puritans in Boston hoped to retain at least some control over the fledgling communities by dictating the structure of their governments. In March 1636, then, they empowered eight men to "make & decree such orders for the present, that may be for the peaceable & quiett ordering of the affaires of the said plantacion, both in tradeing, planting, building, lotts, militarie dissipline, defensive warr, (if neede so require) as shall best conduce to the publique good of the same."[37]

Puritan fears of frontier disorder were not unfounded. The 250 English settlers living in three towns along the Connecticut River threatened Pequot hegemony in the region. The newly appointed Connecticut magistrates responded to rumors of Pequot hostility by establishing a nightly watch and requiring that every male inhabitant secure a firearm and a ready supply of powder and shot. Anyone who traded weapons with Indians would suffer "such heavie penalty as ... the Courte shall thinke meete." Militias in each of the river towns drilled once a month.[38]

It is not surprising that the small but rapidly growing English settlements generated conflict with the Pequots and their tributaries. "The Massachusetts men are coming almost daily," seeking land to plant and a secure livelihood, wrote Jonathan Brewster, from Plymouth's post on the Connecticut. The limited productive capacity of the land, coupled with the different strategies Indians and Englishmen used to exploit it, quickly drew the two populations into conflict. Natives and newcomers in the valley made use of identical ecological resources, but did so in ways that seldom were compatible. Free-roaming English livestock, for instance, grazed in unfenced Indian cornfields, creating tensions between the two groups that raised questions of the survival of each. English pigs rooted for clams on mud flats, depriving Indians of a vital source of food during the lean months of the year.[39] English settlers could not survive without acquiring Indian land. This land they needed for garden crops, pasture, timber, and firewood, and for growing grain and corn. Given their agricultural strategies, an English town of 250 people could use as much land as an Indian village of 400. Such stress on the land, in a region where Indians and non-Indians lived in close contact, required repeated accommodations in order to avoid open conflict, and in every accommodation the Pequots and their allies lost ground.[40]

Even worse from the Pequots' perspective was that the English had obtained their title to those lands from disaffected Pequot tributaries. Settlers at Wethersfield, for example, purchased their lands from Sowheag, a River Indian sachem. Arramament, a Podunk, and Sheat and Congronosset from the tributary village at Poquonnuc put their marks to the deed for the English settlement at Windsor. The Mohegan sachems Wonochocke, Towtonemon, and Foxon also signed the document. The English presence had loosened the Pequots' already tenuous grasp on their tributaries. Other English settlements, at Springfield to the north and at Saybrook at the mouth of the Connecticut River, increased pressure on the Pequots and gave their tributaries additional opportunities to free themselves from their battered overlords.[41]

Indeed, though the Pequots still retained the power to drive Nipmuck bands that lived along the Blackstone River in Massachusetts "from the sea coast with ease," their system of tributaries and subject peoples had clearly begun to unravel. Wequash, an important rival of Sassacus, renounced his allegiance to the Pequots and placed his followers under the protection of the Narragansetts. Sassasaw, the sachem of a village on the western shore of the Pawcatuck River, wavered in his loyalties between the Pequots and Narragansetts during much of the 1630s, fighting, at times, for both sides. He, too, would defect from Sassacus's control after chopping the head off a Pequot war leader, reflecting the fluidity of "tribal" identity in southern New England. Even before hostilities with the English commenced, the pressure from the Dutch, the Narragansetts, and ultimately the Mohegans began to tear the Pequot network of domination apart.[42]

Like Wequash and Sassasaw, Wahginnacut and Natawante, Uncas appears to have grown increasingly resentful toward his Pequot overlords. His father's alliance with Tatobem had been premised upon a certain reciprocity, a balance between two native communities that were closely linked through marriage and kinship, and that saw each other as rough equals. After the death of Owaneco, his father, the tenor of the relationship changed. Uncas seemed unwilling to challenge the powerful Pequot sachem's authority openly. When Sassacus, a weaker and less effective leader than Tatobem, became chief sachem, however, Uncas aggressively began to contest Pequot authority over the Mohegans. On at least five separate occasions, he attempted to undermine Sassacus's authority. Observers at the time, and many historians since, have described these poorly documented acts of resistance as "a coup," "succession attempts," "defections," or "usurpations," but there likely was more to them than that. With the support of Narragansetts who long had been working to destabilize Pequot hegemony in the region, Uncas and other Mohegan sachems began an expansionist drive westward from Shantok and the Thames to secure control of Pequot hunting grounds "almost to the Connecticut River." The Pequots counterattacked each time and drove Uncas and his followers into exile.[43]

The life of an exile among the Narragansetts suited Uncas poorly. He always returned to his homelands and ritually humiliated himself before Sassacus. The Pequot sachem, though he reduced the amount of land under Uncas's control, reinstated him at Mohegan.[44] The leniency of Sassacus toward Uncas suggests that the Pequot sachem could not generate the support necessary to execute his Mohegan rival, no matter how treacherous his behavior. Southern New England Algonquian leaders could take their subordinates only where they willingly would follow, and Uncas, through bonds of kinship and marriage, maintained close ties to many high-status Pequots. For Sassacus to kill his sister's husband, a Mohegan sachem, without a strong consensus that Uncas's actions warranted so harsh a sanction, raised the prospect of a series of retaliatory strikes that could further sunder Sassacus's already tattered chiefdom. Accepting Uncas's submission and reinstating him at Mohegan, on the other hand, apparently secured Uncas's allegiance, at least for a time. Miantonomi, the Narragansett sachem, told Roger Williams that "when the Dutchmen and we fought with the Pequts the Mogia-neucks joyned against us." Uncas, he suggested, was playing both sides of the fence. Indeed, Miantonomi added that Uncas and his men "had a hand in the death of all the English" along the river, killing colonists even as he aided the English during the war.[45]

It was, if true, an alarming charge. Uncas may have backed up his submission to Sassacus with real action in the Pequots' behalf, fighting against their growing number of enemies, both red and white. His failed challenges to Sassacus left him with a dwindling number of followers and little land. Those who had supported him may have shifted their loyalties to other sachems, better able to defend and promote their people's interests. Roger Williams of Rhode Island guessed that Uncas had no more than fifty men left, suggesting a Mohegan population of somewhere between 250 and 400 persons.[46]

Weakened by Sassacus, Uncas enlisted English power to pursue Mohegan objectives. He began to develop relationships with important Englishmen in Connecticut. These efforts have earned for Uncas the contempt of historians who saw in his actions the work of a crass opportunist more interested in currying the favor of imperialistic invaders than in promoting the cause of beleaguered native peoples. Herbert Milton Sylvester, for example, who wrote early in the twentieth century, viewed Uncas's attempt to establish relations with the Connecticut English as the desperate act of a man "selfish, jealous, and inclined to play the tyrant," who sought to "save himself from the vengeance of Sassacus."[47]

Uncas's behavior, however, need not be interpreted solely in these terms. Uncas, indeed, may have sought political power and wealth. He may have been avaricious and ambitious as well. Without question he sought alliances with English colonists in Connecticut. Yet if we are to arrive at a richer, more nuanced, and complex understanding of Uncas's actions, we must, in the words of the anthropologist Greg Dening, attune ourselves to "the multiple meanings in an act" undertaken by an individual. We must recognize "the processes and fluidities in any definition." We must consider, seriously and deeply, the possibility that the strategies Uncas devised to challenge Pequot authority made perfect sense in a Native American context entirely foreign to the Englishmen who left behind the records from which we reconstruct his past.[48]

Consider, for a moment, the situation confronting Uncas as the English began to settle Connecticut. By any standard of native political leadership, Uncas was a failed sachem. His repeated attempts to free his people from Pequot domination had ended in failure, and his supporters were drifting away to other sachems. As the Mohegans' world rapidly swung out of balance, Uncas must have found it increasingly difficult to meet the needs of his followers. With his land base, power, and access to European trade goods reduced by Sassacus, Uncas could not provide his supporters with the material items they desired and expected. Smallpox had ravaged the Mohegans in 1633 and 1634, and many of Uncas's followers died. The survivors must have questioned Uncas's ability to defend them from malevolent spiritual forces.

Uncas thus needed to devise new strategies to protect the interests of his community, and so he began to cultivate relations with the English. The decision to do so made sense on a number of levels, and was by no means inconsistent with traditional Algonquian political practices in New England. With the Pequots under attack by the Narragansetts and the Dutch, and ensnared in an increasingly tangled web of controversy with the English, Uncas saw alliance with the newcomers as a means to increase both his own power and that of the Mohegans. Native alliances could be quite brittle as sachems shifted their allegiance from one leader to another. By proving their worth to their new partners, sachems could bring significant benefits to their people. Uncas and the Mohegans no longer received anything from their ties to the Pequots; they were now a subject people, sequestered on a tiny parcel of land around Shantok. In this sense, indeed, by courting alliance with English settlers in Connecticut, who showed their great power through their immunity to epidemic disease, Uncas demonstrated his growing mastery of "the exercise of seventeenth-century *realpolitik*."[49]

"Upon the first coming of the English," an early chronicler of Connecticut's history wrote, Uncas "fell into an intimate acquaintance" with Captain John Mason, a "tall and portly veteran" of England's wars in the Netherlands. Uncas and Mason must have quickly found some solution to the vexing challenge of intercultural communication. Perhaps Mason, who "had roughed it for years in the Low Countries," had learned to speak enough Dutch to communicate with the Mohegan sachem, who could have picked up bits and pieces of the language from West India Company traders. It is possible, as well, that Uncas had acquired some facility with a pidgin variant of English. Voices speaking such languages can be heard in the colonies as early as 1634, though it is impossible to determine with any certainty from whom Uncas would have learned English. Whatever the case, Uncas and Mason established a partnership that would endure for three and a half decades.[50]

Mason came to New England in 1630, and his military experience gained for him some status in the Massachusetts Bay Colony. In 1632 he helped capture a pirate who had terrorized the coast of Massachusetts, and in 1634 he assisted in the design and construction of fortifications around Boston Harbor. In 1635 he joined his brethren from Dorchester, the Bay Colony town in which he lived, in migrating to the Connecticut River. With the Dorchester men, he began to build a settlement at a site that ultimately became Windsor. With his martial bearing and responsibility for the immediate defense of the new settlement, not unlike Captain John Smith at Jamestown, Mason might have looked to Uncas very much like the sachem of the English village community. He would have seemed like the natural person with whom to form an alliance.[51]

In addition to dealing with the English sachem on the Connecticut, Uncas worked equally well in developing partnerships with those newcomers, like Plymouth's Jonathan Brewster, who contacted him at Shantok. Son of one of the founders of Plymouth Plantation, Brewster settled in Plymouth in 1621. By the middle of the 1630s, he had taken charge of Plymouth's outpost on the Connecticut River. Like his brother-in-law John Oldham, Brewster had spent considerable time in Connecticut as he explored the river, traded with Indians, and looked after his colony's interests there.[52] In June 1636 he sent one of his agents "who hath the Indian language" to Shantok. Trade was on Brewster's mind, but he was also interested in discovering the "Proceedings of the Pequents, as also there present abode." We shall never know the name of Brewster's messenger, or what he saw at the place his employer called "Munhicke." What we do know is that he returned to the Plymouth post with news that would send shockwaves through the region.[53]

"In great secrecy," Brewster wrote, "the sachem thereof called Woncase, sent me word" that Sassacus actively had plotted against the English. Late in May, Uncas told Brewster, Sassacus, his brother Sacowauein, and their advisers had hatched a plot to destroy Plymouth's trading ship, "being then in their harbor weakely manned." Sassacus "appoynted 80 men in Armes before Day to surprise hir." The Pequot attackers narrowly missed their prey. Brewster declared that "it pleased the over Ruleing Power of God to hinder them, for as soone as those bloody executioners arose out of ambush with their canoes, the [sic] deserned her under sayle with a fayre wind returning Home."[54]

Brewster learned as well from Uncas what Puritans in the River Valley already had concluded: "that Sasocuse with his Brother, upon consultation with their own men, was an actor in the death of Stone" two years before. Furthermore, Uncas reported that the Pequots had lied to the English when they claimed that all of Stone's killers had died. Five "of the principall actors," he said, were still alive and well under Sassacus's protection.[55]

Uncas painted for Brewster a frightening picture of the fate that awaited English settlements along the river. The Pequots, he said, had heard from the "indiscreet speaches" of settlers in Connecticut "that the English will shortly come against them." As a result of these hostile rumors and the growing pressure from English settlements, Uncas reported, the Pequots, "out of desperate madnesse," had planned "shortly to sett both upon Indians, and English, joyntly." The implication was clear: unless the English took action, Uncas, Brewster, and the Puritan settlements along the river faced the possibility of Pequot attack. Alarmed by the news, Brewster forwarded Uncas's message to John Winthrop Jr., who first founded the Puritan outpost at Saybrook at the river's mouth. The Puritan magistrates, he warned, should act quickly for Brewster considered the information reliable. Brewster found Uncas entirely "faithfull to the English."[56]

Not all Englishmen upon the river believed the charges that Uncas had leveled against the Pequots, but in Boston they generated a determined response. The Uncas-Brewster message raised issues, the Bay Colony's governor, Henry Vane, wrote, that concerned not only Massachusetts "but all the English upon the river." Therefore Vane, the elder Winthrop, and Thomas Dudley, a former governor, commissioned John Winthrop Jr. to confront the Pequots with Uncas's accusations, and "informe us particularly of their severall answers;

giving them to understand that it is not the manner of the English to take revenge of injury untill the partys that are guilty have beene called to answer fairely for themselves."[57]

It must have been a frustrating meeting for the Pequot delegates. In addition to the old demand for the wampum as compensation and the heads of Stone's killers, they found themselves confronted with additional demands. The Pequots, of course, in their own view had withdrawn the offer of wampum as compensation for Stone's murder when the Bay Colony expressed no interest in a defensive alliance. That had been two years ago. Yet now the younger Winthrop threatened that "if they shall not give ... satisfaction ... or shall be found guilty of any of the sayd murthers, and will not deliver the actours in them," the English will consider themselves "free from any league or peace with them, and shall revenge the blood of our countrimen as occasion shall serve."[58]

The same month that Winthrop Jr. delivered his ultimatum to the Pequots, Indians in southern New England killed another Englishman. John Oldham, Brewster's brother-in-law, a successful fur trader, and a prominent member of the Massachusetts Bay Colony, was found dead on his small ship near Block Island, his body badly mutilated. The Pequots had nothing to do with Oldham's death. Indians from the island, tributaries to the Narragansetts, killed him. The elder Winthrop learned that "all the sachems of the Narragansett, except Canonicus and Miantunnomoh, were the contrivers of Mr. Oldham's death." They had killed him because "he went to make peace, and trade with the Pekods last year."[59]

Oldham's death showed how quickly disputes between Indians could involve Englishmen, and his death complicated an already tense situation along the southern New England frontier. The principal Narragansett sachems, Miantonomi and Canonicus, skillfully deflected responsibility for the killing from themselves. Canonicus met with ambassadors from the Massachusetts Bay Colony and their Indian interpreter, Cutshamakin, "clearing himself and his neighbors of the murder, and offering assistance for the revenge of it." Miantonomi blamed his Block Island tributaries for the crime and paid to have a sachem named Anduah executed for his role in the Oldham killing. Miantonomi's wampum bought for the Narragansetts the trust, at least temporarily, of the Bay Colony magistrates.[60]

The magistrates of the Massachusetts Bay Colony had tried since their arrival on American shores to maintain order along the Anglo-American frontier. In Connecticut they failed to achieve that order. The settlers along the River, effectively free from Bay Colony control, threatened Pequot interests in the region, and now the other English colonies found themselves dragged by Connecticut into disputes among Native American communities. The Pequots had never purposefully attacked English colonists. The death of Stone and his men, they consistently asserted, was a case of mistaken identity, and they made a genuine effort to patch up their problems with the English afterward. Still, the tribe's unwillingness to tremble before the Puritan Saints earned for the Pequots the distrust of the English colonial elite. In this environment Uncas, and to a lesser extent Miantonomi and Canonicus, convinced the Puritans that the badly battered Pequots posed a significant and credible threat to the New England colonies.

As "the blood of the innocent called for vengeance," the Bay Colony magistrates sent Captain John Endicott with one hundred men to "put to death the men of Block Island . . . but to spare the women and children, and to bring them away." He would then "go to the Pekods to demand the murderers of Capt. Stone and other English, and one thousand fathom of wampum for damages, etc., and some of their children as hostages, which if they should refuse, they were to obtain it by force." The Bay Colony would have its order, one way or another.[61]

Endicott landed his forces on Block Island late in August, but the Indians would not stand and fight. They fled to the swamps while the English force entertained itself burning wigwams, destroying crops, and killing a few dogs that the Indians left behind.[62] Endicott and his men then moved on to Saybrook, at the mouth of the Connecticut. Lyon Gardener, the commander of the fort, was livid. The Bay Colony's actions, he knew, could provoke a war, and Gardener accused Endicott of coming "hither to raise these wasps about my ears, and then you will take wing and flee away." Gardener tried to reason with Endicott, but Endicott was not a reasonable man.[63]

The Pequots knew Endicott was coming. Roger Williams had learned that the Pequots "comfort themselves ... that a witch amongst them will sinck the pinnaces by diving under water and making holes" in them. They would defend themselves with sorcery.

Pequot warriors shadowed Endicott's ships as they sailed eastward along the coast, from Saybrook toward the Thames and Pequot Harbor. "What cheer, Englishman, what cheer," they cried, using the common Anglo-Indian expression of greeting. When the English refused to answer, the Indians called out, according to John Underhill, "What Englishman, what cheer, what cheer, are you hoggery, will you cram us? That is, are you angry, will you kill us, and do you come to fight?"[64]

They found out the next morning. Endicott repeated the Bay Colony's demand for the heads of Stone's killers. Once again, the Pequots explained that the death of Stone and his crew was an unfortunate mistake. The Pequots had never changed their story, but Endicott remained unconvinced. He wanted to kill somebody, and he ordered an attack. The Pequots fled. The Englishmen "gave fire to as many" of the Pequots "as we could come near, firing their wigwams [and] spoiling their corn," but their enemy got away.[65]

The Bay Colony's neighbors—Plymouth, Connecticut, and Saybrook—wasted no time in declaring "themselves unsatisfied" with Endicott's raid. They feared it would embroil them in a war they were not yet prepared to fight. Certainly the Pequots, in the words of Mason, "grew inraged against the English." Yet the Pequots' situation was desperate. Their magic had failed to stop the English boats. Their tributaries had abandoned them. Uncas encouraged the English against them, as did others. The Massachusetts sachem Cutshamakin fought beside Endicott's forces; he took a Pequot scalp during the attack on Pequot Harbor.[66]

In desperation, the Pequots approached their old enemies, the Narragansetts. They had learned something, they felt, of the fate that awaited Indians in English New England. The English were strangers, the Pequots said, and had begun to overspread the country. Both tribes would lose everything if the newcomers "were suffered to grow and increase" any further. If the Narragansetts assisted the English, the Pequots warned, they would guarantee "their own overthrow; for if they were rooted out, the English would soon take occasion to subjugate them."[67]

The Narragansetts, however, had little interest in assisting their rivals. By October they had formed a firm alliance with the Bay Colony. Miantonomi, at Boston, proclaimed that his followers "had always loved the English, and desired firm peace" with them. According to

Winthrop, Miantonomi pledged that the Narragansetts "would continue in war with the Pequods and their confederates, till they were subdued; and desired we should do so. They would deliver oure enemies to us, or kill them ... That they would now make a firm peace, and two months hence they would send us a present." Miantonomi's gift arrived in Boston on time: forty fathoms of wampum and a Pequot's hand.[68]

Isolated and under assault, the Pequots directed their anger against Saybrook, the base from which Endicott had attacked. Gardener warned officials in the Bay Colony in November that ships should stay away from the River unless they came with "men knowne and fitted with armes suitable charg'd." Facing a war not of his own making, Gardener kept a close watch. Still, the Pequots managed to pick off men who straggled too far from the fort, or who landed carelessly along the banks of the Connecticut.[69]

Early in 1637 Gardener, along with his interpreter, Thomas Stanton, parleyed with the Pequots outside the fort. "Have you fought enough?" the Pequots asked Gardener. The garrison commander said that he "knew not yet." Was it the custom of the English, the Pequots asked, "to kill women and children?" Gardener menacingly assured the Indians that "they should see that hereafter." His answer confused the Pequots, and "they were silent a small space." They had referred to Endicott's attack at Pequot Harbor, not English plans for the future. Still, apparently they had heard enough. "We are Pequits," they said, "and have killed Englishmen, and can kill them as musquetoes, and we will go to Conectecott and kill men, women, and children, and we will take away the horses, cows, and hogs." Gardener was not impressed. He asked Stanton to tell the Pequots "that they should not go to Conectecott, for if they did kill all the men, and take all the rest as they said, it would do them no good, but hurt, for English women are lazy, and can't do their work, horses and cows will spoil your cornfields, and the hogs their clam-banks." They could not win.[70]

When reinforcements arrived from the Bay Colony in April, the Pequots lifted their siege of Saybrook, and shifted their activity to the north. At daybreak on the 23rd, two hundred Pequots attacked the settlement at Wethersfield. They killed several men from the town and a lot of the livestock. They captured two English girls and carried them away.[71]

After the attack, the Pequots taunted the men at Saybrook. Those Indians who had cast their lot with the English anxiously awaited the colonists' response. How would the English react to so bold a provocation? And now, the Bay Colony's John Higginson wrote, "the eyes of all the Indians in the countrey are upon the English, to see what they will doe." Unless the English acted "to tame the pride and take down the insolencie of these now-insulting Pequots," he continued, "we are like to have all the Indians in the countrey about our ears." Indeed, the Wethersfield attack regained for the Pequots the allegiance of some of their former tributaries.[72]

Miantonomi informed Roger Williams that "the Nanhigonsicks are at present doubtfull of Realitie in all our promises." He proposed a plan to Williams for retaliating against the Pequots. Uncas, at the same time, placed pressure upon Connecticut leaders to act aggressively against the Pequots. Bullying the important Puritan divine, Thomas Hooker, Uncas offered a simple and terrifying threat. "The Indians here our frends," Hooker wrote, "were so importunate with us to make warr presently that unless we had attempted some thing we had delivered our persons unto contempt of base feare and cowardise, and caused them to turn enemyes agaynst us." Uncas expected Hooker and other River Colony leaders to behave in accordance with native principles and to act aggressively in response to the Pequots' attack. Uncas pulled the English into his battle with Sassacus. He demanded that they act against his enemy, or face the consequence: a larger and more dangerous Indian opponent that did not fear the Puritans.[73]

Over the five years preceding the Wethersfield attack, the Pequots had struggled to maintain control over intercultural exchange in southern New England. For a brief period they succeeded, but the searing impact of European diseases, coupled with pressure upon native subsistence systems by land-hungry settlers and the willingness of their native rivals to exploit Pequot weakness, destroyed the tribe as a regional power even before the English mobilized their forces. As their tributaries shifted their allegiance to other protectors, and as former subjects like Uncas assisted the English in bringing the Pequots to heel, their ability to resist was seriously compromised. Historians long have looked upon the Pequot War as the product of an English effort to preserve order on the frontier, or as a legitimate, if brutal, response to Pequot savagery.[74] The Anglo-Indian massacre of the Pequots, however, had sources which predated English settlement in the valley. Native leaders like Uncas and Miantonomi, both Pequot rivals, saw opportunity for their followers in the Pequots' growing misfortunes. Together they kept up enormous pressure upon frightened Puritan leaders, in Connecticut and Massachusetts, to act with decision and, ultimately, with violence, against a Pequot "menace" that need not have threatened the Puritans' holy experiment.

•

In the wake of the Wethersfield attack Uncas traveled to Hartford, accompanied by seventy warriors. Most were Mohegans, but some of his followers must have been drawn from the neighboring Indian communities. The Bay Colony's John Underhill, assessing Mohegan motives, wrote that "these Indians were earnest to join with the English, or at least to be under their conduct, that they might revenge themselves of those bloody enemies of theirs." Two centuries later, the Connecticut historian John W. De Forest described Uncas as a "traitor to the Pequot race" who came to Hartford "smarting with disappointed ambition, with mortified pride, and with a desire for vengeance." Both men overstated the importance of revenge to Uncas, and failed to recognize the Mohegans' desire for autonomy. As the eighteenth-century Connecticut governor Oliver Wolcott wrote in a bit of dreadful verse, Uncas

> was that sagamore, whom great Sassacus' rage
> had hitherto kept under vassalage,
> But weary of his great severity,
> He now revolts and to the English fly.[75]

The English sachem to whom Uncas offered his assistance had already begun preparing for war when the Mohegans arrived. On May 1 the Connecticut General Court had ordered "that there shalbe an offensive warr against the Pequoitt." The three River Colony towns—Hartford, Wethersfield, and Windsor—would raise a combined force of ninety men, under the command of John Mason. They would attack the main Pequot village, Weinshauks, on the Thames River.[76]

The leaders of the Connecticut force quickly recognized the usefulness of Mohegan allies, who would "best know the Pequots holds and holes." Though Mason had military experience, his men were anything but professional soldiers; Gardener would later ridicule their chances for success. They needed all the help they could get. The combined Mohegan-English force left Hartford in mid-May, ninety English colonists and seventy Mohegans. They proceeded down river together in three boats.[77]

Every moment with the English offered Uncas an opportunity to learn about his new allies. A man of little patience, he became increasingly exasperated as the overburdened ships continually ran aground. Mohegan canoes handled the river so much better than the English boats, and Uncas wanted to fight. "Impatient of Delays," Mason wrote, the Mohegans "desired they might be set on shoar, promising that they would meet us at Saybrook."[78] Uncas led his men overland as Mason and the English floated clumsily down river. Near Saybrook, Uncas saw an opportunity to attack and prove his usefulness to Mason. A group of thirty to forty Pequots had camped close to the fort, watching English movements. Uncas and his men attacked the Pequots. They killed seven. Uncas delivered the severed Pequot heads to the English at Saybrook. Mason viewed the attack as "a special Providence, for before we were some what doubtful of his Fidelity."[79]

As Connecticut's forces moved down river toward Saybrook, the Massachusetts Bay Colony made some small efforts to prepare for war against the Pequots as well. They accomplished little. Religious conflict, the Antinomian Schism, occupied the magistrates. Underhill remained with the small Bay Colony force earlier sent to reinforce Saybrook.[80]

Roger Williams at Providence informed the Narragansett sachems, Canonicus and Miantonomi, of the Bay Colony's plans, hoping to secure their allegiance against the Pequots. Canonicus, Williams wrote, "was very sour, and accused the English and myself for sending the plague amongst them," but Miantonomi offered advice on strategy and tactics. Assuming that the Puritans wanted to attack the main Pequot village at Weinshauks, Miantonomi warned that the campaign would take time, at least three weeks or a month. Quick raids like that launched by Endicott simply would not do. If the Pequots saw the English approach they would flee to "a marvellous great and secure swamp, which they called Ohumowauke," near present-day Groton. To avoid this, they should be attacked at night, "by which advantage the English being armed, may enter the houses and do what execution they please." The Narragansetts would provide the English with guides and warriors, but it was their wish "that women and children be spared."[81]

Mason and his Mohegan allies arrived at Saybrook in mid-May. The fort's commander, Lion Gardener, may have been pleased with the security that came from having nearly one hundred more armed Englishmen at the post, whatever their value, but he clearly was uncomfortable with the large number of untried Indian allies in his midst. Gardener demanded of Mason "how they durst trust the Mohegan Indians, who but that year came from the Pequits." It was a good question. Brewster and Mason might have thought Uncas "faithfull to the English," but Gardener had his doubts. Uncas looked like a Pequot and spoke what sounded like the same language, Gardener noticed, and some of the Pequots he knew spoke better English. To what extent, Gardener wondered, were the Mohegans and Pequots separate peoples, and was the divide deep enough to warrant risking the lives of inexperienced English settlers?

Mason said that he had little choice. His men needed Indian guides. The answer failed to satisfy Gardener. He called Uncas over and addressed him through the interpreter, Thomas Stanton. "You say you will help Major Mason," Gardener said, "but I will first see it." He demanded of the Mohegan sachem an additional demonstration of loyalty. Gardener knew of a group of Pequots nearby. "Send you now twenty men to the Bass River, for there went yesternight six Indians in a canoe thither; fetch them now dead or alive," he told Uncas, "and then you shall go with Maj. Mason, else not."[82]

Others in the fort shared Gardener's fear "that the Indians in time of greatest trial might revolt, and turn their backs against those they professed to be their friends, and join with the Pequeats." In an atmosphere in which "the hearts of all" were "in general ... much perplexed" over the question of Indian loyalty, Uncas sent twenty warriors to assault the Pequots. He may have anticipated having to prove his faithfulness to the new English sachems; Sassacus, too, apparently had expected of Uncas an act of allegiance after accepting his submission, and Uncas certainly by now saw that he could achieve much through alliance with the newcomers. His warriors returned, a short time later, with the heads of five Pequots and one prisoner. God had provided the Puritans with a sign of the Mohegans' fidelity. The English could now take advantage of this "occasion to rejoice and be thankful to God."[83]

Yet as the Puritans praised the power of the Lord's divine providence to bend the heart of a savage toward their cause, Uncas and the Mohegans gathered in another part of the fort. Uncas demanded of Gardener the right to deal with the prisoner, a Pequot named Kiswas, as he chose. Gardener recognized Kiswas. The Pequot spoke English. He had spent much time in the vicinity of Saybrook, watching the activities of the garrison. He had played some role in the killing of Englishmen along the river over the preceding months. So treacherous a savage, in Gardener's view, had forfeited his right to live.[84]

Kiswas knew his fate. The Mohegans kindled a large fire. They tied one of the captive's legs to a post. Kiswas tried to die well. "He braved the English," wrote Peter Vincent, and contemptuously taunted his Mohegan captors, "as though they durst not kill a Pequet." After burning Kiswas, and cutting off pieces of his flesh, the Mohegans tied a rope around his free leg and "pulled him in pieces." Earlier Underhill "did not judge it prudent to interpose," but this barbarism was unbearable. Underhill stepped through the crowd of Mohegans as they sang and danced "round the fire in their violent and tumultuous manner," pulled out his pistol, and shot Kiswas in the head.[85]

Accounts written long after the fact agreed that the Mohegans then consumed Kiswas raw, "while yet the flesh was quivering between their teeth." None of the eyewitnesses described such an event. John Mason wrote his account several decades after the war, and by that time his own economic interests were tied closely to Uncas's claims to Pequot lands. It is unlikely he would have included anything in his *History* unflattering to the Mohegan sachem. But Mason was not unique. Indeed, John Winthrop, learning of affairs at Saybrook second-hand, wrote that the Mohegans had taken a prisoner "whom the English put to torture." Early chroniclers of the Pequot War embellished the documentary record with macabre and sensational accounts of Mohegan savagery. Doing so could not be justified by the evidence, but it unquestionably made for good reading.

Amoral enough to sell out his people to the Puritans, some of these early writers seemed to suggest, Uncas could easily have been the type of Indian who delighted in eating human flesh.[86]

Yet much in the accounts of the killing of Kiswas rings true. Eastern Woodland Indians did torture their captives, killing them on occasion in extraordinary displays of communal violence that possessed ritualized significance. To kill animals, hunters followed certain protocols; so, too, with enemies. The condemned tried to withstand all that his persecutors could bring to bear. In a brutal contest that could only conclude in his horrible death, the captive attempted to prove that his power was greater than that of his captors, and that his people possessed the power to avenge his death. Hence Kiswas's "braving" speeches toward the Mohegans and the English. And as Uncas and his warriors wielded their firebrands, stabbed at Kiswas's flesh, burned his remains and, perhaps, consumed part of his body, they brutally demonstrated Mohegan power over the Pequots.[87]

The killing of Kiswas proves that Uncas was not a Pequot traitor or an English pawn. Uncas was Mohegan. He had involved the English in a struggle the origins of which predated English settlement in Connecticut. In the ensuing war, Uncas would be forced to reap a whirlwind of change, as vengeful Puritans determined to make the land they had settled a New England.

CHAPTER 3

The Rise of the Mohegans

As Uncas and the Mohegans sent the soul of Kiswas to wander alone and cold in a barren spirit world, Connecticut's John Mason wondered what to do next. The River Colony magistrates had ordered him to attack Sassacus's main village, Weinshauks, near Pequot Harbor. Now, at Saybrook, Mason considered disobeying his superiors. The English girls who had been captured at Wethersfield had been ransomed by the Dutch and returned to the fort. They told Mason that the Pequots had fifteen guns, and enough powder and shot to inflict casualties on inexperienced English soldiers. The Pequots, furthermore, expected an assault and so "kept a continual Guard upon the River Night and Day." This watchfulness, Mason feared, would allow the "swift on Foot" Pequots to "much impede our Landing" and "dishearten our Men." Mason had little confidence that his untried colonists could prevail in a stand-up fight with the Indians.[1]

Advised by Uncas and Underhill, Mason hatched an alternative plan. Instead of landing as expected at Pequot Harbor, he proposed to his cohorts sailing eastward past the Thames to Narragansett Bay. From there, the combined English and Mohegan force, augmented, he hoped, by Narragansett warriors, could march overland to Weinshauks and "come upon their Backs and possibly surprize them unaware." Some at Saybrook questioned the wisdom of the plan, and Mason himself was uncomfortable with ignoring his orders. A good Puritan, he asked his chaplain, a Mr. Stone, "to commend our condition to the lord, that night, to direct how in what manner we should demean ourselves in that respect." Stone did so. The minister also asked God for a sign, "one pledge of thy love," to convince the English once again of "the fidelity of these Indians toward us, that now pretend friendship and service to us, that our hearts may be encouraged the more in this work of thine." Stone reported to Mason the next morning that the Lord was "fully satisfied" with the revised plan, and that his assistance in the coming campaign against the Pequots was assured.[2]

Mason sent twenty of his weakest men home to protect their towns and replaced them with Underhill and his nineteen men from Massachusetts. Ninety Englishmen and seventy Mohegans sailed from Saybrook on Friday, May 19, arrived in Narragansett Bay on Saturday, and spent an uncomfortable Sabbath aboard their ships. Foul weather prevented their landing, near Miantonomi's village, until the night of the 23rd.[3]

That evening, Mason apprised Miantonomi of the colonists' intent. The Narragansett sachem permitted the English to pass through his territories, but he warned Mason that the English numbers "were too weak to deal with the Enemy, who were (as he said) very great Captains and Men skilful in War." Miantonomi's "somewhat slighting" comment exacerbated Mason's fears that he was outmatched by an enemy whose "numbers far exceeded ours."[4] Mason's sense of insecurity increased the next day. On Wednesday, the Anglo-Mohegan force marched twenty miles westward from the bay, arriving at a Niantic fort. The Indians there, led by their sachem Ninigret, "carryed very proudly toward us." Mason feared that they might alert the Pequots of his approach. He ordered Uncas to surround the fort, with orders that no Indian "should stir out . . . upon peril of their lives." The Mohegans ensured that their English allies retained an element of surprise.[5]

Only in the morning did Mason at last begin to feel some confidence. "There came to us," he wrote, "several of Myantonomo his Men, who told us, they were come to assist us." The Narragansett warriors made "solemn protestations how galliantly they would demean themselves, and how many men they would kill."[6] Yet the Narragansetts were cautious allies, and Mason himself did not trust them entirely. Several hours after leaving the Niantic fort, the invaders came to the Pawcatuck River. They crossed at a ford where, according to Uncas, the "Pequots did usually fish." Unwilling to cross the river into Pequot territory, some Narragansetts, "manifesting great fear," refused to go any farther. After three more miles, and af-

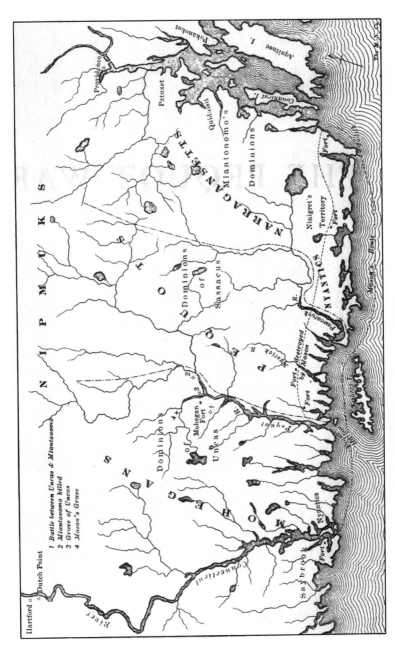

Fig. 4   Map of the Pequot War. From Charles Orr, ed., *The History of the Pequot War* (Cleveland, 1897).

ter passing through the Pequots' fields of green corn, Mason, Underhill, and Uncas met together. Mason asked Uncas if he could trust the Narragansetts. He could not, Uncas replied. "The Narragansetts will all leave you," he said. Mason must have expressed some disappointment, and Uncas tried to shore up the sagging spirits of the English commander. "But as for myself," he added, "I will never leave you." The Narragansetts deserted the English in droves, but Uncas stuck with them. He needed the English.[7]

Those Narragansetts who departed may have disagreed with Mason's objectives. For with the Englishmen "exceedingly spent in our March with extream Heat and want of Necessaries," Mason, Underhill, and Uncas revised their plan once again, opting to attack a Pequot fort on the Mystic River, closer than Weinshauks. Yet the Pequots there had created a formidable defensive position. According to Philip Vincent, they had encircled their village with palisades "ten or twelve feet high," and "as thick as a man's thigh or the calf of his leg." Between the palisades, Vincent continued, "are divers loopholes, through which they let fly their winged messengers." The Pequots' houses stood inside the walls, providing shelter for several hundred men, women, and children.[8]

Mason hoped to surprise the Pequots, "destroy them by Sword and save the Plunder." He gave to the Mohegans yellow bands "for their heads" so that the English could easily identify their allies. He did not have enough to give to the Narragansetts. Uncas guided the English toward the sleeping fort in silence, warning Mason that the remaining Narragansetts had moved to "the rear, very much afraid." The rest of the Mohegans encircled the Pequot fortress. The English forces had approached nearly to the palisades when a dog barked, alerting the Pequots to the coming attack. As the inhabitants of the Mystic fort called out the warning, the warriors in the village rushed for their arms. The English fired a volley and attacked the northern entrance of the fort, overwhelmed the warriors on guard, and began to slaughter Pequots. Despite the evident success of the assault, Mason feared that he would not be able to finish the bloody work before Pequot reinforcements, alerted by the sound of English gunfire, arrived from Weinshauks. He found it difficult, in his heavy armor, to run down the fleeing women and children. Looking to end the battle quickly, Mason told two soldiers that "we must burn them." They set fire to the mats that covered the wigwams and the flames "swiftly over ran the Fort, to the extreme amazement of the Enemy, and great Rejoycing of our selves."[9]

As Mason slashed and burned his way in from the north, Underhill, along with Uncas, attacked at the south entrance. They, too, initially met stiff resistance, and Underhill may have wavered. According to one account, he hesitated as he approached the opening. One of Underhill's men was killed. Uncas received a slight wound to the hip. "Seeing the fort was too hot for us," Underhill recalled later, "we devised a plan how we might save ourselves and prejudice them." Using his remaining powder to feed the flames, Underhill, too, set fire to the Mystic fort.[10]

With both ends on fire, the carnage was horrible. "Down fell men, women and children," wrote Underhill. Those that escaped the fires "fell into the hands of the Indians that were in the rear of us." No more than a handful of Pequots from the fort survived. "Great and doleful," Underhill continued, "was the bloody sight . . . to see so many souls lie gasping on the ground, so thick in some places, that you could hardly pass along." Plymouth's William Bradford learned from eyewitnesses that "it was a fearfull sight to see them thus frying in the fyer, and the streams of blood quenching the same, and horrible was the stinck and sente ther of." Those that escaped the fires of Mystic, he continued, "were slaine with the sword, some hewed to peeces, others rune throw with ther rapiers, so as they were quickly dispatchte, and very few escaped." For Bradford, and for other Saints, the victory "seemed a sweete sacrifice, and they gave prays thereof to God." The Narragansetts who stayed long enough to witness the attack drew another lesson. They cried out to Underhill, "Mach it, mach it; that is, It is naught, it is naught," condemning the English for their viciousness. Their fighting, the Narragansetts charged, was evil "because it is too furious, and slays too many men."[11]

The Bay Colony commander reflected upon the Narragansett charge. "It may be demanded," he wrote, why the English should be "so furious. Should not Christians," he continued, "have more mercy and compassion?" Underhill found his answer in the Old Testament. "Sometimes," he wrote, "the Scripture declareth women and children must perish with their parents. Sometimes the case alters, but we will not dispute it now. We had sufficient light from the word of God for our proceedings." He was, after all, as Underhill saw it, on the Puritans' side.[12]

The slaughter of the Pequots at Mystic took less than an hour. The English suffered few casualties. Two men died. Twenty received wounds, but only four or five had to be carried. Some of the Narragansetts, John Winthrop learned later, were "hurt by the English, because they had not some mark to distinguish them from the Pequods," but nobody seemed too concerned about that. Between four hundred and seven hundred Pequots died in the fires at Mystic.[13]

Mason, Underhill, and Uncas knew nonetheless that they did not have the time yet to celebrate their victory. "Our provision and Munition near spent," Mason wrote, and with "all our Indians except Onkus deserting us," the English feared the imminent assault of Pequots from Weinshauks. Indeed, Pequot warriors, "much inraged" by the horrible sights they discovered at Mystic, shadowed Mason's men as they marched toward their rendezvous with their boats at Pequot Harbor. The English and Pequots exchanged shots, bullets for arrows. When a Pequot fell, Mason wrote, "the Mohegans would give a great Shout, and then would take so much Courage as to fetch their Heads."[14]

Uncas played a vital role in ensuring the safety of Mason's force after the Mystic attack. Without him the English would not have made it. He and his men skirmished with the pursuing Pequots, buying the slow-moving and exhausted Englishmen time as they struggled toward their boats. The Mohegans carried the few Englishmen too badly wounded to walk on their own. And, after Mason sent most of his forces home by boat, Uncas guided Mason through western Niantic country as they marched the twenty miles overland from the Thames River to Saybrook.

The Englishmen who later remembered the Pequot War praised Uncas's loyalty and dedication to the Puritan cause. Yet they never seemed to have understood his motives. Uncas had entered into alliance with the English in order to free himself from Pequot domination. All his actions—developing a partnership with the English sachems Mason and Brewster, killing the Pequots on the march to

Saybrook, and torturing Kiswas—made sense in the context of an indigenous struggle between Mohegans and Pequots that predated English settlement in Connecticut. His behavior remained consistent with native political practice in southern New England.[15]

Nothing in the Mohegan tradition, however, could have prepared Uncas for the carnage he witnessed, and engaged in, at Mystic, a truly savage massacre of unprecedented ferocity. Nothing like it had ever occurred in New England. Native warfare traditionally had been fought for limited and specific purposes: to exact revenge, to extend a sachem's authority, to contest a territorial boundary, or to acquire, but not destroy, another people. Indians tried to keep casualties to a minimum, since village communities simply did not have the population to sustain huge losses of life. To the English, as a result, Indians seemed to fight "more for pastime than to conquer and subdue enemies." To them Indian warfare hardly deserved the name of fighting.[16] But the style of total war employed by the English, involving the killing of men, women, and children alike, seemed utterly and horribly remarkable to southern New England Algonquians. The English had always acted with horrid violence against people they considered savage and barbaric, and in southern New England their actions carried with them dramatic consequences. The Mystic massacre seared into the consciousness of southern New England Algonquians the knowledge that Englishmen could behave in unpredictable and deadly ways, and the belief that their warfare was "naught" and evil for its wanton destruction of human life.[17]

Uncas learned much at Mystic. English force was deadly, the Puritan desire for revenge great. They killed anyone in their way. Uncas certainly knew that Mohegan and English interests would not always complement each other, but Mystic taught him that he must work to remain always a "friend to the English." Maintaining this friendship, he realized, could not be done from a position of weakness: the battered Pequots, in their attempts to make amends for the killing of Stone and his crew, had offered the English all they had. It got them nowhere. Uncas would follow a different course. As he worked to convince the English that he was an ally they could trust, and that they could obtain their colonial objectives most easily with the assistance of friendly Indians like himself, he also maneuvered to acquire enough strength and power to demonstrate to the colonists that he could pose a dangerous threat should he become disaffected.

•

The Mystic attack shattered the Pequots. Some of the tattered survivors sought revenge. They turned on those few Mohegans who had not followed Uncas into the English orbit. Most they killed. Seven escaped, making their way eventually to Saybrook to tell their story. Other Pequots "came in revenge upon the Nanhiggonsicks" but abandoned their plans to attack at the last minute. Some blamed Sassacus for the troubles that had befallen them. The most dangerous enemy, the English, the Pequots knew they could not defeat. They "concluded there was no abiding any longer in their Country, and so [they] resolved to fly into several Parts."[18]

The Pequots "became a Prey to all Indians." Wequash, a rival of Sassacus who earlier had offered his assistance to the colonists, provided Lyon Gardener at Saybrook with the names of those Pequots "yet alive that had helped to kill Englishmen." Waiandance, a Montauk sachem from Long Island and a former Pequot tributary, agreed to help Gardener track down the surviving Pequots in exchange for trading opportunities at Saybrook and protection. Sequassen, a sachem in the Connecticut River Valley, Roger Williams wrote, "cut of twenty Pequot women and children" who had tried to flee westward toward the Mohawks in what is now upstate New York. "Happy were they," John Mason noted, "that could bring in [Pequot] heads to the English: Of which there came almost daily to Windsor or Hartford." The Puritans indeed thought it unwise "to give breath to a beaten enemy," and so they encouraged those Indians willing to help them hunt down the Pequots. Uncas readily joined in the pursuit. The surviving Pequots had killed some of his kin; this was, after all, his struggle that the English had joined. He knew he could not have peace unless the Pequots were eliminated as a viable and autonomous native community.[19]

A month after Mystic, Massachusetts sent forces to aid in rounding up the remaining Pequots. Israel Stoughton, with eighty men, sailed from the Bay Colony to the Thames River. There, with the assistance of some Mohegans, he attacked some scattered Pequot bands that had remained in the area. He then moved toward Say-brook. Mason and forty men from Connecticut, along with Uncas and a sizable Mohegan force, met him there. Together they pursued those Pequots who had fled westward, with Uncas leading the chase. With two Pequot sachems Stoughton had captured earlier, and a handful of Englishmen, Uncas kept close on the heels of the fleeing Pequots. The refugees moved slowly, Mason said, "by reason of their children, and want of provisions." They hugged the coastline, digging clams and procuring "such other things as the wilderness afforded." The Mohegans picked off the stragglers, adopting women and children and killing sachems and warriors. The head of one Uncas fixed "securely in the crotch of an oak tree, where the grinning skull withered and bleached in the sun for many years."[20]

The chase ended near Quinnipiac. Eighty Pequot warriors and perhaps as many as two hundred women and children took refuge in a swamp. The Mohegans and Englishmen attacked but were driven back. Several of the Englishmen received serious wounds. The allies then surrounded the swamp and opened fire. Shortly before night fell, the English interpreter Thomas Stanton delivered an offer from Stoughton to spare those Pequots who had not shed English blood. Slowly, the women and children emerged and surrendered themselves to their pursuers. The men—Pequot warriors—said their farewells to their wives and children, resolving to stay in the swamp and fight. They recognized that this likely was the end. They fought all night. Outgunned, they made a break for freedom at first light. Only a handful got out. The rest were driven back into the swamp, fought until they could fight no longer, and at last were shot down "in heaps at Pleasure." The Puritans killed everyone left behind, firing "their Pieces, loaded with Ten or Twelve Pistol Bullets at a time, within a few yards of them." It was a massacre. Meanwhile, Sassacus and about twenty others headed for New Netherland, hoping to find shelter among the Mohawks. They never made it. The Mohawks killed them all, and delivered their heads and hands to the Puritans.[21]

Estimates as to the number of Pequots killed at Mystic and in the swamp fight vary widely. John Winthrop, late in July, estimated that seven hundred had been killed, but a week later he revised that figure upward to at least eight hundred. John Underhill believed that "fifteen hundred souls" had been slain "by the sword of the Lord." A much more recent student argued that the Pequots had "lost almost half of their pre-war population of four thousand" by the time the war ended in 1637.[22]

But not all the Pequots died. The survivors would play an important role in the intercultural politics of the region as Englishmen and Indians worked to reshape the postwar world. Uncas, whose followers had almost doubled in number by August 1637, adopted Pequot survivors into newly formed "Mohegan" communities. He expressed to the Bay Colony's Richard Davenport a wish "to make women of all the Pecotts, except the sachems and captains and murtherers," whom he would kill. Davenport never recognized that the reason the "Mohegans" he encountered were "much afraid" of his English troops was because up until recently they had been "Pequots." Meanwhile, Miantonomi and Canonicus expressed their wish that surrendering Pequots "be not enslaved ... but ... be used kindly, have howses and goods and fields given them." Uncas and the Narragansett sachems, then, hoped to supplant the Pequots by adding the strength of the survivors to their own network of village communities. They each hoped to place themselves at the center of the Pequots' network of intercultural trade, to dominate the wampum economy as the Pequots had done, and incorporate the remaining Pequots into their disease-ravaged populations. They did not want the Pequots to disappear, but they did want to absorb them into their emergent "tribes." Their struggles to do so would threaten the interests of Puritans who believed that they, and not Indians, ought to control the Pequot country.[23]

•

It is easy to overstate the unity of Puritan New England. No centralized authority existed to oversee Indian-English relations in the region until 1643; in the meantime, the fiercely localistic Puritan commonwealths clashed with each other as frequently as they cooperated in their attempts to control what had been the Pequots' homeland. Faced with the challenge posed by assertive, determined, and powerful native leaders like Miantonomi and Uncas, territorially aggressive colonies like Massachusetts Bay and Connecticut struggled to bring order to the region.

The Massachusetts Bay Colony enacted legislation controlling the behavior of its colonists that could jeopardize frontier order. It regulated the trade in alcohol, fur, and firearms. It required a ready supply of match, powder, and shot in each town in case Indians attacked. Connecticut did likewise, regulating trade with its Indian neighbors and attempting to secure an orderly frontier. The River Colony prohibited acts of vigilantism against Indians and made some effort to mediate disputes between natives and newcomers. To clarify what seemed to them the hazy lines of political authority in Indian village communities, the Connecticut magistrates required that Indians living "neere any English plantacions" "declare who is their Sachem or Chiefe & that the saide Chiefe or Sachem shall paye to the saide English such trespasses as shalbe committed by any Indian in the saide plantaticion adjoyninge."[24]

Both colonies claimed the Pequot country by right of conquest. The Massachusetts elite, who thought of the settlers in Connecticut as "poore rash headed creatures" who "rushed them selves into a warr with the heathen" and who had "been utterly undone" "had not we reskued them at so many hundred charges," wanted the Pequot lands for the settlement of the colony's rapidly growing population and control of wampum production in the area for the economic benefits it could bring. Connecticut, as early as June 1637, had sent a small number of troops into the territory "to maynteine our right that God by Conquest hath given to us."[25] Neither colony, however, could hope to achieve its objectives without the assistance of the native communities that had already been working to shape the region in ways that accorded with Indian political and social practice. Massachusetts, initially, lent its support to Miantonomi and the Narragansetts. Connecticut looked to Uncas in its attempts to bring order to the southern New England frontier.

Uncas welcomed the assistance Connecticut gave him. With the River Colony's support, the Mohegans under Uncas's leadership emerged as a regional power. Janus-faced, increasingly competent in dealing with both native and English authorities, Uncas created a powerful chiefdom that included the surviving Pequots and their former tributaries, Indian villagers in southern and eastern Connecticut, in the Connecticut River Valley, and on Long Island. He creatively exploited the opportunities presented in a world thrown out of balance by English disease and warfare.[26]

Other southern New England Algonquian leaders also sought to carve for themselves positions of influence in the postwar world. Wequash, for instance, a Niantic Indian, had accompanied the English into battle at Mystic. He joined Uncas in raiding Long Island in the fall of 1637 in an attempt to capture Pequot survivors living there. Wequash carried thirty of these Pequots home with him to "Nayantaquit," where they provided their captors with additional population as their villages recovered from the ravages of virgin soil epidemics, and with wealth in the form of wampum. Whether Wequash acquired access through these captives to Pequot shellfishing areas, merely put them to work manufacturing wampum, or profited from some combination of the two, the results were dramatic. Pequot captives strengthened and enriched those native leaders who incorporated them into their communities.[27]

Ninigret, the Niantic sachem, also worked to acquire Pequot captives and to increase his power by subjecting former Pequot tributaries to his authority. Late in the spring of 1638, Ninigret attacked the Montauks on Long Island. His force totaled some eighty men, "whereof twenty of them were a kinde of Pequoitt." Ninigret demanded that the Montauks pay to him the tribute that until recently they had paid to the Pequots. He told the Montauk sachem, Waiandance, to "plant your corne and weede it well and I will come att harvest and eate it." The Montauks, he continued, should not rely on Lyon Gardener's offers of protection. The English, Ninigret said, "are liars," who wanted "onely to gett your wampum."[28]

Ninigret's attempt to extend his power over a group of former Pequot tributaries deeply disturbed the Connecticut magistrates, for if Ninigret "be soe forward against the Indians our frends, whoe knowes how soone they may doe the like against our selves[?]" Connecticut demanded that Ninigret restore to the Montauks all the wampum he took, "or else they were resolved for war." With the conflagration at Mystic a recent and frightening memory, Ninigret backed down. The Montauks paid their tribute now to Connecticut, and the English colony was not willing to allow so brazen a challenge to its authority. Ninigret could not have escaped the conclusion that the Puritans hoped to take the place of the Pequots as a regional power in southern New England.[29]

Far more aggressive than Ninigret in exploiting the opportunities presented by the Pequots' defeat were the Narragansett sachems Miantonomi and his uncle Canonicus. Roughly the same age as Uncas, Miantonomi represented the Narragansetts in matters of war and diplomacy, but he could not act in these capacities, apparently, without Canonicus's support. Both wanted the Narragansetts to supplant their Pequot rivals as the dominant native power in the region. Miantonomi hoped to obtain a "Pequot Squaw" to allow him to establish ties of marriage to the Pequots. They adopted into Narragansett communities other Pequot captives and collected tribute from the survivors. None of these Pequots, the Narragansett sachems consistently argued, were "murtherers of the English," so Miantonomi and Canonicus believed that these innocent captives should "be used kindly, [and] have howses and goods and fields given them." The Narragansetts, Roger Williams observed, inclined "toward mercy and to give them their lives."[30]

Through messengers and in person, Miantonomi tried to assure the English that his actions did not threaten Puritan interests in the Pequot country. The Narragansetts, he pointed out, did not want to control all the captives, but merely "desired that there might be a division made of these surviving Pequots (except the Sachims and murtherers) and let their share be at your owne Wisedomes." Miantonomi would split the Pequots' corn with the English and, with his eye on trading opportunities, encouraged John Winthrop to "send some English to take possession of the Pequot country and there to inhabite."[31]

Yet Miantonomi's attempts so clearly to dictate the terms of his relationship with the English did not sit well with the Puritan leadership. Israel Stoughton complained that the Narragansetts were "so eagerly sett upon their owne ends, to gett booty etc. and to augment their owne Kingdome" that they could not easily be controlled. As a result, Roger Williams was told, there existed "a great itch upon the Souldiers to fall fowle upon" the Narragansetts.[32]

The English worried too much. The power of the Narragansetts had been weakened badly by the Pequot War and the epidemics that preceded it. Narragansett tributaries began to slip away from the tribe, making deals on their own with the English. They did not need Miantonomi any longer to protect them from an English population he seemed unable to control. Miantonomi did not passively watch his power dissipate, however. He cultivated relationships with Englishmen who he thought could promote and protect Narragansett interests in the provincial capitals and translate for him the foreign lexicon of Puritan politics. Roger Williams, the exile from the Bay Colony who settled the English colony at Rhode Island in 1635, genuinely respected the Narragansett leader and worked to clear Miantonomi of the many charges leveled against him.[33]

Williams flooded John Winthrop at Boston with information gleaned from his observations on the frontier and from his conversations with Miantonomi and his messengers. "Concerning Miantunnomu," Williams wrote two months after the Mystic fight, "I have not heard as yet of any unfaythfulnes toward us." He detected in the Narragansett sachem "some sparkes of true Friendship," and "could it be deeply imprinted into him that the English never intended to despoile him of the Countrey I probably conjecture his friendship would appear in attending us with 500 men (in case) agst. any forreigne Enemies." If they treated Miantonomi well, Williams wrote, the English need not fear the Narragansetts, and they could rely upon them to help bring order to the Anglo-American frontier.[34]

Miantonomi acted as well in his own behalf, attempting to convince the Bay Colony leadership that his pursuit of Narragansett interests represented no threat to the English. In November 1637 he traveled to Boston to meet with John Winthrop. According to the governor, Miantonomi "acknowledged that all the Pequots country and Block Island were ours and promised that he would not meddle with them but by our leave." In exchange for recognizing Massachusetts's claims, Miantonomi received permission to hunt in the Pequot territory and "leave to right himself for the wrongs that Ninegret and Wequash Cook had done him." He thus obtained Bay Colony support for his pursuit of Narragansett objectives.[35]

Miantonomi, indeed, had learned much about how the English functioned. When, in 1638, a colonist from Plymouth murdered a Nipmuck Indian loyal to the Narragansetts, Miantonomi expressed his desire "that the English would be carefull on the high wayes," and he worked hard to restrain his tributaries from exacting revenge, sending them "himselfe expresse threatnings" if they did so. Telling his followers that Governor Winthrop "would see Justice done," he forced them to accept English ways, preventing them from carrying out actions that Narragansetts would have considered natural and obligatory and that would have likely, in the wake of the Mystic massacre, provoked a vicious Puritan retaliation.[36]

That Miantonomi had to use force, or at least the threat of violence, to restrain his revenge-minded tributaries, demonstrates the extent to which these village communities defined their interests in terms different from his. As his ability to control his tributaries lessened, he cultivated English support for his efforts to extend his power over Pequot tributaries. The execution of the Englishmen accused of killing the Nipmuck must have vindicated, for a time, his belief that English and Narragansett interests need not stand in opposition. Miantonomi was proud of the assistance he and his people had given to the English. He never imagined that he would be placed on the same level as Uncas. The Mohegans, he told Roger Williams in 1637, "are but as a twig," while "we are as a great tree." Uncas and his followers had joined the English only the year before, while "we have bene ever friends" and "have continued in friendship and love ever since they landed."[37]

Like Miantonomi, Uncas worked diligently to earn English support. Uncas served as the eyes and ears of the Connecticut magistrates, regularly relaying to them rumors and reports of developments that threatened the safety and stability of the New England frontier. In this sense, he was indispensable to the colony's plans to establish an effective dominion along the periphery of its settlements. Uncas was also not above forwarding false information. He told Thomas Hooker, for example, that Miantonomi had hatched a plot to kill Thomas Stanton. Roger Williams assured John Winthrop that no such plot existed, but Uncas's motives were clear: recognizing the potency of Puritan fury as a weapon against his native rivals, Uncas exacerbated Puritan fears of Indian "treachery" by implicating his opponents, Miantonomi in particular, in plots against the English.[38]

Uncas also sought bridges across the cultural divide between Indians and Englishmen that he could cross on his own terms. In the fall of 1637, the Narragansetts reported to Roger Williams that a trader from Plymouth's post on the Connecticut, William Baker, had begun living with the Mohegans. Baker, a fugitive from Puritan justice for having committed "uncleanenes with an Indian Squaw," had "turned

Indian in nakednes and cutting of haire, and after many whore-domes, is there maried." A white Indian, an English adoptee into Mohegan culture, Baker offered Uncas the prospect of an adept and trustworthy interpreter and intercultural broker. The English, however, had always been uncomfortable with the idea of Puritans going native, and Connecticut wanted Baker brought to justice. Uncas bowed to the demands of the River Colony magistrates, but he did so without enthusiasm. He and Wequash reluctantly delivered the "renegade" to William Holmes at Plymouth's post on the river. Baker, however, would not remain in custody long. He soon escaped and returned to Shantok, where he "was hid againe ... by Okace." But Holmes was able to recapture him and delivered him "to Hartford where he had suffered for his much uncleanenes, 2 several whippings." Uncas was learning—slowly—the limits of what the English would allow. Indians, he recognized, must not obstruct the exercise of Puritan justice.[39]

Missteps like this were few and far between, and Uncas learned enough of English culture and society to convince the Puritan elite that he was a valuable and trusted ally. His relations with Connecticut always had been strong. He recognized, however, that he still must have seemed largely an unknown quantity to Puritans in Massachusetts Bay. Accompanied by Connecticut's governor John Haynes and forty men, Uncas traveled to Boston in June 1638, approached Governor Winthrop and the other Bay Colony magistrates, and presented them with a gift of twenty fathoms of wampum. Winthrop, relying on information from Williams and, indirectly, from the Narragansetts, refused to accept the present until Uncas gave "satisfaction about the Pequods he kept." Uncas denied that he had any Pequots with him. They were, he said, "Monahigges all." From the perspective of a southern New England Algonquian sachem, Uncas spoke the truth: the Pequot survivors, in his view, had been adopted and incorporated into Mohegan village communities. Winthrop and other Puritans, who viewed native politics through a lens clouded by their own understanding of European statecraft, could not accept this logic. The discussions broke down, and Uncas left, according to Winthrop "much dejected."[40]

Two days later, Uncas tried again. He returned to Boston and promised Winthrop that he would "submit to the order of the English touching the Pequods he had." He also pledged his willingness to allow the English to intervene in his growing struggle with the Narragansetts for power in southern New England. The Bay Colony governor was pleased. He accepted Uncas's present, and Uncas pledged his loyalty to the Bay Colony. "This heart," he told Winthrop, laying his hand on his breast, "is not mine, but yours; I have no men; they are all yours; command me any difficult thing, I will do it; I will not believe any Indians' word against the English; and if any man shall kill an Englishman, I will put him to death, were he never so dear to me."[41]

Uncas knew what Winthrop wanted to hear, and his offer meant a lot to the Bay Colony's leaders. They acquired for themselves the assistance of an Indian ally who seemingly welcomed English involvement in the Pequot country. Uncas's offer raised the prospect of the orderly and peaceful expansion of Puritan settlement in southern New England and the Bay Colony's domination of wampum production in the region. The grateful governor gave to Uncas "a fair, red coat, and defrayed his and his men's diet, and gave them corn to relieve them homeward, and a letter of protection to all men." Uncas, Winthrop noted, "departed very joyful."[42]

Roger Williams, however, continually urged Winthrop not to trust Uncas. Williams pointed out that among the forty Indians who accompanied Uncas to Boston, six were Pequots. One of these, Pametesick, had killed one of Gardener's men outside of Saybrook in 1636. One of Williams's messengers, furthermore, found the largest wigwam at Shantok "mingled full of Monahiggins and Pequots," who told him "that they had heard that the English were coming agst them." The Mohegans and Pequots, the messenger reported, had armed themselves with English guns.[43]

Winthrop may have been disappointed to learn that Uncas had so completely outmaneuvered him at Boston, but the reality is that the governor had little choice. The Bay Colony could not extend its influence over the Pequot country unilaterally; it needed Indian allies to do so. Winthrop had already made a deal with Miantonomi. Now, in an attempt to bet on all sides, the Massachusetts governor negotiated an accord with the Narragansetts' principal rival. Uncas seemed like one of two possible options to Winthrop if the Bay Colony were to extend its influence into the Pequot country. Still, Uncas continued to pursue his own interests, regardless of what the English desired. The events surrounding Uncas's visit to Boston demonstrate that he was no stooge: that his relationship with the English in Connecticut and Massachusetts Bay was informed by a desire to pursue Mohegan interests in southern New England. Winthrop had given his blessing to Uncas's efforts to dominate the Pequot country.[44]

•

English support would have meant little to Uncas without the firm allegiance of his followers. In addition to linking himself to the sources of English power in the region, he worked to establish his legitimacy as the leader of a growing number of Pequot adoptees and other tributary peoples. One way he did so was by providing his new followers with protection. The five hundred "Mohegans" Richard Davenport encountered in August 1637 seemed "to feare the Naregansick men." They may have fought against the Narragansetts during the Pequots' war with Miantonomi's followers, and may have feared further Narragansett assaults. Uncas provided them with security in the face of Miantonomi's effort to extend Narragansett influence westward. But many of Uncas's new tributaries clearly had been coerced into that position. Roger Williams reported that Uncas had three hundred men with him along the Thames, "most of them Pequts and their confederates the Wunnashowatuckoogs and other Inlanders," who remained loyal to Uncas only because he ordered them "under paine of death not to come to Canonicus, and with whome he hath made himselfe great."[45]

Uncas, indeed, considered it his essential right to incorporate Pequots and other southern New England Algonquian peoples into newly emergent Mohegan communities. That he welcomed into the villages under his control in some cases Pequots suspected of killing Englishmen, however, shows that he intended to play the high stakes game of intercultural politics at least in part upon his own terms. When, for instance, the always suspicious Roger Williams sent a native messenger to demand that Uncas turn over to the Bay Colony those Pequots settled among his followers, the Mohegan sachem responded angrily. He already had an agreement with Winthrop. Now, Uncas said, the Mohegans "found the English so false that the last night they were resolved to fight it out." Williams may have recognized his mistake. He had offended Uncas, and his aggressive request left the Mohegan sachem, in fact, with little choice. The Pequots expected his protection. That, after all, was his responsibility as a sachem. To have sold out those who came to him seeking shelter would have discredited Uncas in the eyes of his potential tributaries. Williams left Uncas with no middle ground between complete submission and resistance. In this sense, what the Puritans wanted could not matter to him. "Although the English bound him and killed him," Uncas reportedly said, "he would not yeald."[46]

Strategic marriage alliances provided Uncas with an additional tool for securing the allegiance of his new tributaries and establishing his legitimacy as a native community leader. His 1626 marriage to Tatobem's daughter had been intended to tighten the bonds of friendship between the Mohegans and Pequots. *That* marriage had not had the desired effect, but the strategy still was sound. In 1638 he married one of Tatobem's widows. By the end of the year Uncas had as many as six or seven wives, most of them women of high status. He even had the audacity to encourage several high-ranking Pequot women held by John Winthrop as servants to escape to his protection. These marriages, Roger Williams added, were "one reason beside his ambition and neerenes that he hath drawne all the scattered Pequts to himselfe and drawne much wealth from them." Marriage to powerful Algonquian women, who themselves must have possessed considerable sway with their followers, allowed Uncas to establish networks of kin relationships that could help him carry his authority with greater ease into ever more native village communities in southern New England. These marriages helped him legitimize his claim to lead the Pequots and their former tributaries, and to construct a new native political entity upon the ruins of Tatobem's chiefdom.[47]

Archaeological evidence suggests that Uncas may have tried to encourage the development of a new, Mohegan identity at Shantok. His new tributaries and followers were a diverse lot, brought together in a relatively short span of time. Yet pottery styles in the Mohegan heartland surprisingly demonstrate a remarkable degree of homogeneity. "Shantok ware" has been found only in southern Connecticut, west of the Thames, in Mohegan territory. Distinct from the

Hackney Pond and Niantic wares found in neighboring parts of Connecticut, Shantok ware, with its unique design, signaled Mohegan group identity. Its prevalence suggests that Uncas had forged increasingly unified Mohegan communities out of a great diversity of southern New England native peoples.[48]

Uncas's power had increased dramatically in the year since the close of the Pequot War. Large numbers of Pequots had settled under his protection. At "Pequot Nayantaquit," Roger Williams reported, a village of twenty wigwams stood. Uncas spent much of his time away from Shantok at this location. Further up the Thames at a location called "Maugunckakuck" eight houses stood. Ten more stood at "Sauquunckackock" and fifteen at "Paupattokshick." At Tatuppequauog, in the northern part of what is now Waterford, twenty more houses could be found.[49]

His strength considerable, Uncas had emerged from the wreckage of the Pequot War, a war he helped to precipitate, as the most influential native leader in Connecticut. He had replaced the Pequot sachems at the center of a new and powerful native chiefdom comprising native villagers from a variety of communities. Uncas, in 1638, had acquired the power requisite to dictate, to a tremendous degree, the nature and quality of his relationships with the English in Connecticut and Massachusetts Bay.

•

Massachusetts, under the direction of Governor Winthrop, had worked out agreements with both the Narragansetts and the Mohegans. On their surface at least, these legitimized the Bay Colony's claims to the Pequot territory. Connecticut, as yet, had not formally established such accords, and feverishly wanted to extend its own dominion over the lands it felt it justly had acquired through conquest. The River Colony magistrates deeply distrusted the Narragansetts, but feared that the growing hostility between Uncas and Miantonomi could flare into warfare that could ravage Connecticut's settlements and cut off the colony's access by land to its neighbors to the east. To secure its own claims to the Pequot country, Connecticut would have to treat with both the Narragansetts and the Mohegans.

Connecticut's demand that he appear at Hartford "to answer for proud Speeches which they heare of" puzzled Miantonomi, who thought that "all the English in the land were wrapt up" in the agreements he had negotiated with Massachusetts. Connecticut objected to these agreements, wrote Thomas Hooker, because they had been "prejudiciall" to Connecticut's interests. Miantonomi, traveling with Roger Williams and 150 men, began the journey to Hartford in September 1638 to meet with Uncas and the River Colony men. As the Narragansetts moved westward, Uncas encouraged his followers to harass them. Many Narragansetts complained "of robbery and violence, which they sustained from the Pequots and Monahiggins in their travel from Qunnihticut." Later, some Wunnashowatuckoogs who had remained loyal to Canonicus, Williams said, "came to us and advertised, that . . . about 600 and 60 Pequts, Moahiggins, and their confederates had robbed them, and spoiled about twenty-three fields of corn." Four of the men who survived this attack warned Williams that the Mohegans planned to "lay in way and wait to stop Miantunnomues passage to Qunnihticut, and divers of them threatened to boil him in a kettle."[50]

Despite the company of the Narragansetts, Williams was afraid. He was no soldier, and did not relish the possibility of being caught in a Mohegan ambush or watching them eat the Narragansett sachem. He suggested to Miantonomi that they return quickly to Narragansett Bay and make the journey to Connecticut by water. Miantonomi, however, was determined to continue. He put plenty of men on his flanks to prevent ambush by day, kept a close watch at night, and arrived safely at Hartford. Miantonomi believed that the Connecticut men would recognize what he considered his long-standing devotion to the colonists and that when he presented to the Connecticut magistrates the facts of Uncas's behavior, they would rein in the Mohegan sachem.[51]

From the outset of the gathering, it became evident that Miantonomi and Uncas intensely disliked each other. Each accused the other of harboring Pequot refugees who had played a role in killing colonists. Each accused the other of dealing falsely with the English, of being disloyal, and of plotting treachery. The Englishmen overseeing the gathering—Williams, Connecticut's governor John Haynes, and the interpreter Thomas Stanton—tried to persuade the two to shake hands, a custom that may have meant little to the sachems. At

long last they did so. At Roger Williams's suggestion, Miantonomi invited Uncas and his advisers to dine with the Narragansetts, to share
some of the venison his men had killed, but Uncas refused. Friends
might eat together, but Miantonomi and Uncas did not.[52]

Uncas was no more conciliatory when the discussions began. Governor Haynes asked him to provide the magistrates with a list of the
names of those Pequots who had settled under his protection. Uncas
claimed not to know their names. He had forty on Long Island, but
only a score on the mainland. Ninigret and three other Niantic
sachems, he said, had many more. Thomas Stanton knew that Uncas
was lying. You "fetched thirty or forty from Long Island at one time,"
he pointed out. Others nodded their heads, confident that Stanton
was correct. Reluctantly, Uncas conceded that he did have thirty, but
he did not know their names. Governor Haynes gave Uncas ten days
"to bring in the number and names of his Pequts and their run-
aways." If he did not, the Connecticut men would march out on their
own "to fetch them."[53]

The Connecticut men listened to Uncas's explanations with little
patience. They knew Uncas had incorporated Pequot survivors into
Mohegan communities, and they knew that he encouraged these Pequots to continue their raids against the Narragansetts. They could
hardly mistake the enmity Uncas showed Miantonomi. The Connecticut magistrates, however, were less interested in attributing
blame for the poor relations that existed between the Narragansetts
and Mohegans than they were in bringing order to their frontier. The
treaty that they dictated to Miantonomi and Uncas can be understood only with this goal in mind. The "Covenant and agreement
made between the English inhabitants within the jurisdiction of the
River Connecticut," Miantonomi, and "Poquiam or Uncas, the chief
sachem of ye Indians called the Monhegins, in the behalf of himself
and others, ye sachems under him," announced "a peace and familiarity" between the two leaders and an agreement that "if there fall
out injuries or wrongs . . . they shall not presently revenge it." Rather,
they must "appeale to the said English and they are to decide the
same." Uncas and Miantonomi, the Connecticut men demanded,
would "doe as is by the said English set downe and if they one or the
other shall refuse soe to doe it shall be lawfull for the English to com-

pell them and to rise and take part . . . agaynst the obstinate or refusing party."

Uncas and Miantonomi, as well, acceded to the Connecticut demand that they not shelter any enemies of the English, that they not trespass upon the other's lands, and that they not "take away one or the others corne nor rob nor steal from another either skins, beaver, or ye like or burn or spoil one or the others wigwams." Further, in a provision that implied that this early both the Mohegans and Narragansetts had to contend with English livestock upon their lands, the Connecticut magistrates required "that they, nor their men, nor doggs, nor trapps, shall kill nor spoile or hurt any of [the] Englishmen's hoggs, swine, or cattle."

Regarding the Pequots, the Connecticut men expected Uncas and Miantonomi immediately to behead those "that had the chiefe hand in killing the English." Neither the Narragansetts nor the Mohegans were to "possess any part of the Pequots country without leave from the English." The Connecticut men concluded the meeting by dividing evenly between the two sachems the Pequot survivors and receiving in return from them promises to pay to Connecticut an annual tribute in wampum for the Pequots under their protection. The Pequot name, they said, would no longer exist.[54]

At Hartford Miantonomi found himself forced to sign an agreement on equal terms with Uncas. Connecticut's support of Uncas, wrote Plymouth's governor William Bradford, "did much increase his power and augmente his Greatnes, which the Narigansets could not indure to see." Miantonomi and Canonicus, Roger Williams reported, complained often of "the English Partialitie to all the Pequots at Monhiggin." The Narragansett leaders felt their ambitions in the Pequot country had been frustrated by Connecticut, a colony willing to follow the deceptive lead of Uncas.[55]

As for the Mohegans, today their tribal historian argues that they "and the English recognized one another's sovereignty in the Treaty of 1638." Nothing in the language of the document supports this claim. The agreement rendered the Mohegans tributary to the River Colony. It established a relationship between the governor of Connecticut and Uncas akin to that between a superior and inferior sachem. The treaty dictated that Uncas could pursue his interests in the Pequot country only with the explicit approval of the Connecticut English. Uncas conceded much, on paper, to the colony's magistrates.[56]

Yet whatever the terms of the Hartford agreement, and however subservient Uncas became on paper, he remained to a great extent a free agent, acting as the colony's eyes and ears along the frontier. Connecticut needed him, and that gave him a significant degree of power, the ability to influence colonial officials, and the opportunity to maintain his and his people's autonomy. If the Hartford treaty showed that Connecticut expected to dominate the Narragansetts and Mohegans in the Pequots' former territories, it also significantly increased the Mohegans' strength relative to the Narragansetts, and demonstrated that the River Colony viewed Uncas at least as Miantonomi's equal. Uncas, by 1638, had achieved the goals he had struggled to attain over the course of the five preceding years. He emerged, at Hartford, as the recognized leader of a regional power.

CHAPTER 4

Killing Miantonomi

Through the Hartford Treaty, Connecticut had done much to support Uncas's attempt to fulfill his ambition of assuming the mantle of authority once worn by Tatobem. Despite the River Colony's claims of dominion over its Indian neighbors, the initiative in Anglo-Indian relations remained at Narragansett and at Shantok and at other less well-known communities lining the waters pouring southward into Long Island Sound in the years following the treaty. Native leaders like Uncas and Miantonomi struggled to preside over these villages and the networks of tribute and obligation they had formed from the wreckage spawned by the Pequot War and European settlement.

A complex and multilayered frontier resulted: neither a line nor the "outer edge of the wave" and the "meeting point between savagery and civilization," as Frederick Jackson Turner once described it. Rather, it was a zone of intercultural contact and conflict where no one of the participants could unilaterally determine the nature of the relationships that developed. It was far messier than New England's founders ever envisioned. Here, on this frontier, "Mohegan" and "Narragansett" villagers were not always what they seemed. Indians who had been Pequots could be Mohegans, Narragansetts, or Niantics, while remaining Pequots. Niantics could sometimes be Narragansetts, and vice versa, as they shifted their allegiance or became subject to competing sachems. The most astute colonial observers recognized something of this complexity, but they could not prevent Uncas, Miantonomi, and others from continually dragging their colonies into conflicts that had their origin in Indian country. Colonial magistrates constantly found the question of how to react to Indian crises dominating their colony's public agenda. The struggle between Uncas and Miantonomi for control of the Pequot country and its resources commanded the attention of the New England colonies in the years following the 1638 agreement, led directly to the formation of the New England Confederation in 1643, and threatened the security of native and colonial villagers throughout the region.[1]

Connecticut tried to establish an effective dominion over the Indians who lived within the colony's claimed boundaries. The River Colony men worked to secure their title to Indian lands and collect tribute from those communities willing to submit to their authority. They carefully watched the functioning of a colonial economy dependent upon Indian corn and wampum for its currency, and tried to regulate those occasions where natives and newcomers came into contact. Colonists who sold alcohol or ammunition to Indians, the magistrates believed, threatened the colony's security, and were punished. Indians, who as a result of a "lenity and gentlenes" on the part of the colony that "hath made them growe bold and insolent, to enter into Englishemens howses, and unadvisedly handle swords and peeces, many times to the hazard of the lymbs and lives of Englishe or Indeans," and who stole things while visiting, would pay "for every such default halfe a fadom of wampum." Indians visiting English farms, playing with guns and pilfering goods, Puritans selling rum and repairing Indian weapons, all shortly after a tremendously violent war—little wonder that the Puritan fathers enjoyed such small success in acquiring control over the southern New England frontier.[2]

Indians continued to react creatively to the newcomers and to develop strategies for coping with the growing numbers of English settlers. A few, like the Pequot Wequash, were "astonished at the success of the English . . . and attributed it to the superiority of the English God." As a result of his belief in the great manitou possessed by the English, according to John Winthrop, Wequash converted to Christianity and "became a preacher to other Indians, and labored much to convert them, but without any effect," until his death in 1642.[3] Not all natives so fully accommodated themselves to the ways of the newcomers, however. Wequash was poisoned, after all, by one of his non-Christian brethren.[4] Ninigret, despite English protests, continued his raids against the Long Islanders.

Miantonomi worked to secure a preeminent position for the Narragansetts in regional trade networks and in the Pequot country. This required that he maintain his bruised relationship with the English authorities at Boston. The Narragansett sachem, however, found himself consistently outmaneuvered by Uncas, who rose to power at Miantonomi's expense. So in addition to sending messengers with wampum to visit Governor Winthrop and publicly following the dictates of the Puritan elite, the increasingly disenchanted Miantonomi also sent emissaries to visit native communities throughout the region, urging them to unite in a war against the newcomers who had set the world so out of balance.[5]

For his part, Uncas recognized that the English would remain a part of the southern New England landscape, and he believed that their strength was too great to justify the type of armed resistance increasingly contemplated by Miantonomi. English *manit*, he believed, was considerable, and the English had the capacity to do tremendous damage to those who became their enemies. Still, Uncas, whose people at Shantok had comparatively little contact with English settlers, and who appear to have liked it that way, walked a fine line between the Connecticut English and his Indian neighbors. He managed to become indispensable to the English, meeting the colony's deeply felt need for security along its frontiers. At the same time, he worked to acquire and maintain enough strength to defend himself against his rivals and to convince the River Colony magistrates that he could pose a significant threat to the English should he become unhappy with the settlers.[6]

Uncas continued, for example, to employ strategic marriages to extend his influence into other Algonquian communities in Connecticut. By the summer of 1640 he had married the daughter of Sebequanash, the "Squa Sachim" of Hammonasset. The union, apparently, gave Uncas some claim to the Hammonassets' lands, which lay along the coast between the Connecticut River and present-day Guilford. He promptly sold these lands to the English. The Hammonassets, then, moved eastward, settling on Niantic Bay, a long day's walk from Shantok, but close enough to be protected and controlled by Uncas. They became Mohegans.[7]

As Uncas extended his sway over native neighbors, he also worked with the English. In the fall of 1640, for instance, in an ambiguously written deed, he gave to the Connecticut English "all the land that doth belong, or ought of right to belong, to me by whatever name soever it be called, whether Mohegan, Yomtoke, Aquapanksuks, Pork-tannocks, Wippawocks, Massapeake, or any other, which they may hereafter dispose of as their own." According to the deed, Uncas reserved for himself only "that ground which at present is planted and in that kind improved by us."[8] Clearly, something is strange about the document. Uncas, who over the preceding four years had extended his power over neighboring native communities, suddenly and without any compensation gave up nearly all of his claimed lands to the English. It makes little sense, and has led many of those who have studied his life to conclude that indeed, he had truly compromised Indian interests in a desire to please the Connecticut magistrates, or that he had become a pawn in the "deed game" played by land-hungry English settlers. Yet there are other explanations. Uncas and the Mohegans likely saw the deed not as a transfer of property but as something akin to a recognition of the colony's right of preemption over Indian lands within its borders. The agreement was conditional, and brought Uncas certain benefits. He did, after all, "promise and engage myself not to suffer, so far as I have the power, any English or any other to set down or plant within any of those limits which before this grant did belong to me, without consent or approbation of the said magistrates or governor at Connecticut." His possession of the lands in question remained undisturbed. Uncas gave up nothing in the deal. He acquired for himself, however, English blessing to keep these lands—lands that he had acquired through "conquest" of the Pequots and their former tributaries—clear of intruders. He gained as well the confidence of a colony that increasingly viewed him as the only Indian they could rely upon in their efforts to bring order to the colony's frontier.[9]

And with the firm support of the Connecticut magistrates, Uncas continued to pursue his people's conflict with Miantonomi and the Narragansetts. The colonial authorities at Hartford relied upon Uncas for information, and this gave him tremendous influence. He acted, and Connecticut reacted. He played the dynamic role in this Anglo-Indian exchange. Few Englishmen, after all, had arrived at a thorough understanding of the complex political alignments in Indian country, and fewer still had mastered native languages well enough to gather information independently of their Indian allies. The River Colony was in need of a go-between, and Uncas fulfilled that function, sending ambassadors and messengers to the English authorities with information concerning every possible hint of Indian conspiracy. Whether he was engaging in "an effective smear campaign against the Narragansetts," as one scholar put it, relaying word of real plots, or something else, he drew the colony into situations it otherwise would not have confronted. The River Colony, in reality, had little choice: it believed, and usually convinced its partners, that the safety of Connecticut depended on Uncas, and that Miantonomi's Narragansetts posed the greatest threat to the colony's security.[10]

•

The source of the conflict between Uncas and Miantonomi remained the fate of those Pequots who had survived the war, and control of their former territories. Late in the summer of 1639, Uncas told the Connecticut magistrates that a considerable number of Pequots had settled along the banks of the Pawcatuck River. These Pequots, Uncas pointed out, were tributaries of the Niantics, and they had returned to their old homelands with the support of Ninigret, one of Miantonomi's closest allies.[11]

The magistrates appointed John Mason to lead forty men to drive off what the colony considered intruders on "part of the land which was conquered by us" during the war. They would also destroy the Pequots' wigwams and gather their corn. Uncas volunteered to accompany Mason's force, contributing one hundred men and twenty canoes to the enterprise. With English assistance, Uncas would drive the tributaries of one of his most important rivals out of the Pequot country.[12]

As Mason, Uncas, and their men approached the village, the Pequots fled, well remembering the lessons of Mystic, but they did not travel far. Uncas and the Mohegans began to gather the abundant supplies of corn they found in the abandoned wigwams. As they did so, sixty of the Pequots emerged from cover and charged at them. Uncas and his men had expected an assault. They waited until the attackers closed to thirty yards. Then, giving a war whoop, the Mohegans rushed to meet the charging Pequots. The fighting was light in terms of casualties, providing the English observers with more entertainment than apprehension. Mason slowly moved his men to cut off the Pequots' avenue of retreat, and as soon as the attackers saw this, they fled once again. Seven Pequots were captured. Uncas insisted on keeping the prisoners.[13]

By now the hour was late, and proper plundering took time. Uncas and Mason decided to spend the night in the village. The next morning they awoke to find a combined force of three hundred Narragansetts and Niantics on the opposite side of the river. A Narragansett translator yelled across the water to Mason. "The Pequots who live here are good men," he said, "and we will certainly fight for them and protect them." Mason, despite being badly outnumbered, was not in the least bit intimidated. "It is not far to the head of the creek," he yelled back. "I will meet you there, and you may do what you can at fighting." But to the Narragansetts and Niantics, this was not about the English, and they had no interest in a fight with Mason. "We will not fight the English," the Narragansett interpreter replied, "for they are spirits; but we will fight with Uncas." They wanted the Mohegans. Mason and the Connecticut men, they tried to point out, had intruded into an Indian conflict, with Uncas at its center. The Narragansetts and Niantics had, however, emerged from the Pequot War with a heightened respect for English manitou, a power that made the colonists seem "spirits." If the newcomers protected Uncas, the Narragansetts and Niantics recognized that there was little that they could do at this time. They watched helplessly as Mason torched the Pequots' village and returned with Uncas and the Mohegans—a force that together included far more Indians than Englishmen—westward to the Connecticut Valley.[14]

The Pawcatuck attack deeply upset the Narragansetts and Niantics. The prisoners Uncas took at Pawcatuck would, Mason hoped, be exchanged by the English with Ninigret for Pequots suspected of killing colonists during the Pequot War. Ninigret, supposedly, provided shelter to four Pequots accused of murdering Englishmen. A year later, however, Uncas still held these captives. Ninigret wanted them returned, but Mason was not able to persuade Uncas to consent to an exchange. According to Roger Williams, "the Hurries of the Natives thoughts and Consultations so continue" on how best to respond to Uncas's decision to hang on to the captives.[15]

The Niantics, who kept a "constant wach sence Conectecute took their men," felt that they had been treated unjustly. When Connecticut demanded that he turn over those Pequots suspected of killing Englishmen, Ninigret refused. William Coddington, the Antinomian follower of Anne Hutchinson who planted the English settlement at Newport in Rhode Island, told Governor Winthrop that the Niantics "would deliver up their 4, but they would have Ocas first deliver up his 8." Ninigret, Coddington said, needed to see "its Justice the English seekes."[16]

Miantonomi, hoping to preserve what remained of his relationship with the English while at the same time attempting to protect his Niantic allies, tried to persuade Ninigret and the Niantics "to be wise and yeald up their Pequts." The Connecticut men, after all, "intend present Revenge upon them." Only by surrendering the suspected killers could the Indians avoid the risk of war. Justice, Miantonomi pointed out, had little to do with it. Still, Ninigret refused. He told Miantonomi "that for so many lives as are taken away by the English or the Monhiggins or Pequts with them they will take revenge upon Mr. Throckmorton at Prudence, or Mr. Coddington etc. or Providence or elsewhere."[17]

When Roger Williams learned of Miantonomi's failure, he urged the Narragansett sachem "to desert the Nayantaquits in this business." From Miantonomi's perspective, however, Ninigret had done nothing wrong. He may have been "greedie upon the Prey against the English mind" and he may have spoken in a threatening manner, but the Niantics never "had shedd the blood of the English" and "never hurt the English." Furthermore, Miantonomi told Williams that "the English partialitie to all the Pequts at Monhiggin is so great and the Consequences so grievous" that all his appeals to persuade the Niantics to hand over the suspected Pequots "returne back . . . as Arrowes from a stone wall."[18]

Miantonomi soon developed a plan of his own, which was well received in Rhode Island. With Williams's blessings, Miantonomi traveled toward Shantok "with a sufficient company" to take into custody on his own the Pequot killers living under Uncas's protection. The Mohegan sachem preempted this threat through the skillful manufacture and exploitation of rumor. Uncas, the evidence suggests, sent some of his Pequot tributaries eastward carrying word to the Narragansetts of a sinister English scheme to capture Miantomomi. Somehow, Williams reported to John Winthrop, "Onkas sent word that it was your worships plot to bring" Miantonomi "into the snare at Monhiggin, that there the Qunnihticut English might fall upon him." However it was conveyed, the rumor must have seemed at least plausible to Miantonomi. The meetings leading up to the Hartford Treaty in 1638 had convinced him that the River Colony men thought little of him. And certainly Miantonomi had seen plenty of evidence demonstrating the close working relationship between Uncas and the "Qunnihticut English." He and his men turned back, fearful of the consequences that might come with attacking Shantok.[19]

While Uncas continued to outmaneuver his rivals, he informed John Winthrop at Massachusetts Bay and Governor John Haynes of Connecticut of "Indians plotting mischief against the English." Haynes heard of this plot directly from Uncas. Winthrop learned that his colony was in danger from William Bradford, who likely gathered his intelligence either from some of Uncas's Pequot tributaries or from the Wampanoag (or Pokanoket) sachem Massasoit, an enemy of Miantonomi who lived to the east of the Narragansetts. Bradford refused to say. The Plymouth governor told Winthrop, in June 1640, that the Narragansetts had sent a huge sum of wampum to the much-feared Mohawks, "to entreate their help against you, and your friends, if they see cause." The Mohawks, Bradford reported, had accepted this present and promised to assist the Narragansetts, "bidding them begine when they will, and they will be ready for them, and doe encourage them, with hope of successe."[20]

Connecticut wanted "to begine a warr with the Narragansetts speedilie," a preemptive strike designed to disarm a potentially lethal Indian alliance. The Boston men remained more skeptical about the rumors. Nonetheless, they summoned Miantonomi to meet with them in November 1640.[21] From the outset the meeting was tense. The magistrates rode out to greet Miantonomi at Roxbury. He recognized the Bay Colony's interpreter, a Pequot he did not trust. Miantonomi could not risk miscommunication given the charges he faced and, according to Winthrop, he "refused to treat with us by our Pequot interpreter." The Puritans, however, "being as resolute as he, refused any other interpreter, thinking it a dishonor to us to give so much way to them." The magistrates' arrogant behavior deeply offended Miantonomi, and on the journey from Roxbury to Boston the

Narragansett sachem, the Puritans believed, behaved in "a rude manner, without showing any respect or sign of thankfulness to the governor for his entertainment." The Englishmen refused to permit Miantonomi to dine with them until "he had acknowledged his failing." Miantonomi had attempted to force the English onto a middle ground. He told Winthrop, revealingly, "that when our men came to him, they were permitted to use their own fashions, and so he expected the same liberty with us." But Miantonomi simply lacked the power to persuade the English to behave in a manner he considered courteous and neighborly. He had to back down, to conform in this case, to English expectations.[22] Miantonomi approached the magistrates and agreed, reluctantly, to work with their interpreter, "a Pequod maid who could speak English perfectly" but whom he did not and could not trust. He agreed as well to an unreasonable English demand that he take responsibility for damage done to English livestock in Indian traps, even the traps of natives who did not recognize Miantonomi's authority. And then, after receiving so much abuse, Miantonomi finally addressed the accusations against him. He knew that Uncas was the source of the rumors. Miantonomi sensed that the Bay Colony officials did not trust Uncas entirely, and he asked that his accusers be brought before him. He demanded that if they could not prove their charges they should be put to death. His earnest defense convinced the Bay Colony men that there was little to worry about at this time from Miantonomi, and they let him return home. They did recognize his anger. Miantonomi carried with him a growing hatred of Uncas and, "in his breast, as an injury, the strict terms he was put to both in this, and the satisfaction he was urged to for not observing our custom in matter of manners."[23]

News of possible Narragansett conspiracies continued to circulate through the region. Dutch sources indicate that in 1641 Miantonomi traveled throughout Long Island with one hundred men, asking the Indians there to join him in "a general war against both the English and the Dutch." Some of the villagers Miantonomi visited afterward tried to destroy Dutch powder supplies. Then, reportedly, they tried to poison the Dutch West India Company's director-general, William Kieft, and to "enchant him by their devilry."[24]

The next year brought even more alarming news. An anonymous "relation" published in the summer of 1642 contained charges that

Miantonomi had attempted to forge an alliance with Indian bands "upon the maine from the Dutch to the Bay and all Indian sachems from the Eastward." Lion Gardener confirmed these reports. He had journeyed from Saybrook to the Montauk village at Meantecut on the eastern end of Long Island. Gardener knew that Miantonomi was in the village, but he did not learn of the Narragansetts' business until the Montauk sachem, his friend Waiandance, approached him.[25] "They say I must give no more wampum to the English," the sachem said. He wanted Gardener's advice. The Narragansetts, according to Waiandance, had combined themselves with Indians throughout the region "to cut off all the English." They would do so the next year, after harvest. They would go "by small companies to the chief men's houses by way of trading ... and should kill them in the houses and seize their weapons, and then others should be at hand to prosecute the massacre." The English commander recognized the seriousness of the situation, and he urged Waiandance to stall. He should promise Miantonomi an answer in one month's time, after his people considered the Narragansetts' proposals at length.[26]

Waiandance did as he was told, and Miantonomi returned one month later with gifts for the Montauks. His behavior shows that he had come to accept the Pequots' earlier bleak assessment of the Indian future in southern New England. Miantonomi called upon the Montauks to be "brethren and friends" with the Narragansetts, "for so are we all Indians as the English are, and say brother to one another." Only if Indians united could they effectively counter the English and their Indian allies. The Narragansett sachem reminded the Montauks that English settlement devastated and divided native communities. Unless they worked together, Miantonomi warned, "we shall all be gone shortly, for you know our fathers had plenty of deer and skins, our plains were full of deer, as also our woods, and of turkies; and our coves of fish and fowl." The English, having taken their land, "with scythes cut down the grass and with axes fell the trees; their cows and horses eat the grass, and their hogs spoil our clam banks, and we shall all be starved."

Some Indians had already lashed out at the European colonizers. Munsees in the Lower Hudson Valley, whom Miantonomi had visited in 1641 and 1642, pressed by expanding Dutch settlements and the heavy taxes of Director-General Kieft, attacked the Dutch West India

Company's settlers. The Dutch retaliated, beginning a series of raids and counter raids that continued for several years. Waiandance of the Montauks, however, had only five years before freed himself from domination by the Pequots, and had little interest in subordinating himself to the Narragansetts. Seeking to preserve his autonomy, he refused to join Miantonomi and promptly relayed the details of the "Plott" to Gardener at Saybrook.[27]

Other Indians spoke out as well. Uncas was among them. English magistrates in Connecticut, Massachusetts Bay, Plymouth, and New Haven "had many strong & concurrent Indian testimonies, from Long Island, Uncoway, Hartford, Kennibeck, and other parts, of Miantonomo's ambitious designes ... to make himselfe their universal Sagomore or Governour," by combining with the Mohawks and other Indians against the Mohegans and the English.[28]

In all these accounts the possibility of a Narragansett-Mohawk alliance loomed large, and Miantonomi often invoked the threat of Mohawk intervention in southern New England. The easternmost of the powerful Five Nations Confederacy in upstate New York, the Mohawks had for several years been sending small war parties into the Connecticut and other New England river valleys in search of furs, wampum, and captives. The English had an almost hysterical fear of the Mohawks and believed that a Narragansett-Mohawk union could seriously threaten the safety of their settlements. Thus the widespread reports of a Narragansett plot against the English terrified the colonists, and Connecticut, Plymouth, and Massachusetts Bay all placed themselves upon a war footing. The River Colony wanted to attack immediately but, again, the Bay Colony men were more cautious, summoning Miantonomi to Boston to answer the charges against him.[29]

The Narragansett sachem once again appeared before the Puritan magistrates. They informed him that they were aware of his plot and of his rumored plans to make his son a sachem over the Pequots, something that certainly would have challenged Uncas. Miantonomi, according to Winthrop, "was very deliberate and showed good understanding in the principles of justice and equity, and ingenuity withal" as he answered their questions. Once again, he demanded to be confronted by his accusers, "to the end, that if they could not make good what they had charged him with, that they might suffer what he was worthy of, and must have expected, if he had been found guilty, viz. Death." Miantonomi made his case well, and he blamed Uncas for spreading these rumors against him. He "offered to meet Onkus at Connecticut, or rather at Boston, and would prove to his face his treachery against the English."[30]

After considering Miantonomi's testimony and the intelligence that came from Connecticut, the Bay Colony men decided that there was "not sufficient ground for us to begin a war." All the turmoil, Winthrop thought, all the rumors, "might come out of the enmity which had been between Miantunnomoh and Onkus, who continually sought to discredit each other with the English." Winthrop noted that "like reports . . . had been raised almost every year since we came, and . . . they proved to be but reports, raised up by the opposite factions among the Indians." Winthrop also understood the difficulties of waging war against the Narragansetts. English raids, he noted, "might destroy some part of their corn and wigwams, and force them to fly into the woods . . . but the men would be still remaining to do us mischief, for they will never fight us in the open field." This consideration, too, weighed heavily, and ultimately decisively, on the magistrates' decision-making. Winthrop and the Bay Colony Council wrote to the more bellicose Connecticut men "to dissuade them from going forth" against the Narragansetts. "Upon receipt of this," Winthrop wrote, "they forebare to enter into war, but (it seemed) unwillingly, and as not well pleased with us."[31]

Despite his protestations, Miantonomi had embarked upon a path of resistance, attempting to organize Indians throughout the English colonies and New Netherland against the newcomers and their allies. Uncas, who followed a different course, one based more on accommodation than on resistance, had short-circuited Miantonomi's plans at every step. It was the Mohegan sachem after all, who benefited as Connecticut and Massachusetts limited the Narragansetts' claims to lands in the Pequot country and curtailed their autonomy. It was Uncas who informed English authorities of Miantonomi's every move, including his alliance with the Mohawks. Faced with the threat posed by the still more numerous and powerful Narragansetts, Uncas emphasized constantly that Miantonomi's actions threatened not only him but all of New England. Uncas hoped to convince colonial authorities that they faced an imminent attack from a powerful combined native force, thus prompting a preemptive attack against the conspirators. He clearly had convinced the River Colony men of the gravity of the situation, but elsewhere, even with the abundant evidence from other sources corroborating his story, English authorities remained reluctant to attack. Nonetheless, Uncas succeeded in raising suspicions that caused the English to watch Miantonomi closely and to interfere frequently in his conflict with the Mohegan sachem.[32]

In this atmosphere of escalating tension between the Narragansetts and Mohegans, Uncas was wounded in the first of several attempts upon his life. One evening at Shantok an unseen archer fired an arrow at him from out of the darkness. The missile struck him in the arm, but the injury was slight and soon healed. Uncas must have paused to survey the scene around him. There were many for whom his death would have provided cause for celebration. Miantonomi's hatred, by this point, was well known. Ninigret despised Uncas as well. And many Pequots must still have harbored deep within their hearts considerable resentment for the role Uncas had played in the killing of their kin. Uncas's suspicion quickly fell upon a young Pequot tributary who resided at Shantok and, Uncas's advisers noted, had been seen with an unusually large sum of wampum. Someone, they reasoned, must have paid the Pequot to assassinate Uncas. But who? Before Uncas could obtain an answer to that question, the suspect fled to the Narragansetts.[33]

Uncas reported all of this to authorities in the Bay Colony, who summoned Miantonomi and the suspected Pequot to Boston to explain what had happened. The Pequot, who had reportedly boasted that he had killed Uncas, according to Winthrop now argued that the Mohegan's wound was self-inflicted; Uncas, he said, "had hyred him to say he had shot and killed him." The Bay Colony magistrates did not believe this for a second, and they requested that Miantonomi allow them to turn the Pequot over to Uncas for punishment. The request placed Miantonomi in a difficult position. The Pequot had fled to him seeking his protection. To leave him with the English would look like a sign of weakness, and would have given the Pequot's kin good cause to question the value of their submission to the Narragansetts. After debating the matter with the authorities for some time, Miantonomi agreed that if the Bay Colony allowed him to carry the Pequot back to Narragansett, thus fulfilling his promise of protection, that he would then "send him safe to Uncas to be examined and punished." To this all parties agreed, and Miantonomi and the Pequot departed Boston.[34]

The Bay Colony magistrates suspected that Miantonomi had paid the Pequot to assassinate Uncas. Certainly he had motive. Uncas had grown rich from wampum, and had proven far more successful in collecting tribute from the Pequot survivors and incorporating them into Mohegan village communities. As reports arrived in Boston of attempts "to take away Uncas life by poyson and by sorcery," and that Miantonomi "and his confederates have both secretly and openly plotted and practised against the life of Uncas," the Puritans' suspicions and sense of insecurity grew.

•

By the summer of 1643, Uncas and Miantonomi had gone to war. The conflict began along the Connecticut River. There a sachem named Sequassen, an ally "and an intimate confederate with Miantonimo," ambushed Uncas and a company of Mohegans as they paddled down river. One prominent Mohegan warrior was killed. Uncas complained of what he considered an unwarranted attack to Governor Haynes of Connecticut, who promptly summoned both him and Sequassen to Hartford. Haynes hoped that he could work out a peaceful solution to the conflict. He feared that Connecticut colonists might be caught in the crossfire should an Indian war erupt. At the meeting, however, Uncas treated Sequassen with scorn and contempt. He demanded six of Sequassen's men as compensation for his slain kinsman. This was an unreasonable demand, and Haynes recognized that it would hardly play well with Sequassen. After some arm-twisting, he managed to persuade Uncas to reduce his demand to the Indian who had committed the crime. Sequassen, however, was now in no position to compromise. He had seen in alliance with the Narragansetts a means to resist Uncas's attempt to extend Mohegan influence over Indians in the Connecticut Valley. The assistance Miantonomi provided helped Sequassen preserve a considerable degree of autonomy, but now the Narragansetts wanted something in return. The Indian who had killed Uncas's man was a favorite of Miantonomi's. Sequassen, "expressing his dependence on Miantonimo," refused to surrender the suspect to Uncas. Haynes thus gave Uncas permission to right his wrongs in his own way.[35]

The Mohegan sachem did so quickly, leading a war party westward toward Sequassen's village. He and his men attacked, killing seven or eight of Sequassen's men and wounding several more. Thus they avenged the loss of the warrior Sequassen's men had killed along the river. They had, by a strictly Algonquian standard, restored balance to the world. But Uncas did not stop there. The Mohegans burned to the ground the wigwams in Sequassen's village. Uncas had incorporated into the Mohegans' way of war the scorched-earth tactics the English had first employed at Mystic.[36]

Miantonomi had to respond to Uncas's attack. Sequassen had done what he demanded. He was obligated to protect his allies, and Miantonomi already found others of his tributaries slipping away. Saconoco and Pumham, two sachems near Providence who had under them nearly three hundred men, "finding themselves overborne by Miantunnomoh," traveled to Massachusetts Bay and asked Governor Winthrop "to receive them under our government." A failure to defend Sequassen might cause him and others to drift away as well. With his eye on the Treaty of Hartford and his earlier agreement with Massachusetts Bay, Miantonomi inquired of Winthrop whether the Puritan elite "would not be offended, if he made war upon Onkus," fulfilling, as he thought, his obligation to seek Puritan approval before attacking the Mohegans. If he could attack the Mohegans with English support, he would. The Bay Colony governor replied that "if Onkus had done him or his friends wrong and would not give satisfaction, we should leave him to take his own course."[37]

Miantonomi had attempted to follow the rules of intercultural diplomacy that the English had dictated following the Pequot War, but Uncas sent word to the English that Miantonomi had never surrendered the Pequot suspected in the assassination attempt against him. Miantonomi, he revealed, had in fact killed the culprit. The magistrates could draw only one conclusion. "Fearing that his owne treachery would be discovered," Winthrop wrote, Miantonomi had "stopped the Pequot's mouth by cutting of his head." This convinced Winthrop of Miantonomi's involvement in the plot to assassinate Uncas, and caused him to withdraw his already qualified endorsement of Miantonomi's plan to attack the Mohegan sachem.[38]

The aggressiveness of Uncas and Miantonomi in pursuing their own objectives convinced colonial leaders of the necessity for a union to oversee Indian and frontier affairs more efficiently. The Confederation of New England, formed in 1643 directly in response to the conflict between the Mohegans and Narragansetts, defined itself as "a firme and perpetuall league of frendship and amytie for offence and defence, mutual advice and succour upon all just occations both for preservinge & propagating the truth and liberties of the Gospell and for their own mutuall safety and wellfare." Eight Commissioners of the United Colonies, drawn equally from Plymouth, Connecticut, New Haven, and Massachusetts Bay, would determine "how all the Jurisdiccons may carry it towards the Indians, that they neither grow insolent nor be injured without due sattisfaccon, lest war break in upon the Confederates through such miscarryages."[39]

But the commissioners could do little to prevent warfare between the Narragansetts and Mohegans. Late in the summer of 1643 Miantonomi, acting with what he considered Winthrop's consent, "took his owne course" with Uncas. He assembled a huge invasion force. Some accounts say as many as one thousand warriors joined Miantonomi to attack the Mohegans at Shantok, suggesting that Miantonomi had brought together a considerable number of allies. Uncas expected an assault to come, and he had posted sentinels in the hills that make up much of present-day Norwich. These scouts watched Miantonomi's huge force break from "the shadows of the woods" and cross the Shetucket River, a short distance above its junction with the Quinebaug. Some of the scouts rushed to Shantok to notify Uncas of the invasion; others moved through the tributary villages, gathering whatever warriors were available.[40]

Uncas knew from the reports his scouts carried that Miantonomi's force vastly outnumbered anything he could hope to put together. He hurried out of Shantok with perhaps four hundred warriors. They met Miantonomi at a site known as the "Sachem's Plain," about four miles from Shantok. There Uncas called for a parley. It was the first time the two sachems had spoken to each other since the signing of the Hartford Treaty, five years before. Uncas, described as a "tall and robust man in the prime of life," whose stature and strength often inspired comment, sized up the Narragansetts' sachem. Miantonomi, impatient of delays, and dressed in the chain mail corselet that had been given him by a Rhode Island settler, appeared confident. Uncas, according to a version of the battle written down in 1769, told Mian-tonomi that "you have got a Number of Brave men with you & so have I." He challenged his rival to personal combat, for he thought it "a Pitty that such Brave men should be Kill'd for a Quaril Between You and I. Come Like a Man as you Portend to be," Uncas continued, "and we will fight it out." If I lose, Uncas said, "my men shall be yours but if I kill you your men shall be mine."[41]

It was the legendary haughtiness of Uncas at its purest. He never expected the Narragansett sachem to accept his offer. Miantonomi had twice the number of warriors. The entire scheme was part of a larger plan by Uncas to regain some element of surprise, to begin the fight as much as possible on Mohegan terms. As soon as Miantonomi refused to stand and fight with Uncas alone, "the Mohegan sachem dropped to the ground, and his warriors," at this signal, "let fly a shower of arrows upon the Narragansetts." Miantonomi's forces "were taken by surprise, especially when Uncas, leaping to his feet in a shrill war whoop, led his men against the astonished Narra-gansetts, who at once took refuge in flight."[42]

As Miantonomi's men broke and fled, the Mohegans pursued them "through tangled thickets," one source said, "like wolves in chase of timid deer." Thirty Narragansetts died and many more were wounded in the rout. Miantonomi, burdened by his coat of mail, was overtaken with some of his closest advisers by a lesser Mohegan sachem named Tantaquidgeon, who held them until Uncas arrived.[43]

Miantonomi, expecting to die, sat down. He said nothing. Uncas taunted him. The captive's silence was troubling. "If you had taken me," Uncas said, "I would have besought you for my life." Still, Miantonomi said nothing, asked for nothing. He treated the Mohe-gan sachem with silent contempt. Uncas's anger grew. Miantonomi was demonstrating his power. He showed no fear of Uncas. The Mo-hegan sachem grabbed a tomahawk from one of his men. He broke open the skull of one of Miantonomi's followers and then another. Amid the slaughter Miantonomi remained silent.[44]

Uncas carried his prisoner to Shantok. There he received presents of wampum from the Narragansetts to ransom their leader. Uncas would not free his captive, but the evidence suggests that the two sachems spoke at some length during Miantonomi's short stay. The

Narragansett sachem, who likely had watched the Mohegans kill more of his men, proposed that Uncas join him in his alliance against the newcomers. If they worked together, he said, the Indians could drive out the Europeans who had set the world so far out of balance. Perhaps Miantonomi told Uncas of the Munsee raids against the Dutch to the west. He had visited those villages earlier and now, after finding their lands pressed upon by a growing Dutch population, their corn fields trampled by Dutch livestock, and their lives subject to Kieft's mind-numbing violence, they had destroyed farms along the lower reaches of the Hudson and sent the settlers scurrying for safety to the fort at New Amsterdam. The Mohegans could join in this resistance movement. Miantonomi would marry one of Uncas's daughters to cement the alliance. Meanwhile, Miantonomi's younger brother, Pessicus, would marry the daughter of the powerful Pokanoket sachem Massasoit. If consummated, the alliance would have brought together Indians from the Hudson River eastward to the Massachusetts Bay in a powerful union against the English and the Dutch. Uncas accepted more Narragansett wampum, suggesting that he at least considered the possibilities inherent in Miantonomi's offer.[45]

Yet in the end Uncas delivered his prisoner to the English authorities at Hartford, an act consistent with his 1638 agreement to wait for "advice from the English how to proceed against him for sundry treacherous attempts against his life." Uncas knew the newcomers well, understanding them better, perhaps, than any of his contemporaries. He had witnessed the fury of Puritan violence. He could not convince himself that an uprising against the English could succeed. And if it did bring some type of success, he did not see how it could serve the interests of his people. It would have been difficult for Uncas to trust Miantonomi, who had tried to assassinate him, and who had invaded his territory with an enormous fighting force. Few would have surrendered the power Uncas had at this moment, as he listened to Miantonomi desperately try to save his neck. Uncas chose to preserve the ties to the Connecticut English that thus far had served him and his people so well.[46]

At their first meeting in Boston in August, the Commissioners of the United Colonies, founded primarily with the goal of bringing order to the New England frontier, decided Miantonomi's fate. According to John Winthrop, one of their number, the commissioners were "all of opinion that it would not be safe to set him at liberty," but they also agreed that "neither had we sufficient ground for us to put him to death." The heart of the matter for the commissioners was the dispute between Uncas and the Narragansett sachem. And considering Miantonomi's "ambitious designes to make himself universall Sagomore or Governor of all these parts of the Countrey, of his treacherous plotts by guifts to engage all the Indians at once to cut of the whole body of the English in these parts which were further confirmed by the Indians Generall preparations, messages, & sundry insolencies and outrages by them committed against the English and such Indians as were subject or friends to the English," the commissioners concluded that "Uncas cannot be safe while Myantenemo lives." And without Uncas, they suggested, the commissioners feared for the security of their settlements.[47]

The commissioners as a result ruled that Uncas might "justly put such a false and bloodthirsty enemie to death." Once they all had safely returned to their homes, the Connecticut men would surrender Miantonomi to Uncas, who "should put him to death so soon as he came within his owne jurisdiction." They warned Uncas "that in the manner of his death all mercy and moderacion be shewed." Pilate-like, the commissioners repeatedly emphasized that Miantonomi would be put to death by a Mohegan sachem, and not an English court. The colonists would send observers to witness the execution, and the commissioners agreed that "if any Indians should invade him for it, we would send men to defend him."[48]

Many historians have found the commissioners' decision abhorrent. As one early historian of eastern Connecticut wrote, in words echoed by numerous later students of the period, the sentence passed upon Miantonomi was "one of the most flagrant acts of injustice and ingratitude that stands recorded against the English settlers."[49] The decision, however, accorded with the provisions of the Treaty of Hartford, negotiated five years earlier. Uncas, after capturing Miantonomi, had turned his prisoner over to the English before taking any action, as required by the treaty. Miantonomi had pursued Narragansett interests along the New England frontier. He had challenged

FIG. 5 "Killing Miantonomi," a depiction of the death of the Narragansett sachem, showing Uncas and his brother in the most unflattering terms. From G. H. Hollister, *The History of Connecticut*, 2 vols. (New Haven, 1855), 124. Reproduced by permission of The Huntington Library, San Marino, Calif.

the power of the united English in the region. He threatened English control of the frontier, providing the commissioners with cause to "take part . . . agaynst ye obstinate or refusing party." By sanctioning his murder, they demonstrated the violent lengths they would travel to secure some sense of order along the Anglo-Indian frontier. Uncas, in this sense had allowed himself to become the instrument of Puritan frontier management, helping the Saints as he eliminated a dangerous rival.[50]

Uncas traveled to Hartford to collect his prisoner. With several of his men and two English escorts, he marched Miantonomi eastward toward the Mohegan territory. When they reached "the Sachem's Plain," where Miantonomi had been captured, Uncas ordered his brother Wawequa to club the Narragansett sachem to death. A blow to the back of the head ended Miantonomi's life late in August 1643. And then, according to sources generally hostile to the Mohegan sachem, and originating well after the fact, Uncas cut a piece of flesh from Miantonomi's shoulder and ate it "with savage exultation." It was "the sweetest meat I ever ate," Uncas said. "It makes my heart strong."[51]

•

By killing Miantonomi, John Winthrop wrote, Uncas "slew an enemy, but not the enmity against him." Miantonomi's brother and successor, Pessicus, early in October sent a present of wampum to the Bay Colony governor, desiring "peace and friendship with us, and withal that we would not aid Onkus against him, whom he intended to make war upon in revenge of his brother's death."[52]

The commissioners believed that they must protect Uncas. If they did not, and "if Uncas be ruined," Winthrop wrote, the Indians of New England would "foresee their head, upon the next pretence shall be delivered to the wil of the Narrowgansets, with whom therefore they shall be forced so to complye (as they may) for theire future safety; & the English may not trust any Indian in the whole Country." Uncas, a "frend to the English," the commissioners promised "to assist and protect . . . as farr as they may against such vyolence." The Mohegan sachem, in the commissioners' eyes, had done their bidding. If he fell victim to Narragansett vengeance, other Indian leaders, potential allies, would be reluctant to provide assistance. Connecticut sent eight men, led by John Mason, to Shantok "to defend Uncas, and to doe such service in building or otherwise as shall be thought meet." New Haven sent six men more "to assist Unkas against the Narragansett Indians, whom he expects shortly to warr upon him."[53]

Uncas had defused what potentially might have been a lethal Indian conspiracy. He eliminated a native leader whom the English did not and could not trust. But killing Miantonomi, more than any other act, fixed Uncas's reputation in the eyes of his many detractors as a blood-drenched errand boy who relished the dirty work of his Puritan overlords, a serpentine manipulator who through lies and deceit brought down his chief native rival, or a hapless pawn in a vicious game of intercultural politics. For those inclined to such harsh assessments of Uncas's character, that he allegedly engaged in cannibalism after killing Miantonomi was not surprising.

Uncas always walked a treacherous path between the English, his native rivals, and his numerous tributaries. Each expected something from him, and the middle ground he occupied between these forces Uncas must have found a most fragile place. Intercultural violence was always a possibility, whether from the English or his native rivals, and Uncas took steps to insulate himself and his people from it. He worked to maintain the strength of the Mohegans through strategic marriage alliances with tributary peoples and the incorporation of others into "Mohegan" village communities. And he worked to harness the tremendous power of the English.

Mohegan interests and those of Connecticut had become closely intertwined since the close of the Pequot War. The River Colony leaders depended upon Uncas to keep them informed of conditions along the frontier, to provide them with intelligence on the actions of Indians who threatened the colony's security, and to furnish them with military assistance, as at Pawcatuck, in their attempts to establish English dominion. This gave Uncas certain benefits. He received Connecticut's support as he extended his influence over the Pequot survivors, and the River Colony men were always more willing to believe him than they were any of his rivals. Uncas fully recognized the power of the English, and he welcomed their intervention in his struggles against the Narragansetts. If the newcomers saw these actions as an attempt to bring order to the Anglo-American frontier, they also served Uncas's interests. That Uncas drew Connecticut, and then the United Colonies, into his conflict with the Narragansetts, however, should not mask the fact that he had become increasingly reliant upon the English for military assistance and protection. As Narragansett fury descended upon Shantok and as Miantonomi's successors sought to avenge their fallen leader, Uncas would find the challenge of balancing Mohegan and English interests increasingly difficult.

Chapter 5

To Have Revenge on Uncas

As the leaves fell and the first frosts appeared in 1643, hostile rumors once again circulated through the English colonies. The Narragansetts, led now by Canonicus and Pessicus, Miantonomi's young successor, needed to avenge their fallen leader. John Mason, late in 1643, whispered to Governor Winthrop news of "strong plottings and endeavours" by Sequassen and the Narragansett sachems to enlist the assistance of the much-feared Mohawks. "The thing certaine beyond scruple," he wrote, is "that theire intendments and resolucions are as well against the English as the Monheage." The Narragansetts, he believed, held both responsible for killing Miantonomi. Certainly Mason gathered this alarming news from Uncas. But other Englishmen, beyond Uncas's reach, chimed in as well. Edward Winslow of Plymouth, like Mason, heard "that the Narr. prepare for war, [and] that the Mowhakes have promised to aide them with a thousand men in the spring." The Mohawks expected Uncas to flee to his colonial protectors. "That done," Winslow concluded, "they purpose to send a message to the Engl. and demand Uncas." He feared the violent consequences should the English not comply. William Pynchon, from Springfield, who knew conditions along the frontier well, doubted that the Mohawks would aid the Narragansetts against the Mohegans but he was sure that the Narragansetts wanted war. Pynchon counseled patience and "delatory meanes," and he hoped that if such "meanes of delay be used but a while the edge of their revengefull desyer will soone be cooled."[1]

Not all colonial observers agreed about the immediacy of the Narragansett threat. The Rhode Island colonist and trader Benedict Arnold, who knew the Narragansetts well, wrote to Governor Winthrop that Canonicus was "in a sadde conditione" owing to "the distractions of his countrey" and the death of four of his children, including one "slayne this last sommer in fight by the Monaheagans." Canonicus, Arnold said, wanted the governor to know that the Narragansetts had not allied themselves with the Mohawks against the English. Arnold was a sympathetic observer, convinced that the Mohawks "will have noe hand in this bussinesse." Nonetheless, even he recognized "the vehement shew of desire that the Nanheaganssitts have to reveng on Woncas."[2]

Just two days after Arnold wrote to Winthrop in February 1644, Pessicus again sent a messenger to the Bay Colony governor. The messenger, Wahose, told Winthrop that the Narragansetts had done nothing yet to avenge Miantonomi, but that spring rapidly was approaching. Their sachem's soul wandered alone, unavenged, and they needed to act. Presenting the governor with a gift of wampum, Wahose asked Winthrop if the Bay Colony men "would grant their request, and suffer them to fight with Onkus" in the spring. Winthrop returned the wampum. He told Wahose that even if the Narragansetts "sent us 1000 fathom of wampum and 1000 skins, yet we would not do that which we judged to be unjust, viz to desert Onkus." Whether they liked it or not, Winthrop said, if the Narragansetts "made war upon Onkus, the English would all fall upon them."[3]

Frustrated by the Puritans' determination to insulate Uncas from Indian vengeance, the Narragansett sachems acted to free themselves from the controlling and oppressive hand of the United Colonies. In May Winthrop received word that the Narragansetts intended finally to wage war upon Uncas, their "inhumane and cruell adversary," and that they had formally submitted themselves "unto the protection, care, and government of that worthy and royal Prince, Charles, King of Great Britaine." Assisted by the Rhode Island colonist Samuel Gorton, a heretic from Puritan orthodoxy with his own reasons for undermining the Saints' authority, Canonicus and Pessicus informed Winthrop that the Narragansetts were "subjects now ... unto the same King and State yourselves are" and as such, that in any dispute "neither yourselves nor we are to be judges; and both of us are to have recourse and repair unto that honorable and just Government." They had gone over the commissioners' heads, in hopes that their direct submission to crown authority and claim to the equal protection of the munificence of the king would persuade the Puritans not to meddle in their conflict with Uncas and the Mohegans.[4]

The Bay Colony magistrates were not impressed, and they quickly sent messengers to the Narragansetts to demand an explanation for so brazen an act of Indian autonomy. Canonicus let the Puritan messengers stand in the rain, miserable and soaking, for two hours. After allowing them to suffer that indignity, Pessicus then announced to the Englishmen his intent to wage war upon Uncas by sending out raiding parties "to catch his men, and keep them from getting their living, etc."[5]

In June the Narragansett attacks began. The Narragansetts first fell upon an outlying group of Mohegans at a seasonal camp, killing six of Uncas's men and five women. They called upon their allies to join in assaults against the Mohegans. Uncas appealed immediately to the English for assistance. The commissioners sent ambassadors to the Narragansetts and the Mohegans in the fall, haplessly reminding them of their obligations under the Hartford Treaty. The Narragansetts told them once again that Uncas had treacherously accepted a ransom to spare Miantonomi's life, and then killed their sachem anyway. They wanted revenge. Uncas, who came before the commissioners with some of his principal advisers, denied the accusation and convinced the gathered Englishmen of his innocence. The commissioners "did not fynd of any proofe of any ransome agreed" and once again announced that if the Narragansetts "assault Uncas the English are engaged to assist" him. The commissioners did express willingness to listen to further complaints against Uncas should the Narragansetts uncover any evidence of his guilt, but it is clear that they did not expect any such information to surface.[6]

By the spring of 1645 the Narragansett sachems were willing to run the risk of defying the commissioners. Nothing more could be achieved through diplomacy. Pessicus and the other Narragansett sachems guided a series of war parties into the Mohegan homeland. Tantaquidgeon, the Mohegan who had captured Miantonomi in 1643, first felt the hard hand of vengeance when he received a life-threatening wound from a Narragansett warrior who attacked him in the night. Perhaps they had targeted him for special treatment. The raids overwhelmed Uncas and threw him on the defensive. Only once did he order a counterattack, and that ended badly as his men barely escaped from a well-executed Narragansett ambush.[7]

Uncas sent messengers to Boston, Hartford, Saybrook, and New

Haven, again pleading for assistance. By late spring Roger Williams could report that "the Flame of Warr rageth next dore unto us," as the Mohegans and Narragansetts had "deeply implunged themselves in Barbarous Slaughters." The Narragansett raids had taken an enormous toll, and the number of their allies grew with each success. Indians from Long Island had joined in the attacks upon Uncas, as had Ninigret and the Niantics. Some of Uncas's Pequot tributaries, lured by promises of wampum, had also shifted their allegiance to the Narragansetts. Uncas's enemies, moreover, had acquired more guns than the Mohegans, giving the Narragansetts an important tactical advantage. Thus when Thomas Peters and John Winthrop Jr. arrived at Shantok in May, the two Englishmen spent their time helping Uncas bury six warriors and treat the injuries of thirty-four others, "most of which were wounded with bullets." Uncas's Mohegan chiefdom, like that of Sassacus before him, seemed to be falling apart.[8]

English authorities in Hartford and Boston discussed possible courses of action. They decided to call an emergency meeting of the Commissioners of the United Colonies to gather in Boston late in July, specifically "in regard of the danger Uncas was in, & our Engagement to save him harmlesse from any damage for Miantonomo his deathe." A small force of River Colony men helped Uncas strengthen fortifications at Shantok. The Massachusetts Bay Colony sent messengers to order the Narragansetts "to desist from warr upon Uncas." Once again, Uncas and the dangers he and his followers confronted dominated the attention of the Puritan elite.[9]

Pessicus received the English messengers with "scorn and contempt." He told them he would "have no peace without Uncas his head." If the English intervened further, Pessicus warned, he would enlist the aid of the Mohawks against them. Together, "they would lay the English cattle on heaps as high as their houses." "No Englishman," he warned menacingly, "should stir out of his door to piss, but he should be killed."[10]

Threats of this temper inspired the commissioners to provide Uncas with the help he needed. Before the English could send any additional assistance, however, the Narragansetts settled into a siege of Shantok. Pessicus's attacks had driven Uncas and the Mohegans behind the palisades of their beleaguered fort. Now they had no place else to go, and they clearly were losing the war. Pessicus only needed to wait until the Mohegans' food ran out. Then he would have his enemy.

No one knows how long the siege lasted. The entire incident is shrouded in a veil of myth. On several occasions, we know, Uncas sent out messengers westward toward Saybrook, looking for English assistance in breaking the siege. Many of them did not make it, captured by Narragansett sentries. Uncas also left the fort at night, according to one old story, creeping southward along the banks of the Thames to a rocky point just above Massapeag Cove. There he waited on a ledge of rock known as the "Sachem's Chair," until nearly daybreak, listening for the sounds of English oars upon the water.[11]

Meanwhile the Narragansetts continued to snipe at any Mohegans who dared to show themselves. Wounded warriors filled the wigwams of Uncas and his brother Wawequa. According to a Mohegan oral tradition, one Narragansett warrior had climbed a tree that looked down upon Shantok, and from this height rained a destructive fire upon Uncas's followers. The Mohegans, who had a few guns of their own, shot back, but they failed to dislodge the sniper. The Narragansett taunted the Mohegans and continued to fire from this advantageous position. Uncas's men concluded that their assailant was a *moigu*, a witch. At length, according to the Mohegan interviewed by the anthropologist Frank Speck early in the twentieth century,

> a Mohegan who possessed power equal to that of the Narragansett appeared and ordered the others to desist. Taking a bullet from his pouch he swallowed it. Straightaway it came out of his naval. He swallowed it again and it came out of his naval. Again he did it, with the same result. Now he loaded his rifle with the charmed ball, and taking aim, fired at the man in the tree. The Narragansett dropped out of the branches, dead.

Mohegan warfare still existed in a realm of ritual and manitou.[12]

The Narragansetts lifted their siege of Shantok sometime in July. Thomas Leffingwell, an Englishman from Saybrook, learned of Uncas's desperate situation from a Mohegan messenger and managed to sail up the Thames and enter the fort undetected. The next morning Uncas ordered his men to raise a huge piece of beef above the palisades on a pole. The Narragansetts saw that supplies had arrived, and they saw the English boats on the river next to the fort. English assistance had saved Uncas from almost certain defeat.[13]

The Narragansetts failed to take Uncas at Shantok, but they continued to raid Mohegan villages into the summer. The Commissioners of the United Colonies, gathered finally at their emergency meeting in Boston, agreed that they must act decisively to assist Uncas and that they need not limit this aid to defending him in his fort. The present crisis justified whatever offensive action would preserve Uncas in "his liberty and estate." The commissioners quickly dispatched Lieutenant Humphrey Atherton and Sergeant John Davies from the Bay Colony to help garrison Shantok. Connecticut would send additional forces under John Mason. They would secure Uncas's fort, colonizing it in effect, until the commissioners assembled a military expedition to punish the Narragansetts.[14]

The commissioners ultimately gave Edward Gibbons of the Bay Colony command of the expedition against the Narragansetts and their allies, "who in making warr upon Uncas the Mohegan Sachem . . . became as well our enemies as his." A veritable who's who of New England's military history—Miles Standish of Plymouth, John Leverett of the Bay Colony, and Mason—would accompany Gibbons as the expedition's council of war. The commissioners ordered them "to provide for Uncas his future safety that his plantations be not invaded, that his men and Squawes may attend their planting, fishing, and other occasions without feare or injuries." Gibbons would demand a truce from the Narragansetts, and secure it by either taking the sons of their sachems hostage or acquiring "some considerable pt. of the Countrey" for "plantations wherein there may be a fort, built by the English and maintained (at least in part) by a tribute from the Narrohigganets." If Pessicus would not agree to these terms, the commissioners authorized Gibbons "to prosecute with force of Armes the said Narrohiganets & Nyanticks and all such as shall assiste them untill you may (through the Lords assistance) have subdued them or brought them to reason."[15]

The dispute between Uncas and Miantonomi's successors had now brought the Narragansetts and the English to the brink of war. The United Colonies had committed themselves to the defense of Uncas with the creation of a three hundred-man army. Pessicus and Canonicus, despite their threats and obvious defiance, remembered the fury Puritans could show in war, and must have considered that they would suffer a fate similar to that of the Pequots should the English invade. They backed down, reluctantly. Pessicus, two Narragansett interpreters, and Ninigret traveled to Boston before Gibbons's army could march. They were still angry. They began once again to "charg Uncas with sundry injuries he had donn them and particularly they alleagd his takeing a ransome for their Sachim's life." The commissioners had heard it all before. They told the sachems that "the charge trouble & disturbance which they had brought upon the Colonies by their unjust proceedings was great beside the damnage Uncas had sustayned." To purchase peace, the commissioners demanded that Pessicus pay a fine of two thousand fathoms of white wampum to the United Colonies (Uncas would get a share) and return to Uncas "all captives and canowes they had taken from him with repairation for his corne spoyled and destroyed in this war." Looking down the barrel of a gun, the Narragansetts and Niantics signed a coercive and humiliating treaty of peace, promising to "keep and mayntaine a firme and perpetuall peace both with all the English united Colonies . . . and with Uncas the Mohegan Sachem."[16]

•

Uncas's close alliance with Connecticut and the Commissioners of the United Colonies allowed him to survive the Narragansett raids of 1644 and 1645. The English considered, after all, his security as essential to their own. Yet even as Uncas fought off outsiders, the Mohegan sachem, presiding over a loose chiefdom of numerous village communities—many of these consisting of Pequots or former Pequot tributaries—had to withstand significant challenges from within.

In the spring of 1646 John Winthrop Jr. and Thomas Peters began to lay out a settlement at Nameag in the Pequot country. Uncas at first welcomed the English planters. He saw in the younger Winthrop and in Peters, who had helped treat the wounds of battle-weary Mohegans the year before, yet another English ally and, importantly, one willing to take up lands in between the Mohegan and Narragansett homelands. Uncas sent to Winthrop Jr. a gift of twenty-five fathoms of wampum to cement an alliance.[17]

The younger Winthrop had other ideas. He cultivated and expanded his own relationship with Robin Cassacinamon, the leader of the Nameag community. Cassacinamon had not participated in the Pequot War, and the Winthrop family trusted him. Some years before, he had lived with them in some capacity as a servant. That he and Winthrop Jr. would later develop so close a partnership suggests that Cassacinamon influenced the decision to plant the Puritan outpost at Nameag. With a deep-water port, lush natural resources, and friendly Indians, Nameag certainly must have appealed to Winthrop. And the presence of an English settlement guided by Englishmen who trusted him must have appealed to Cassacinamon. The Hartford Treaty had rendered the Nameag Pequots tributary to Uncas, and the Mohegan sachem was no easy overlord. Uncas, apparently, expected considerable sums of wampum from his subjects, and discontented Pequot tributaries had been slowly gathering at Nameag in the years after the war. Cassacinamon saw in alliance with the younger Winthrop a means to free himself from Uncas's control.[18]

The English settlers at Nameag spent their first winter living in Indian wigwams, in close proximity to Cassacinamon and his slowly growing number of followers. The presence of the settlers apparently emboldened the Pequot leader, who began to seek opportunities to defy Uncas and challenge his authority. His chance came early in the summer of 1646. The English settlers found themselves short of food. Thomas Peters asked Cassacinamon and Wequash Cook, the sachem of the Pequot community at Pawcatuck that paid its tribute to Ninigret, to hunt for them on the east side of the Thames River.[19]

These lands Uncas claimed by marriage to a Pequot woman, and he regarded the hunting party as trespassers on territory he controlled. Uncas gathered together a considerable number of warriors, at least three hundred, and set an ambush. He and his men fell upon Cassacinamon's unsuspecting party, terrifying the Pequots, who broke and ran. The Mohegans pursued them "with great clamor and fierceness back to the Plantation," beating those they caught and wounding a small number of those who failed to keep pace.[20]

Uncas and his warriors followed the fleeing Pequots into the settlement. The residents of Nameag, Pequot and English, awaited their fate. Some of Cassacinamon's men tried to hide in their houses. Uncas paced slowly, eyeing the frightened colonists. He gave an order in Mohegan, and his warriors rushed into the wigwams, and dragged the cowering Pequots out into the open. They plundered the Pequots of their goods, "takinge there wampum, there skins [and] there baskets." The Mohegans destroyed the wigwams, and then they began to humiliate the Pequots. They tore "there breaches there hose from there legs." They cut the Pequots' hair, a symbol of humiliation, and beat them "in a sore maner which was a sad sighte to the beholders." They shot at them, too, and forced them into the English houses, beating them some more, "friteinge the women and Children" still inside. They then began to threaten the English, pointing their guns at them, gathering their corn, plundering their wampum, and driving off their livestock. As the terrified English women and children cried, as Winthrop Jr. and the others said silent prayers, and as the Pequots cowered waiting for whatever came next, Uncas addressed his victims. He spoke in English, something he seldom did. Uncas wanted everyone at Nameag to understand him. "I am the victor," he said.[21]

No one was killed, though Uncas could easily have slaughtered every person in Nameag had he so desired. With the Nameag attack, he intended to send a clear message to the English, to his Indian tributaries, and to his native opponents. Uncas punished Cassacinamon for trespassing into Mohegan hunting territories, but also demonstrated to the Pequots that it was he, and not the English, to whom they must look for protection and security. They would not get away with doing what he had done. The younger Winthrop and his fellow settlers in the Pequot country learned that Uncas viewed them as a threat to the tributary relationship he had established between the Nameag Pequots and the Mohegans. They would interfere with it at their own considerable risk. At Nameag, Uncas expressed contempt for the English in word and deed. In so doing, he demonstrated to any who cared to see that he was much more than "a little dog" of the English.[22]

Uncas's assault upon Nameag clearly rattled the younger Winthrop, who asked his father for help. The Bay Colony governor responded to Uncas's provocations with threats of his own. If Uncas continued in this behavior, the elder Winthrop warned, "we shall leave you and your brother to shift for yourselves and then (we knowe) the Naragansets wilbe well pleased, and doe what we will require of them." Only if Uncas carried himself well "towards those of our new plantation and the Indians there" will the English "still re-

maine your friends." Thomas Stanton translated the letter "into Indian" so that it could be read to Uncas "by any Englishman and yet
hee understand it."[23]

Uncas worried little that the Narragansetts would join the English
against him, but he did fear diplomatic isolation. Although his attack
in the short term demonstrated his power over the Pequots at
Nameag, the Mohegan sachem nonetheless found himself with a
need to prove his fidelity to the English once again. In September the
Commissioners of the United Colonies met in New Haven. Uncas
made a point of joining them.

At New Haven Uncas confronted charges leveled by the supporters of John Winthrop Jr. that he had ruled tyrannically and cruelly
over the Nameag Pequots. He had transcended, with English support,
the usual constraints on a sachem's power. Now he must be reined
in. The younger Winthrop's intentions were clear: he wanted to separate the Nameag Pequots under Cassacinamon from Uncas's control. If the Pequots remained "under Uncas command, there wilbe
noe living for the English there," he wrote to Thomas Peters. For the
"greater security" of the plantation, the Indians must "have their
chiefe dependence upon the English."[24]

Before the commissioners, Uncas "acknowledged some miscar-
riages in vindicatinge his owne right soe neare the English plantations," but he also complained of the many wrongs he had suffered.
His Pequot tributaries, Uncas told the commissioners, "were drawne
from him under colloure of submitting to the English plantation at
Pequat." Others, with English encouragement, had "hunted within
his proper limits without his leave." Herein lay the heart of the matter for Uncas: the younger Winthrop and Peters were the real trouble-
makers, in attempting to destabilize and disrupt the network of
tributaries he had assembled since the close of the Pequot War.[25]

No Pequots were yet in attendance, so the commissioners decided
to delay any action until they could gather additional information.
Two days later, on September 16, a settler from the younger Winthrop's plantation named William Morton arrived with three Pequots from Nameag. Uncas had stayed in New Haven, and returned
again to meet with the commissioners. Morton brought forth a new
accusation against him. Wampushet, a Pequot shaman, had according to Morton been paid by Uncas to attack an Indian and lay the

blame for it on Wequash Cook. Wampushet did his job and collected his wampum, but soon felt himself overcome with guilt. "Troubled in conscience," Morton said, Wampushet "could have no rest until he had discovered Uncas to be the author" of the plot.[26]

The commissioners expressed their interest in Morton's charge, but the evidence against Uncas was terribly weak. Morton had heard none of this himself. Wampushet had told his story only to Robin Cassacinamon, Uncas's rival, and the leader of the Nameag Pequots did not attend the meeting of the commissioners. Thus the entire claim would rest upon the testimony given by Wampushet in New Haven. With Uncas staring at him intently, and with Thomas Stanton acting as his interpreter, Wampushet told his story. It was not the story that Morton and the Pequots expected. Much to Morton's surprise, Wampushet "cleared Uncas & cast the plot & guilt upon [Wequash] Cooke, & Robin Mr Winthrops Indyan." Stanton, stunned, repeated his questions. Morton, watching his credibility in the commissioners' eyes dissolve, angrily questioned him as well. The two Pequots who accompanied Wampushet to New Haven, one of whom was Cassacinamon's brother, were also infuriated, but Wampushet stuck to his story. The Pequots, he testified, had "promised him 25 fadome of wampum to cast the plot upon Uncas, & that the English Plantation & Pequots knew it." Uncas must have felt some sort of satisfaction, for Wampushet had vindicated Uncas's claims that the Pequots had wronged him. This sort of confusion and conflict, however, the commissioners hated, and they expressed their frustration to all at the meeting. They could not tell whether Uncas or Cassacinamon had hired Wampushet. They warned Uncas "if he expected any favore & respect from the English to have no hand in any such designes or other unjust wayes." Uncas certainly would have responded by assuring the English of his fidelity. He needed to say little else. Morton and the Pequots had wasted the commissioners' time. The commissioners sent them home without further hearing, and abandoned any effort to determine whether Wampushet had worked for Uncas or the Nameag Pequots.[27]

The commissioners finally proposed a solution to the conflict between Uncas and the Pequots in February 1647. They ruled that Cassacinamon and his followers would pay tribute to Uncas, "as is sett down by the Englishe in the Covenants betwixt them," and that they would "not offer wrong in word or deed to Uncos or his." Uncas apologized for his actions at Nameag, but did nothing more. After attacking an English settlement in the Pequot country and asserting his dominance over the tributary peoples there, he escaped with little more than the mildest of reprimands from the Commissioners of the United Colonies.[28]

The younger Winthrop, however, would not rest. Despite his father's advice to the contrary, he continued to pester the commissioners with complaints about Uncas. The English settlers at Nameag, he wrote, have been "most barbarously injuriously and unchristianly dealt withal" by the Mohegans, who "unnecessarily provoked and forced upon" them "a condition of absolute despaire." The younger Winthrop did not believe his settlement could prosper as long as Uncas dominated the Nameag Pequots.[29]

Certainly Robin Cassacinamon understood Winthrop's concerns, and saw in the Nameag English an ally in his struggle against Uncas. In July 1647, Cassacinamon, Obechiquod, also from Nameag, and other Pequots, who had no "hand in the shedding of English blood" during the Pequot War, petitioned the Commissioners of the United Colonies to take the Nameag Pequots "under the subjection of the English."[30]

Winthrop presented Cassacinamon's petition to the commissioners at their meeting in Boston. Foxon, Uncas's principal diplomat, attended the meeting to defend Uncas, who stood once again accused of a number of offenses. Uncas, the Pequots charged, had unjustly collected their wampum. He allowed his Mohegans to bully the Pequots, cheating them in games of chance. He also roughed up Pequot women. Sanaps, one of the petitioners, complained "that Uncas had abused his wife," and "that after she was soe defiled, she grew forward & he had little peace with her." Obechiquod "complained that Uncas had taken away his wife, defileth her, & keepeth her away per force." Finally, Cassacinamon accused Uncas of forcing his people to live in constant fear of violence.[31]

Sometime during the spring of 1647, Cassacinamon's petition continued, one of Uncas's children died. To allay his own grief and that of his wife, Uncas "commanded" that the Pequots give her a gift. The Pequots did so, one hundred fathom of wampum, which "pleased Uncas, & he promised thence forward to esteeme them as Mohegans."

According to Cassacinamon, the Nameag Pequots hoped that they finally had brokered a lasting peace with Uncas. Yet Cassacinamon was probably less than forthcoming, and he was not an obedient subject. He continued to pursue Pequot autonomy, so "a few days later," according to Cassacinamon's account, Uncas's brother Wawequa "came & tould them that Uncas & his Councell had determined to kill some of them. Cassacinamon and the Pequots were "much amased." He and his followers then "resolved to with draw from Uncas, & to submit themselves to the English" for protection. Uncas's behavior, the Pequots suggested, violated the traditional constraints placed upon the exercise of power by a sachem. When he learned that the Pequots had collected a gift of wampum to present to the English for this purpose, Uncas had escalated the conflict. He came with his warriors to Nameag and "called for those who promoted that businesse, threatninge to kill them." Uncas would employ force and coercion to keep his tributaries in line and maintain his power over them.[32]

The commissioners listened to these complaints. Foxon told Thomas Stanton, the commissioners' interpreter, that some of Cassacinamon's followers "were in Misticke fort in fight against the English & fled away in the smoake." Now they were Uncas's subjects, "an under people," Foxon said, who owed their sachem tribute and obedience. He denied Cassacinamon's charge that Uncas had ruled over them in a tyrannical manner, explaining that Uncas felt "justly offended" when the Pequots attempted to place themselves under the protection of the English. Though he conceded that the Mohegans had been "foolish and faulty in that rash assault" of the year before, Uncas, Foxon said unapologetically, was within his rights to punish the Pequots and maintain his authority over tributary communities.

Questioned about the "base and unsufferable outrage" that Uncas stood accused of committing upon Obechiquod's wife, Foxon "denied that Uncas either tooke, or kept away Obechiquod's wife by force, & affirmed that Obechiquod withdrawinge with other Pequats from Uncas, his wife refused to goe with him." Indian marriages operated on different assumptions from those of the English, and native women had considerable freedom when it came to dissolving a union. Obechiquod's wife, Foxon said, had left her husband, and Uncas could not be faulted for that. In response to a complaint from the younger Winthrop on behalf of the "Nepnet," or Nipmuck Indians that Wawequa and 130 men had "plundered them, takeinge from them 35 fathom of wampum, 10 copper kettles, 10 greate hempen baskets, many beare skins, deere skins, & other things to great value," Foxon asserted that this attack took place while Uncas and his closest advisers were at New Haven for the meeting of the commissioners. Uncas had nothing to do with Wawequa's raid, nor had he the power to prevent it, and he received no share of the plunder that his brother collected.[33]

Foxon served Uncas well. He had an answer to every accusation. The commissioners "founde no proff" to support Sanaps's accusation. Though they ordered Uncas to return Obechiquod's wife, they required that the Pequots "assist Uncas in his wars." They also required of Uncas "satisfaction for the outrages committed" by his brother. Uncas must learn to control Wawequa or "els wholly disert & leave him, that the Narragansett & others may require & recover satisfaction as they can." The commissioners did not, however, honor the Pequots' petition. They were to continue to pay tribute to Uncas. As long as they did so, Uncas should leave them alone.[34]

Uncas appears to have tried to live by the agreement. He got what he wanted from the commissioners. Still, a year later, he complained that the Pequots "resideing neere the English Plantations settled at Nameach" had not returned "to their former subjection." The commissioners called upon the younger Winthrop, whom in May the colony had commissioned "to execute the place of a Magestrate at Pequoyt," to assist in enforcing their order of the previous year.[35]

Winthrop Jr., however, was little help. He despised Uncas and had committed himself to Cassacinamon, aiding and abetting the latter's attempt to break free from Uncas. John Mason told Winthrop Jr. that he worried too much about the Mohegans, that they "are lymitted and cannot goe beyond their tether." Winthrop's father, from his deathbed, asked that his son "would strive no more about the Pequod Indians but leave them to the commissioners' order." No argument registered.[36] The commissioners had little choice but to give "Uncus leave by violence and constraint to enforce them," provided that he did not "disturbe" the English. The English were in no way "to hinder Onkus in the prosecution of this service." The Pequots should remain in "subjection" to Uncas.[37]

But the younger Winthrop interfered even in this, and by June 1649 Uncas complained that the English at Nameag refused to allow Mohegans to fish at their traditional sites along the Thames River. Settlers from the town had destroyed two Mohegan canoes, and their harvest from the spring spawning runs had been badly disrupted. Winthrop Jr. responded with countercharges. He petitioned the commissioners, making his strongest case yet as to why the English should support a Pequot community independent from the Mohegans. At some point in the future, Winthrop Jr. warned, the English will need help in "the discovery of . . . particular injuries to the persons, cattle or other goods of the English" and in "the discovery of any treacherous plots or what ever dangerous designes" Indians may contemplate. The southern New England frontier, he insisted, was still a dangerous place. If the Pequots remained subject to the Narragansetts or Mohegans, their dependence "should make them afraid to comply cordially and solely with the English eyther in discovery or any matters as above, or affording ther labours and helpe for hire, or principally in attending to any dispensations of such light of the glorious Gospell, which it may please the Lord in his good time to send amongst them." The English could prosper, plant secure settlements, and spread the reformed religion most easily with the assistance of reliable Indian allies.[38]

Winthrop Jr. asked that the commissioners might permit the Nameag Pequots, few in number, to live "free from tyranny and oppression." The commissioners recognized the need for some sort of compromise. They authorized Connecticut to set aside land for the Nameag Pequots to plant "under the shadow of English justice." They would remain, however, subjects of Uncas, who at last agreed that he would "carry himself towards them in a loving way" and "not tyranise over them."[39]

•

Uncas certainly had benefited from his close relationship with the Commissioners of the United Colonies. With their support and assistance, he had withstood the invasions launched by the Narragansetts. In his dispute with the younger John Winthrop and the Nameag Pequots, the commissioners had stood by him firmly until

1649. The compromise worked out that year, granting a sliver of autonomy to Cassacinamon's followers, still preserved the network of tributaries Uncas had assembled since the end of the Pequot War, twelve years before. Nonetheless, problems and challenges continued to present themselves to the Mohegan sachem, who confronted a growing number of opponents intent on disrupting his connections to the English.

For example, as Uncas struggled to maintain his dominance over Cassacinamon and his followers at Nameag, he faced challenges to the west, along the Connecticut River. There, Sequassen, whom Uncas had attacked three years before, concocted a plot to take revenge upon the Mohegan sachem and his English defenders.

In September 1646, the Commissioners of the United Colonies learned that Sequassen had hired Watchibrok, an Indian who "was almost ruined, & the English at Hartford the cause of it," to kill Edward Hopkins, John Haynes, and Joseph Whiting, all River Colony magistrates. Sequassen gave to the desperate Watchibrok three girdles of wampum, and promised him more once he committed the crime. Afterward, Watchibrok would "give it out that Unkus had hired him for so much wampum," in hope that doing so "would sett the English against Unkus" and "the said Sequassen should rise again."[40]

Watchibrok, it seems, had little left to lose, but at some point it dawned on him that following Sequassen's lead posed a significant threat to his health. He recognized that if he killed an Englishman "he should goe in feare of death all the dayes of his life." Turning coat was much safer. By revealing the plot to the English, Watchibrok hoped to find favor with them, "and he thought the favoure of the English with security would be better to him than Sequason's wampam with feare and danger."[41]

The commissioners summoned Sequassen to answer Watchibrok's accusation, but he refused to appear. Uncas knew that Sequassen had found shelter among the Pocumtucks. At the commissioners' behest, he led a band of warriors northward, "surprised" Sequassen "in the night, and brought him to Hartford, where he was kept in prison divers weeks." The Hartford magistrates tried Sequassen but lacked sufficient evidence to convict him. He was released.[42]

While Uncas wrestled Sequassen out of Pocumtuck, the Narragansetts, too, worked to acquire their pound of Mohegan flesh and to have revenge upon Uncas. Ignoring the coercive treaty of 1645, the Narragansetts had never delivered the hostages they had promised to the commissioners, restored Uncas's captives and canoes, or paid the fine in wampum they had been assessed to defray the costs of Uncas's defense. The commissioners needed an explanation. They summoned the Narragansetts to attend the meeting of the United Colonies in Boston in August 1647. They feared that the Narragansetts had "bene plottinge & by presents of wampum, ingaginge the Indyans rounde aboute to combine with them against the English Colonies in war." Pessicus did not attend; the commissioners assumed he was afraid, but he may have been mourning the death of Canonicus, who had died "a very old man," late in May or early in June.[43]

The effective power vacuum among the Narragansetts created an opportunity for the Niantic sachem Ninigret to assume a leading role in the community's affairs. Related by marriage to Canonicus, Ninigret traveled to Boston with a guarantee of safe passage from John Winthrop Jr. Ninigret had ingratiated himself with the promoters of the settlement at Nameag. He told the younger Winthrop that his wife and children need not fear him as they did Uncas. In February he had told Winthrop Jr. "that he was resolved to be acquainted" with the English "and keepe peace with them and doe whatsoever they shall require in reason."[44]

Ninigret's definition of the reasonable always would differ from that of the commissioners. Made to answer for the Narragansetts' failure to pay the fine in wampum, Ninigret feigned ignorance. He tested the commissioners' patience. Again facing threats of violence, Ninigret, acting for the Narragansetts, sent out messengers to collect the wampum. They returned with only two hundred fathoms, a small portion of what the Narragansetts still owed. The commissioners then gave Ninigret twenty days to pay off the debt. He told them what they wanted to hear, left Boston, and made little effort to pay the fine.[45]

Within a year, the commissioners concluded that the Narragansetts' determination not to pay their debt to the United Colonies was only one part of a much larger and more dangerous plot against Uncas and his English allies. The Narragansetts had used their wampum to assemble an enormous anti-Mohegan force. Nearly one thousand Indians, more than three hundred of them armed with guns, bullets, and powder, assembled at Pocumtuck in the summer of 1648. Despite the release of Sequassen two years before, the Pocumtucks in 1648 remained angry that Uncas had led a successful raid against them. According to John Winthrop, they had taken "it so to heart against Uncas as they intended to make war upon him." Mohawks had traveled to Pocumtuck as well. Uncas knew that the powerful Iroquois chiefdom contemplated sending aid to the Narragansetts and their allies, and he let the Mohawks know that if they went to Pocumtuck, he would "set his ground with gobbets of their flesh." His threats carried little weight, however. The Mohawk party arrived. So did large contingents from the Narragansetts and Niantics. Uncas sped this information to the commissioners, who could only conclude that Ninigret and Pessicus "have by wampum hired the Mouhackes and Pocuntock Indians and others to cut of Unquas and his people, and in case the English defend him, then to fight with the English."[46]

The Narragansetts prepared for war, "with draweing theire ould men theire weomen and children into swampes, hideing theire Corne, etc." Frightened, the commissioners sent several agents to Pocumtuck to defuse so dangerous a situation. Roger Williams traveled along, serving as an interpreter. Ninigret, Pessicus, and Mixanno, Canonicus's son, told the Englishmen that the Narragansetts had not given "a peny to hire" the Mohawks. That, they said, had been done by Sequassen. Williams, at least, believed that the Narragansetts wanted "to hould friendship with both the English and the Mauguawogs together." He did not think they ever "intended hurt against the English." As for the Mohegans, the Narragansetts "promised that they would not meddle with Uncas," and that they would "not stir up any other against him, before they had paid all their debt of wampum to the English." They would then "require satisfaction for all the wrongs Uncas had done them, and if the English would not see them satisfied, they would consider what to do." They knew that "if they made war upon Uncas, the English must defend him." Ninigret, Pessicus, and Mixanno told the English messengers that they had decided not to fight at this time. They knew the English "to be a wise and warlike people, and they intended not to fall out with them," and that "therefore for the present they would desist, and consider further of the matter." They would not challenge the Anglo-Mohegan alliance. This satisfied the elder Winthrop. "The Lord," he wrote with obvious gratitude, "delivered us from that war, which must needs have been very dangerous, especially to our brethren of Connecticut."[47]

Ninigret backed down when confronted by the commissioners in 1648, but he continued to challenge Uncas for power in southern New England at every opportunity. Uncas had worked out an accord with the Pequots who lived at Pawcatuck, and their leader, Wequash Cook, to hunt together on their lands while excluding other Indians. Ninigret had since 1638 claimed these Pequots as his tributaries and claimed a right to hunt on their lands. He believed that Wequash Cook, like Uncas, had elevated himself to a status that he did not deserve, and was using the Mohegan sachem to break free from Niantic control.[48]

Ninigret had few friends in the colonies, and Wequash Cook had the support in this instance of both John Winthrops, John Mason, and Uncas. When word arrived that Ninigret would hunt at Pawcatuck anyway, Mason angrily wrote to Roger Williams demanding that he "forbid the Narigansetts to hunt at Pequot, and to assure them of his visiting of them if they so did." The younger Winthrop was less worried. He told Mason that rumors of Ninigret's activity in the region had been stirred up by Uncas, who claimed a right to hunt Pequot lands "from hence to New Haven." One must listen more critically to the "surmises and jealousies of the Mohegans." Better to rest satisfied, given that there was little the English could do to prevent Narragansett hunting in the lands in question, that Ninigret had at least asked for permission and announced his intent in advance.[49]

The English must have felt exasperated as they looked out at the frontiers all about them. Since the end of the Pequot War they had tried to bring order to the region and to work out some type of agreement between Uncas and his many rivals. Nothing worked, and at every meeting of the United Colonies, the commissioners found themselves struggling to protect the Mohegans from a myriad of enemies. In 1649 Uncas again complained that the Narragansetts and their allies had plotted against him. Early in the year they had tried to kill him using witchcraft, he said. In April they tried more direct and violent means. An English ship under the command of a Captain Smith sailed up the Thames River, anchoring near Shantok. Uncas, expecting to trade with the voyagers, paddled out with several of his men and boarded the vessel. A Narragansett Indian named Cuttaquin, already on board the English craft, lunged at Uncas and "suddenly ran a sword into his breast." Uncas "groaned and cried out that the Narrigansett had killed him."[50]

The wound initially appeared serious, and Uncas by all accounts lost a lot of blood. Still, he survived. His followers seized Cuttaquin. They cut off the forefingers on both his hands, ensuring that he would never hold a sword against their sachem again. John Mason interrogated the would-be assassin, and learned that he had been hired to kill Uncas two years before by Ninigret, Pessicus, and Mixanno. He "was to have for his paynes 1000 fathom of wampum of which he already received two hundred." Cuttaquin also told Mason "that hee was frequently urged by them to doe the thing especially seaven dayes before the act."[51] Roger Williams smelled a rat. He believed that "many circumstances look earnestly toward a plot of Onkas." The wound was small, Williams argued, and located in a safe place. Perhaps it was self-inflicted. Williams could not help but think of the assassination attempt in 1642 when, the Narragansetts believed, Uncas feigned injury to implicate Miantonomi. Cuttaquin, moreover, Williams knew "to be of a gentle and peaceable spirit and ... never forth with them in their wars." And even if Cuttaquin wanted Uncas dead, it made little sense to attack him in broad daylight on a boat at Mohegan, where capture and death were certain. The Narragansett sachems denied that they had ever paid Cuttaquin to assassinate Uncas, and they advanced an explanation of their own that Williams, at least, found plausible. The Narragansetts by 1649 had nearly paid off their debt to the United Colonies, freeing them, they believed, to attack Uncas. "Knowing how neere he is to a Triall (after the payment finished) (according to the English sachems promise)," the Narragansett sachems argued that Uncas "projected this villanie, etc., to render the Narigansetts still odious to the English."[52]

The commissioners thought Williams's theory far-fetched. Cuttaquin, after all, had confessed. They summoned Ninigret to Boston to explain himself. He continued to deny any involvement in a plot against Uncas. Indeed, Ninigret conceded, Cuttaquin had confessed and had accused the Narragansetts of hiring him, but only after he had been "drawen thereunto by torture from the Moheges." Ninigret pointed to Cuttaquin's hands, to the two missing index fingers. The commissioners did not believe him. Ninigret had no credibility left with them, and Cuttaquin himself "affirmed hee was necessitated to attempt that murtherous acte by the desperateness of his owne condition." The commissioners decided to turn Cuttaquin over to the Mohegans. Uncas could punish him as he saw fit. Uncas carried his prisoner back to Shantok, where he and his followers put the would-be assassin to death.[53]

Yet another near miss. Uncas enjoyed the support he received from the English colonial authorities, but neither the River Colony magistrates nor the Commissioners of the United Colonies could provide him with peace and stability. Indians in southern New England feared Puritan military might, but they did not otherwise respect English authority. Repeated demands that Indians leave Uncas alone continually fell upon deaf ears.

In September 1650, for instance, Uncas complained to the commissioners that one of his tributaries, a Long Island sachem named Ascassasotic, "had killed som of the said Uncus his men, bewitched divers others, and himselfe allso." The same month Sequassen asked the commissioners for permission to return from an exile among the Mohawks to his lands above Hartford. The commissioners' decision to allow Sequassen to return angered Uncas. The Mohegan sachem "overcame him and Conquered his Countrey." Now Uncas felt himself wronged "in that Sequassen, as hee is enformed, is set up and endeavoured to bee made a great Sachem, notwithstanding hee hath refused to pay an acknowledgement of wampum to him according to Engagements." Without English assistance, Uncas exerted little real control over outlying tributary communities.[54]

Still, Uncas always viewed his relationship with the colonists in conditional terms, and he always weighed the costs and benefits of alliance with the English. In September 1651, the commissioners met with "Uncus the Moheggin Sagamore with severall of his men, Wequash Cooke came allsoe and som of Ninnacrafts men with Robert [Cassacinamon] a Pequot Indian sometimes a servant to Mr. Winthrop and some with him, and some Pequots living on Long Island." The Indians brought to the commissioners arrearages in wampum they owed as tribute. None of them paid it gladly, and Uncas, especially, "demaunded why this Tribute was Required; how long it should continew and whether the children to bee born hereafter were to pay it."[55]

The English documents surviving from these years can allow one to sketch an outline of Uncas's activities: where he was, with whom he met, with whom he fought, and, at times, what he talked about. The challenge comes in trying to see in Uncas more than the sum of his appearances before the commissioners and various colonial magistrates. The evidence is there, but it is fleeting, allowing us only glimpses into Uncas's world. We can see, for instance, if we look carefully, a father and husband who mourned, with one of his wives, the death of a child carried away, perhaps, by one of the European diseases that continued to prey upon southern New England Algonquians with a ruthless efficiency. We can see Uncas fail to find a husband for a daughter mutilated by disease, left with "sore eyes" that made her odious to potential suitors. We can see a factionalized Mohegan "tribe," as Uncas's brother Wawequa aggressively and violently pursued his own interests along the frontier with a considerable degree of freedom. We can listen to Uncas struggle to deliver his boastful message in English to the Nameag Pequots and their Puritan protectors, but the rest of the time watch him speaking comfortably his own language, leaving it for the English to scramble and find interpreters. We can look at the mark of Uncas, the glyph he used in place of a signature on many historical documents. The figure he drew is that of a powerful man, with an enormous upper torso and a strong heart beating inside. The mark of Uncas denotes power, that here is a man with whom the English must reckon carefully. And yet, as we listen to a boastful and prideful sachem we can watch as English troops garrison and fortify Shantok. We read of Uncas's frequent appeals to the commissioners and the River Colony men to defend him from his attackers.

The relationship between Uncas and the English defies easy categorization. Clearly no pawn, Uncas nonetheless by the early 1650s relied upon the English for protection, and he maintained his influence and power over the wampum-producing communities in southern New England with Puritan assistance. The English, whether in the

Massachusetts Bay Colony, Connecticut, or in the meetings of the Commissioners of the United Colonies, were never entirely comfortable with Uncas, and they feared the consequences of his autonomy. But they had few alternatives. Uncas still had many followers, and he had demonstrated his allegiance to the English on a number of occasions. To inform themselves about affairs in the Indian communities lining the periphery of their settlements, to ready themselves for whatever threat awaited, they needed Indian allies. Uncas willingly and ruthlessly played that role, but his price for doing so was high.

•

Take, for example, a series of events that began to unfold in 1652. Ninigret and his followers complained of the abuses, real and imagined, that they suffered at the hands of Uncas. Ninigret presented before the commissioners at their annual meeting Pemumbans, a Pequot he accused of "being hired by Uncas to poison" him. Awashaw, a Narragansett, complained at the same meeting that Wawequa had "robbed Ninigrett's men, and some other of the Sachems' men of Narragansett, and took from them much goods, trays, pots, pans, &c so many as they cannot name." Wawequa and his followers, Awashaw added, had killed a Narragansett warrior. Awashaw also repeated the Narragansetts' older claim that Uncas had accepted a ransom for Miantonomi's life.[56]

The commissioners showed little sympathy toward the Niantic and Narragansett complaints. The evidence against Pemumbans was too weak to proceed against him. The commissioners did not trust Ninigret, and he never managed to rise above their suspicions. As with Miantonomi, Uncas reported every move Ninigret made, creating an atmosphere of considerable fear and distrust. In the spring of 1653, for example, the commissioners learned from Governor John Haynes in Connecticut of a plot directed by Peter Stuyvesant, the director general of the Dutch Colony at New Netherland. According to Haynes's report, Stuyvesant had encouraged local Indians to join in an attack against English colonists on Long Island and in Connecticut. English suspicion centered immediately upon Ninigret who, Haynes believed, had been provided by the Dutch with guns, powder, and shot. Ninigret, Haynes learned, had spent the winter of 1652/53 on Manhattan. With the Netherlands and England at war on the high seas and in Europe, such reports demanded further investigation.[57]

The Connecticut magistrates already had decided "that the neighboring Indians to the severall Plantatytions within this Jurisdiction should be required to give an evident testimonye of their fidelity to the English" during this time of war, even if that meant they had to deliver "their gunnes & other armes to the Governour or Magistrates." The commissioners followed the River Colony's lead by directing a list of queries to Ninigret, Pessicus, and Mixanno, demanding the sachems' response to reports "that the Duch Govr. Hath stured up youer selfe and severall other Sachems by perswasions and gifts to fight with and make war upon our selves and other English."[58]

The Narragansetts responded in writing, their answers carried to Boston by Awashaw. Mixanno claimed that he knew "of noe such plot that is entended or plotted by the Dutch Governor against the English my frinds." Though he was poor, Mixanno said that "it is not goods, guns, powder nor shott that shall draw me to such a plot as this against the English my frinds." Ninigret, who never seemed intimidated by English colonial officials, responded with questions of his own:

> Doe the English thinke that I thinke they bee asleep and suffer mee to doe them wronge[?] doe not wee know the English are not a sleepy people[?]; the English make queries for guns, powder and shott and swords for such a designe; doe they think wee are mad to sell our lives and the lives of our wives and children and all our kindred and to have our countrey destroyed for a few guns powder shott and swords[?] what will they doe us good when we are dead[?]

Ninigret admitted that he had spent part of the winter at Manhattan. He had been ill and "went thether to take Phisicke for my health." According to Awashaw, Ninigret had visited a French physician on the island, carrying wampum with him to the doctor. He also delivered a gift of wampum as a courtesy to Director General Stuyvesant, but "found noe such entertainment from the Duch Governor when I was there to give mee any Incorragement to sturr mee upp to such a league against the English my frinds."[59]

The Narragansett sachems demanded to know their accusers, and the commissioners made clear that the charges had originated with Uncas, who had relayed news of the plot to Governor Haynes. According to the commissioners, Uncas told Haynes "that Ninnigrett Sachem of the Niantick Narragansetts went this winter to the Monhatoes and the Duch Governor with whome hee made a league himselfe gave the Duch Govr a large present of wampam and the Governor gave him again twenty guns and a great box of powder and bullets." Uncas also accused Ninigret of meeting with Indian leaders from the lower Hudson Valley, where he "made an ample exclamation against the English and Uncas desiring theire Aide and Assistance against them." Ninigret then reportedly hired "an artist both in magic and poison" to assassinate Uncas.[60]

Uncas, for his part, claimed to have learned with certainty of the plot when he and his men captured a party of seven Indians, including "the Powawgh and poisoner." Uncas quickly killed the would-be assassin, "fearing hee might escape and doe mischeife." Two of the other Indians in the captured party, in the presence of Governor Haynes and in real fear for their lives, "confessed" that a plot existed. Many other witnesses came forward, painting an alarming picture of a Dutch-Indian conspiracy directed against the colonists. Addam, an Indian "whoe spake English very well," had seen Ninigret, with a huge sum of wampum, in the presence of Director General Stuyvesant. Other Indians—a "sagamore upon Longe Island whoe professes Respects to the English," and an "Indian squaw in the former war with the Pequots found trusty to the English," corroborated portions of Uncas's account. So too, apparently, did "9 Indian Sagamores whoe live about the Monhatoes." Benjamin Crane, an Englishman who lived with his Dutch wife along the Hudson, testified that Stuyvesant had hired "three sagamores that live up the Countrey . . . to cutt of the English and kill all they could." Henry Ackerly of Stamford pointed out that Stuyvesant had approached Indians in the vicinity of Manhattan and "did sett them on to burne the houses poison the waters and kill the English." Powanege and Ronnessoke, both lower Hudson Valley Indians, testified that Dutch and Indian forces would hit targets in Connecticut. According to an Indian named Coco, Stuyvesant ordered his native allies to see that "Uncas bee killed."[61]

A good number of witnesses had come forward against Ninigret.

His only English supporters could not help him, for they were Rhode Islanders who had been excluded for religious and political reasons from the New England Confederation. Ninigret and the Narragansetts had long been objects of colonial suspicion. They stood accused of plotting against the English in the past, and their hatred of Uncas was well known. Uncas's report, then, was received by commissioners willing to believe the worst about the Narragansetts.

Ninigret, Pessicus, and Mixanno all emphatically denied that they had joined in a conspiracy against the English. Director General Stuyvesant, too, denied that such a plot existed. We can hardly expect him and the sachems to have done otherwise. But is there more to the story? Ninigret certainly was shrewd enough to recognize the grave risks participating in such a plot would entail. And what of the evidence produced to support Uncas's charges? The alleged assassin, of course, never told his story: Uncas killed him before that could happen. The "confessions," of which we hear nothing, were coerced at best. Of the other witnesses, only Ronnessoke said that Ninigret and his followers would attack "Stanford and other smalle plantations of the mayne." Addam said only that he had seen Ninigret with Stuyvesant. The Long Island sagamore who supposedly corroborated Uncas's story said only that "the Duch counseled the Indians to fier some of the English houses in all partes and when the English came forth to quench them then to shot them." All this bore evidence of sinister Dutch activity, certainly, but little from natives in the area linking Ninigret specifically with the plot. The Pequot woman and the sagamores from Manhattan added little, testifying only that Ninigret went to Manhattan but nothing more.[62]

The Dutch director general attempted to lure Indians into an anti-English alliance during a period of Anglo-Dutch warfare; Ninigret, long distrusted by the English, at the same time journeyed to New Amsterdam. Without question, a strong circumstantial case can be made. Still, the best evidence linking Ninigret to the plot came from his embattled archrival, Uncas, who we know constantly reported the misdeeds of his enemies to the English. We must at least consider that Uncas may have embellished or trumped up charges against his principal native rival.

And whatever the truth of Uncas's accusation against Ninigret, the result of his information is clear. Uncas provided the leaders of Connecticut with intelligence that they carried before the commissioners. Uncas, the colonists' ally in their attempt to bring order to the southern New England frontier, prompted an investigation that increased English distrust of Ninigret and brought the United Colonies once again to the brink of war.

The spark occurred in the fall of 1653. Ascassasotic, "a very inferiour sachem" and former Mohegan tributary, whom Roger Williams considered "proud and foolish," killed several of Ninigret's men. The Niantics retaliated in force, drawing upon their alliances with the Pocumtucks and Mohawks.[63] The commissioners sent Thomas Stanton and other messengers in September to demand that the captives Ninigret seized on Long Island be restored to their villages. The Narragansetts and Niantics were in no mood to listen to the English. They insulted Stanton, "using scornfull words saying they cared not for the English nor did they feare them." Stanton's response was vilent and unambiguous: he "struck att the wolfes tayle on the head of a Pequot Indian most active in the said offencive Carriadge" with his sword. He quickly realized his mistake. The Pequot "drew his bow with an arrow in it." "A Narragansett Captaine" pointed a gun at Stanton. With the Niantics and Narragansetts behaving so tumultuously, Stanton resolved to deliver his message, even if it cost him his life. Ninigret heard him out and then responded by asking him pointedly "what the English had to doe to desire or demaund his prisoners and tould Thomas they should neither see them nor have them." While Stanton and Ninigret exchanged words, "the Indians then surrounded them and sum of them charged theire Guns with powder and bullets and some primed their guns." Ninigret had provided many of the commissioners with ample grounds for war.[64]

Only the unwillingness of Massachusetts's two commissioners to commit to an Indian war while England and the Netherlands were locked in combat averted hostilities in 1653. In the meantime, neither Uncas nor the Niantics and Narragansetts sat passively. Uncas, in the spring of 1654, sent messengers to Ascassasotic with word that "if he would send him wampum, he would avenge him upon the Narhigganset, for the blood they shed last year." He offered, in effect, to reestablish a tributary relationship with the Long Islanders and to protect them, as a good sachem should, from their native enemies. In

April Uncas attacked a Nipmuck community that had shifted its allegiance to the Narragansetts. Ninigret responded by sending a gift of wampum to the Nipmucks, as well as to the Pocumtucks and other Connecticut River villages, to enlist their assistance against the Long Islanders and, presumably, Uncas.[65]

Ninigret also continued his attacks on the Long Islanders. He was by now furious. "If [your] governor's son were slain," he asked an English messenger, "would you ask counsel of another nation how and when to right yourselves?" Ninigret well knew that they would not. He pointed out angrily that sixty of his men had been slain. He needed to avenge them to restore balance to his world, and desired "that the English will let him alone."[66]

When the Anglo-Dutch conflict ended in 1654, the commissioners prepared at last to teach Ninigret the lesson they felt he deserved. Roger Williams opposed that decision, arguing passionately that it was "not only possible but very easie to live and die in peace with all the Natives of the Countrey." But he stood alone. Frustrated by Ninigret's long chain of "hostile attempts and outrages" and fully convinced, largely through the efforts of Uncas, that the Narragansetts were no friends to the English, the commissioners sent 270 foot soldiers and forty cavalry under Simon Willard to force the sachem to subject himself once and forever to English authority. Ninigret was to bear the cost of the expedition, pay additional wampum to the English for their trouble, and immediately cease "from warring any further against the Long Island." The commissioners also expected him to surrender "all the Pequots under him or lately living upon his land." They authorized Willard, if he felt a need for military assistance, to "send to Uncas whom wee have prepared to assist you," presumably with a supply of arms and ammunition, and who "may bee very usefull in the service." Willard told Ninigret that he could comply with the commissioners' demands, or have "his head sett up upon an English pole." Once again Ninigret signed a coercive treaty agreeing to turn over his Pequot tributaries within a week. And once again the treaty meant little, for Ninigret did not deliver his Pequots on time. The Long Islanders continued to complain of Niantic and Narragansett raids, and the frontier remained a realm only tenuously controlled by the English.[67]

It would not get any easier for Uncas. The commissioners' assistance had allowed him to survive the plots, assassination attempts, and invasions of numerous foes. They could not eliminate all threats. With military and political support from the United English, his own coercion of subject peoples, and the establishment of a network of kin relations with his tributaries, Uncas unquestionably had transformed the Mohegans into a regional power. Nonetheless, that power rested on shaky foundations. Patterns of alliance could shift rapidly. Uncas's tributaries could attempt to use English power against him to pursue their own interests, as Robin Cassacinamon had done.

Even his brother Wawequa caused Uncas trouble. Always the more bellicose of the two, and far more energetic in his desire for war against the Narragansetts, Wawequa challenged Uncas's authority as Mohegan sachem in the fall of 1654. The heart of the conflict is difficult to discern, but it began in September when the commissioners learned "of some purpose" of the Mohegans "to Invade the Narragansetts or Ninnegret the Nyanticke Sagamore." At the same time they learned also "of some differences lately growne betwixt Uncas and his brother and betwixt them and theire men." Factionalism threatened to sunder the Mohegans. The commissioners summoned both brothers to come before them at their next meeting. That the English sent men to guard Shantok during Uncas's absence, "being informed some sturrs may arise in his absence to his prejudice," suggests that in the commissioners' eyes Wawequa posed a significant threat to Uncas.

The problem, apparently, was resolved. Wawequa does not appear again in the records challenging his brother's authority. Still, the event, however murkily described in the documents, remains significant. Perhaps Wawequa wanted to war upon the Narragansetts and Niantics in ways that Uncas opposed. Perhaps Wawequa objected to the assistance Uncas offered, and the English considered calling upon, during the 1654 campaign. Perhaps Wawequa felt that the Mohegans did not benefit in acceptable ways from befriending the English. We cannot tell. What we can determine is that despite his continued efforts to forge a unified Mohegan identity, Uncas's authority remained subject to challenge in a tumultuous political environment where he confronted a diverse array of external and internal threats.[68]

CHAPTER 6

Amongst the English

The survivors of the Pequot War, whether settled at Nameag, Pawcatuck, or smaller village communities at Noank and Wecapaug, never rested in their efforts to free themselves from Uncas's control. The Commissioners of the United Colonies supported the Mohegan sachem, but at heart they could do little to prevent individual Pequots, or small family groups, or clusters of kin relations, from resettling on their traditional lands between the Mystic and Thames Rivers. Pequot survivors of the war moved readily from villages under the nominal control of Uncas to those of Robin Cassacinamon. Farther east, Ninigret found that his Pequot tributaries shifted their allegiance to Wequash Cook at Pawcatuck. Even if one accepts the arguments of those historians who view the Pequot War as a genocidal conflict, one must also concede that the Pequots, through their own determination and the help of English allies like John Winthrop Jr., quickly reestablished themselves on their old homelands, free from the authority of those sachems who viewed them after the war as a conquered and defeated people. The Pequot restoration was emblematic of a general decline in Uncas's influence that occurred, slowly and steadily, over the course of the two decades that followed the United Colonies' punishment of Ninigret in 1654.

Wequash Cook's followers, tributaries of the Narragansetts and Niantics since the Hartford Treaty, petitioned the Commissioners of the United Colonies in October 1654 for permission to "disowne the jurisdiction of Ninigrett over us." They pledged themselves "hereafter nott to joyne in any war with Ninigritt or any other without the full and free consent of the Commissioners of the United Colonies." The following September, in 1655, the commissioners freed Wequash Cook and Cassacinamon from their tributary obligations to Ninigret and Uncas, stepping in themselves to occupy the position held previously by the Narragansetts and Mohegans. Wequash Cook became "the United Colonies governor" over the Pequots dwelling at Pawcatuck and Wecapaug, essentially a lesser English sachem. He would act "in all things, according to such rules and instructions as you have or shall receive from the said commissioners, and according to their orders." Robin Cassacinamon received a similar commission to govern the Pequots at Nameag and Noank. He would preside in the commissioners' name over a community in which Indians would neither commit blasphemy nor "prophane the Sabbath day." Murder and the practice of "witchcraft" were capital crimes, and Indians who committed adultery, became intoxicated, stole, plotted against the English, or joined an Indian war party would suffer severe punishment.[1]

Uncas attended this meeting of the United Colonies and continued to assert his authority over Indians he considered his tributaries. He fought a losing battle. He paid the commissioners four fathoms of wampum, for instance, as tribute "for one of his Indians Pequots now resideing with Robin incase hee will returne backe to Monhegine," but realizing that his subject was unlikely to return, he quietly asked them to repay the wampum if the Pequot stayed with Cassacinamon. The commissioners, certainly, recognized Uncas's dissatisfaction, and they encouraged his former tributaries "to returne and those with him to continew still at Mohegene." They ordered Cassacinamon, as well, to keep off Mohegan lands and to limit his hunting and fishing to the east side of the Thames River. This was all talk, however, and the United Colonies could do little to back up their words with action. The commissioners, in effect, offered Uncas partial solutions at best. The Pequots clearly had slipped from his control, their freedom from the Mohegans a fait accompli.[2]

Cassacinamon's settlements became an increasingly attractive site for Pequots disenchanted with Uncas as sachem, and the number of Pequots leaving Mohegan villages apparently increased each year. Uncas complained to the Connecticut magistrates about this again in February 1657, but he found little encouragement. The River Colony men, like the commissioners, ruled that Cassacinamon could "keep the Mohegins or others of Uncasses men that are with him," unless "Uncas desires them & they desire themselves to goe to Uncas." Few seemed to want to return. Despite Uncas's best efforts to work with the English, Cassacinamon had managed to reestablish the Pequots in their traditional homeland east of the Thames within two decades of the Hartford Treaty. Within a decade more, he and his followers took up residence on a 2,000-acre reserve at Mashantucket near present-day Ledyard. They had risen from the ashes of the Pequot War, and reemerged this time as friends to the English. The defeated remnants of a once-despised tribe had been transformed into a community under the nominal control of the commissioners, and, like Uncas, a full participant in the establishment of English dominion over the southern New England frontier.[3]

•

The loss of his control over the Pequots did not discourage Uncas from continuing to assert his authority over rivals to his west. In 1656 Uncas and Sequassen, for example, managed to look past their long history of violence and mutual contempt to form a short-lived partnership. A young warrior named Weaseapano provided the occasion for this unlikely union. He killed a sachem living near Mattabesett, an ally of Sequassen, and then took shelter under the protection of the Podunk sachem Tontonimo. Sequassen had made several attempts to persuade Tontonimo to hand over the killer, but failed. Weakened by his defeats over the preceding decade, Sequassen next turned to the agent of his earlier misfortunes. He appealed to Uncas "for helpe, to bee revenged for the said Sachems death." Sequassen desperately needed to satisfy his followers' demand for justice; else, they would have little reason to continue following him.[4]

Uncas had good cause for siding with his former nemesis. Weaseapano, the murderer, had done nothing to the Mohegans, but Tontonimo had done Uncas "severall wrongs." Tontonimo harbored another Indian who had murdered one of Uncas's men. Tontonimo also, presumably through gifts of wampum, had encouraged Uncas's tributaries in the Connecticut River Valley to abandon their allegiance to the Mohegan sachem. The River Colony men, worried that the desire for revenge might flare into warfare, summoned Uncas, Sequassen, and Tontonimo to appear before them at Hartford in May.[5]

The Connecticut magistrates wanted to avoid war. Governor John Webster asked Sequassen and Uncas "what satisfaction they required" from the Podunks. They both told Webster that ten of Wea-seapano's friends should be put to death. After all, he had killed a man of extremely high status. The Podunks protested. Weaseapano, Ton-tonimo argued, was settling a score: the sachem from Mattabesett had slain his uncle. He killed for revenge, an act perfectly justified in Indian communities. The Podunk sachem offered to compensate Se-quassen and Uncas with a present of wampum. Certainly there ex-isted precedents for this in native communities, but Uncas and Sequassen rejected the offer. They reduced their demands, however, and told the magistrates that they would be "sattisfyed with the death of 6 men." Webster attempted to explain to the Indians how En-glish law treated cases of murder—"that onely the murther[er] or any that were accessory to it should bee punished." The Connecticut magistrates insisted that Tontonimo deliver up the murderer. He agreed to this demand, telling them what he thought they wanted to hear, but then "privately stole out of the Court" and fled to his fort. The River Colony men, still trying to preserve peace, appointed a com-mittee to meet with Sequassen and Uncas. They "privately brought Unquas to accept of the murtherer only for full satisfaction." A deal workable to all could be reached, they thought, if only Tontonimo would honor the promise he made before fleeing from Hartford.[6]

The Podunks told the same committee men who had met with Un-cas that they could not deliver Weaseapano, for "his friends were so many & potent within the forte." Like many of the "tribes" in south-ern New England, the Podunks likely were a polyglot community composed of individuals and kin groups with ties to several villages. Weaseapano's kin seem to have tied Tontonimo's hands. At an im-passe, Governor Webster "made a long speech," appealing once again for peace. Attempts at "advising and counseling of Unquas not to fight" failed to dissuade the Indians from going to war. The blood of the slain, Uncas said, must be quieted. Though the Englishmen believed that Uncas had motives for fighting beyond attaining vengeance for the kin of one of his slain followers, Webster recog-nized the futility of any further argument. He agreed, reluctantly, to allow Uncas and Sequassen to resolve the matter in their own way. The English "would not hinder them, but left them to themselves." Webster required only that the Indians not fight on the west side of the Connecticut River, and in the course of their conflict they must not damage English property on the eastern side.[7]

Uncas quickly organized a war party to demand the surrender of Weaseapano. The Podunks learned of the Mohegans' approach, and Tontonimo gathered his forces. He met Uncas at the Hockanum River, east of Hartford, with an equal number of men. Recognizing that the odds did not favor him, Uncas decided to withdraw. The historian Herbert Milton Sylvester, who despised Uncas, attributed this to the Mohegan sachem's "usual cowardice," but avoiding conflict in this case made sense. Uncas hoped to avenge the murder of one of his followers by an Indian whom Tontonimo had sheltered. He hoped to assert his authority over the Podunks and assist Sequassen. If he lost warriors in battle, this would leave more Mohegans grieving and demand further warfare, which Uncas could not expect the River Colony magistrates to tolerate.[8]

With force untenable, Uncas resorted to trickery. He sent a message to Tontonimo. If the Podunks continued to shelter the murderer, Uncas would enlist the assistance of the Mohawks to destroy Tontonimo's village. The Podunks did not believe him, but Uncas had a plan. According to an account written long after the fact, Uncas sent a Mohegan warrior, who carried with him some Mohawk weapons, on a stealthy raid into the Podunks' territory. The Mohegan set fire to a Podunk wigwam in the night and fled. He left behind the Mohawk weapons on the ground, as if he had dropped them during his escape. The Podunks surveyed the scene in the morning and quickly recognized the evidence of Mohawk involvement in the nighttime assault. They concluded that Uncas could carry out his threat. Terrified, they immediately sent a messenger to him desiring peace, and surrendered Weaseapano to the Mohegans for punishment. Uncas had succeeded in obtaining revenge for the kin of his follower killed by Tontonimo's man, asserted his power over the Podunks, and demonstrated to Sequassen the benefits that Uncas's friendship might bring.[9]

If the River Colony men unenthusiastically endorsed Uncas's plans to go after the Podunks, the Commissioners of the United Colonies, at their annual meeting in September 1656, were extremely upset by the Mohegan sachem's behavior. The commissioners, like the Connecticut magistrates, wanted a peaceful and orderly frontier. After disarming Ninigret's conspiracy in 1654, they thought that they had achieved it. But Uncas would not play along. Earlier the commissioners and the River Colony leaders had favored Uncas because the Mohegan sachem promised to help them achieve English dominion along the frontier. Now, however, he seemed to them the source of disorder and a threat to peace along the margins of their settlements. The commissioners had before them "sundry complaints" about Uncas, "all tending to desturbe both his owne peace and the peace of the countrey." They thought his attack on the Podunks reckless, as they did an invasion led by Uncas or Wawequa of the Norwottock Indians, who lived near present-day Northfield in Massachusetts. The Narragansetts, meanwhile, complained that Uncas's son Owaneco had stolen a gun from a Narragansett warrior. Uncas also had taunted the Narragansetts, "sometimes upbraiding them with theire dead Sachems." A powerful taboo existed against public statements of a slain sachem's name, so Uncas, by "naming and jeering" the dead ancestors of Mixanno, had engaged in behavior "which hee knowes they can not beare." Uncas reportedly challenged the Narragansetts to fight, an alarming charge given the time and energy the commissioners had expended to defend the Mohegans from their enemies. The commissioners heard disturbing rumors, as well, that Uncas and Ninigret, after a decade and a half of conflict, finally had worked out "a peace or some agreement" "without the advise or knowlidge of the English."[10]

Puritan officials continued to receive reports on Uncas's activity, and they were not happy with what they heard. From his outpost at Springfield, along the Connecticut River in western Massachusetts, John Pynchon told John Winthrop Jr. that peace could not be attained so long as Uncas failed to restrain himself. The English, Pynchon wrote, had no sooner resolved a crisis by intervening in Indian affairs than Uncas did "presently undo all by his proud and high words." In the months since he had obtained Weaseapano from Tontonimo, Uncas had apparently conducted piecemeal raids against the Podunks that had driven them from their homes. Having frightened Tontonimo, he would not let up. According to the commissioners, Uncas would not "permit the Podunk Indians to returne to their dwellings

& there to abide in Peace & safety, without molestation from him or his," unless they paid him tribute. In the spring of 1657, Tontonimo appealed for help, calling upon the Pocumtucks and Narragansetts to protect him from the Mohegan sachem. He also called upon the Connecticut English, and may have offered at this time to cede a portion of his lands around Hartford to the River Colony in exchange for their services. If he did so, he would have made himself more immediately useful to colonial leaders than Uncas.[11]

In May a group of sachems from the Narragansetts and Pocumtucks requested of the Massachusetts Bay Colony General Court "liberty or consent to make war upon Uncas, sachem of the Mohegins." They expected that Connecticut would protect Uncas, so they never bothered appealing to the Hartford magistrates. The Pocumtucks needed to protect the Podunks, and the Narragansetts felt obligated to assist them. At least that is what they told the English. The Bay Colony men listened to the Indians' arguments. They admitted that they did not fully understand the source of the conflict between Uncas and the Pocumtucks. The Pocumtucks at some point (we do not know when) already had attacked Uncas, and "had so great a victory over him, & kild ... many of his men." Perhaps, the magistrates suggested, the Pocumtucks "may well rest satisfied," at least until the commissioners came together to hear both sides. As for the Narragansetts' request to assist the Podunks, the magistrates could not "by any meanes assent." They reminded the Narragansett sachems "of the covenant made with the commissioners, at Boston, in the year 45, ... not to warr with any Indians that are in friendshipp with the English, without the consent of the Commissioners." The two groups had to wait until the next gathering of the United Colonies for permission to attack Uncas.[12]

Yet within two months Uncas and the Mohegans once again faced the wrath of their enemies. A Pocumtuck war party, including a small number of Pequots, ambushed and killed several Mohegans traveling by canoe on the Connecticut River. Pessicus, meanwhile, invaded Mohegan territory and drove Uncas from Shantok. The sachem fled downriver toward the coast, finding shelter behind the palisades of the tributary village at Niantick. The River Colony men recognized the gravity of the situation Uncas faced. John Mason kept the magistrates informed "about the Narragansetts beleaguering of Uncas, at Niantick." They authorized Jonathan Brewster, another old friend of the Mohegan sachem, to enlist the aid of several men to protect him at his new post. Brewster's soldiers, indeed, made life difficult for Pessicus, as did the actions of English settlers in the area, who warned Uncas of the Narragansetts' approach and gave him time to take shelter. Pessicus easily might have wiped out Brewster's men but decided to withdraw instead. He knew well that the fighting of the English was "naught" and that their desire for vengeance was without limit. It was, Pessicus recognized, the Narragansett dilemma again. His people could not war upon Uncas without drawing down upon them the fury of the English. Uncas, ever the opportunist, sent warriors to pursue and ambush Pessicus's frustrated men as they returned home. The Mohegans killed many Narragansetts, and their retreat became a rout. The Narragansetts died as they fled, "struggling through the thickets or floundering across the streams."[13]

Uncas's territory had been invaded, and he and his followers had been driven from Shantok. He traveled to Boston in September 1657 from his post at Niantick to lay his grievances before the commissioners, as he had done many times before. In this sense, the Mohegan sachem's journey to meet with the commissioners differed little from his earlier visits. Brewster would remain with his small English force to guard Niantick during Uncas's absence. Disorder on the frontier required the attention of the United Colonies, and Uncas had every reason to expect English intervention on his behalf once again.[14]

But Uncas found this time that things had changed. The commissioners clearly viewed him as a trouble-maker. The two from the Massachusetts Bay Colony especially, Simon Bradstreet and George Denison, complained of his "proud, insolent, and provoking speeches and treacherous actions." For the Bay Colony men, Uncas simply was no longer worth the trouble. Defending so rash and "unseasonable" a sachem, and one so unamenable to Puritan control, could "in reason have no other attendance in conclusion then to render us lo and contemptible in the eyes of the Indians or engage us to vindecate our honor in a dangerouse and unnecessary warr upon Indian quarrels." The Bay Colony men had a point. The commissioners ordered the Indians to leave Uncas alone, but announced to them as well that they would attempt to keep Uncas in check. They required Uncas to permit the Podunk Indians to return to their homes, eliminating, they hoped, the initial source of the present conflict.[15]

And despite the Pocumtucks' claim that they "would yield to the English in any Thing but in making peac with Uncas," the outlook for a settlement over the winter of 1657–1658 seemed good. In January Uncas sent messengers with a small gift of wampum to secure his pledge to maintain the peace, and in February John Pynchon reported that "things stand in as fair a way for a peaceable agreement betwixt Uncas and the Pocumtucks as possible." Rather than preparing for war, the Pocumtucks began to ready themselves for a winter hunt. The amicable situation could not last, however, and the opportunity for peace slipped away as quickly as it appeared. First came reports that "divers great sachems from about the Dutch and Wapeages [in southwestern Connecticut] have brought presents to Uncas and made a league with him." The Mohegan sachem had worked out an alliance, apparently, with the Esopus Indians of the Hudson Valley, who found their fields frequently overrun by land-hungry Dutch settlers and their livestock. The strength that these allies brought to Uncas, along with their access to trade with the Dutch at Fort Orange, may have rendered any alliance with the Pocumtucks less useful than it once might have been. Uncas began to use many "high words" in his dealings with his rivals, leaving the Indians at Pocumtuck "very much discontented."[16]

Annapecum, the leader of the Pocumtucks, told Pynchon that war might still be avoided, but only if Uncas behaved himself in a more respectful manner. The Mohegan sachem made many "proud speeches," Annapecum told Pynchon, but if "they find him now to forbear and that he doe send them some good girdle or girdles of wampum from himself that they may see his reality, they do intend a full peace, otherwise not." Pynchon passed this news along to John Winthrop Jr. with the advice that he encourage Uncas to "carry it well." The Mohegan sachem was the problem, Pynchon said, and the choice of peace or war rested in his hands. "I wish," Pynchon wrote, "that Uncas may give them good and loving words and messages and that he would take some convenient tyme to send them some good girdles which they will take as a testification of his reality." If Uncas followed this course, and did so quickly, Pynchon believed that "all will be well and will issue I believe in a firm peace."[17]

But Uncas refused to listen to Puritan advice. Early in the spring of 1658, as a result, Annapecum, with allies drawn from among the Tunxis and the Narragansetts, invaded Uncas's territory. Annapecum's warriors rifled a farmhouse near Wethersfield in search of corn. They roughed up some English messengers from Connecticut and took their Mohegan guides captive. They also laid siege to Uncas at Niantick. When word of the Pocumtucks' invasion arrived, the commissioners sent a messenger of their own to ask the Pocumtucks to withdraw. Annapecum, the commissioners suggested, must act quickly to preserve the friendship of the English. Annapecum firmly requested "the English sachems not to persuade us to a peace with Uncas, for we have experience of his falseness, and we know that, though he promises much, he will perform nothing." Any further messages from the English, Annapecum continued, should be carried by men who are not "liars and tale-bearers, but sober men and such as we can understand." In disturbing ways, Annapecum repeated many of the concerns that Pynchon had raised a short time before.[18]

No evidence exists to tell us about Annapecum's siege of the Niantick fort. Uncas survived, as did the Mohegans, and the Pocumtucks returned home unsuccessfully, but we do not know specifically why. Neighboring settlers may have interfered, as they had before, but there is no direct evidence that they did so. Perhaps Uncas's strength was too great to make a continuation of the effort worthwhile. What is clear is that other sachems joined Annapecum in complaining about Uncas's bellicose behavior. Pomham, the former Narragansett tributary who had subjected himself to the English in the mid 1640s, reported to the commissioners that Uncas had killed one of his men and two women at Cowesett in Rhode Island. Apumps, a Nipmuck sachem from Quinebaug, complained that Uncas in August had taken six hostages, killed one, and wounded another in his village. The commissioners sent Thomas Stanton and George Denison with a message to Uncas, demanding that he appear before them at their next meeting, and that "in the mean time hee forbeare to make any further attempt or assault against them" without "some warrantable grounds." The commissioners needed peace on the frontier and Uncas, on the defensive since 1643, they thought had instigated the warfare. They increasingly looked to control and limit the Mohegan sachem's freedom to act in his own behalf.[19]

Uncas told Denison and Stanton that he would refrain from warring upon the Indian subjects of the United Colonies if those Indians "keepe at home and do him no wrong." He expressed his desire to remain a friend to the English, but he would not be pushed around. Uncas's behavior shows the weakness in the arguments of those historians who have forced his story into one of two static molds, either a treacherous collaborator with the colonial powers in the subjugation of Indian peoples or a trusted and loyal ally of the English. Uncas consistently pursued Mohegan interests, and in this instance his pursuit of these ends brought instability to the Anglo-American frontier. The English could not tolerate it. Uncas recognized that the nature of his relationship with the colonists had changed after 1654, and this realization stirred in him feelings of bitterness. His power to dictate to the English had declined, and he did not like listening to Puritan lectures. He told Denison and Stanton that he "hath a good heart toward the Comitioners still, notwithstanding all the Indians round abought doe bight him." Uncas was frank. He told them that "he hath heard the Comissioners are like Gods," and challenged them to "shew themselves so that the Skie may be cleared and then" he could "conclude that they are so indeed." They were not acting like sachems; they were not now offering Uncas the protection he felt he deserved, and the Mohegan sachem told the Englishmen that he feared for the future. The commissioners, who should help him, "have cast him off for the crow and wolves to feede upon." In Uncas's eyes, they were abandoning the one Indian who could help them achieve frontier order.[20]

And that order indeed remained elusive. In the fall of 1659 the Pocumtucks and their allies again invaded Uncas's territory. They laid siege to the Mohegan sachem in his Niantick fort and raided the house of Jonathan Brewster. The Pocumtucks had heard that "twenty of our enemies were gotten in there," and that Brewster "did furnish Uncas with Guns, powder and shott." Since the earliest battles with Miantonomi, the Mohegans had been outgunned by their adversaries. The River Colony men recognized early their ally's need for weaponry, and in this sense, Brewster made himself a sensible target for Uncas's enemies. Still, attacks of this sort the commissioners could not abide, and they fined the Pocumtucks, Tunxis, and Narragansetts heavily for the assault on Brewster's house. The Narragansetts would pay by themselves an additional fine of eighty fathoms of wampum for gunning down a Mohegan servant at the feet of Mrs. Brewster, a breach of etiquette in the eyes of the English that could not go unpunished.[21]

The commissioners, as always, penalized Uncas's enemies for attacks that jeopardized the security of English settlers. This time, however, the commissioners believed that the conflict had been entirely avoidable. If only Uncas had carried himself more wisely, and with less bellicosity, order might have come to the Anglo-American frontier. Now, settlers remained on their guard, and English lives nearly were lost in Indian raids on Mohegan strongholds. The commissioners took the opportunity to lecture the Mohegan sachem. "Severall injuries and affronts" had been done "to some English by the Pocumtucke and Narragansett Indians whiles they were in the procecution of the quarrels against you." These quarrels, they pointed out to Uncas, "hath been occationed" solely by his "want of attendance to the Councell of the English." Uncas must in the future heed the commissioners' advice more closely.[22]

Uncas would again need English assistance to stave off an Indian invasion. In 1660, the Connecticut magistrates complained to the Commissioners of the United Colonies that some Narragansett Indians, in the dead of night, "shott 11 bulletts into a house of the English there, in hopes, as they boasted, to have slayne him whome wee have cause to honor, whose safety we cannot but take ourselves bound to promote, our Deputy Gov, Major Mason." Native hostility toward Uncas had spilled over, at long last, into attempts to eliminate the Mohegan sachem's closest English allies. The River Colony magistrates were furious. After experiencing the "insolent and proud carriage and manifold abuses" hurled upon them by the "uncircumcised Heathens round about us," they could not "but conceive it is high time to renew upon the memory of these Pagans the obliterate memorials of the English."[23]

The commissioners agreed that the Narragansetts must be punished. They ordered the sachems of the tribe to pay an enormous fine in wampum—five hundred fathoms for the recent attacks on Mason's house and an additional ninety-five fathoms for an earlier assault upon Uncas. They demanded the Narragansetts' land as security for the payment, which they expected in four months. Humphrey Atherton, the leader of a group of Puritan land speculators that included John Winthrop Jr., who was both a commissioner and the Connecticut governor, saw opportunity in the Narragansetts' distress. Atherton and his associates loaned the Narragansetts the wampum due in return for a mortgage payable in six months. When the two additional months did not make a difference, the Atherton Company foreclosed on the Narragansetts, laying claim to all their lands, including a significant chunk of territory in Rhode Island. Uncas had once again received English protection from his enemies; the reason why, however, owed less to his position as an ally than it did to the fact that now prominent Englishmen found themselves caught in the crossfire.[24]

•

Whether or not he had the blessings of the English, Uncas still acted as a traditional sachem, righting wrongs, avenging his people's losses, and extending his influence over rival communities. Exercising these powers, however, became increasingly difficult for him during these years of decline.

Early in the spring of 1661, for example, Uncas and his followers attacked the village of the Quabaugs near present-day Brookfield, Massachusetts. They killed several and took others captive. The Mohegans also took goods from the Quabaugs later valued at £37. Wassamequin, the Quabaug sachem, had earlier submitted himself and his people to English authority. He quickly informed the Massachusetts Bay Colony magistrates of the attack and asked for their assistance.[25]

The Puritans demanded that Uncas hand over the captives and make restitution for the goods he and his men had spoiled. If Uncas failed to comply they would, with "the Lord's Assistance," "right our foresaid injuryes upon him and our said subjects." If it came to war, Uncas would bear "all charges whatsoever" and, if necessary, the Bay Colony would require of him "sattisfaction . . . for the lives of our subjects by him slain." A small Bay Colony force would occupy Wassamequin's fort in case Uncas attacked again. Finally, the magistrates wrote to the commissioners with news of yet another outrage committed by Uncas, and asked for their assistance in forcing him to obey their demands.[26]

The commissioners took the opportunity once again to lecture Uncas on his obligations to the English. The attack on the Quabaugs, they told him, was "contrary to your covenant and promise to the commissioners severall times renewed; not to make warr [against] any of our Tributaryes without the allowance of the commissioners." If Uncas would only follow English rules, the commissioners implied, peace and order might prevail along the frontier. Uncas knew his stock had fallen dramatically with the commissioners. Instead of sending a Mohegan, like the adept translator and courier Foxon, Uncas recognized the importance of having an Englishman represent his interests before the United Colonies. He asked his old friend John Mason to plead his case.[27]

Uncas, according to Mason, did not know that the Quabaugs had subjected themselves to the authority of the Bay Colony. The men Uncas attacked, furthermore, did not belong to Wassamequin. They were supporters of Onopequin, Uncas's "deadly enemie," who "had formerly fought against him in his owne person." Mason tried to explain that Uncas had attacked the Quabaugs to settle an old score. The commissioners, however, had grown entirely frustrated with Uncas, however much his attack made sense in a native political and cultural lexicon. Given their low opinion of him, nothing would justify warfare against English tributaries. Uncas clearly understood this reality and acted accordingly. Mason reported to the commissioners that Uncas already had freed the captives he took at Quabaug, in recognition of the futility in this case of subjecting them to Mohegan authority.[28]

The following years, if in fact the remaining documents accurately reflect the totality of Uncas's activity, were years of relative peace for the Mohegans. We know that the Narragansetts and Niantics left them alone. The Narragansett sachems devoted their attention to hanging on to their Nipmuck tributaries and their southern New England lands. Ninigret continued his raids against the Long Islanders. The Connecticut magistrates oversaw the affairs of the Pequots closely, virtually precluding any chances they might have had for getting in trouble. Only with the Podunks did Uncas experience any difficulty. Arramament, the new Podunk sachem, and Uncas both claimed lands to the east of the Connecticut River for hunting. The evidence does not show how the dispute came before the River Colony magistrates, but in 1666 the Connecticut English intervened to resolve the conflicting claims to the hunting grounds peacefully. Summoning Arramament and Uncas to Hartford, officials appointed by the Connecticut General Court helped the sachems reach a deal. A formal agreement between Uncas and Arramament, Seacutt, and Nessaheagon, "in behalf of the Indian people at Windsor, Podunck, and Hartford," emerged in the summer. Uncas pledged not to "practice any evil or Mischief" against the River Indians and they, in turn, promised to "carry it peaceably towards" Uncas. The magistrates drew a boundary line defining Uncas's and Arramament's hunting grounds. The Connecticut men, dealing with the conflict before it could become a more general war, did not allow Uncas the freedom to resolve the dispute in his own way.[29]

•

In the decade and a half following Ninigret's plot, leaders in the River Colony had less and less use for an Indian like Uncas, and his declining influence in English councils was mirrored in a number of areas. First, as the English population grew and expanded, a significant number of frontier settlers and land speculators coveted the Mohegans' valuable and fertile lands in southeastern Connecticut. As the settlers at the younger Winthrop's plantation expanded their farms into the neighboring countryside, for example, conflict with the Mohegans resulted. As early as March 1654, the River Colony men had learned from Uncas "that the inhabitants of Pequett have taken possession of Uncas his forte & many of his wigwams at Monheag." They drove him out of Shantok. In response to his complaint about aggressive encroachment on his lands, the magistrates sent John Mason to warn settlers "not to mollest the Indyans in their planting ground or other rightfull possessions."[30]

Winthrop's settlers retired, but the pressure on Mohegan lands steadily mounted. The magistrates tried to regulate this expansion, for they feared that hard-pressed Indians might lash out, embroiling their colony in war. In March 1658, they granted permission to Richard Haughton to purchase "a certaine neck of land called Massapeag, betweene Pequot and Mohegin" from Uncas, provided that Haughton use the land only "to plant or sowe thereupon in the summer, and kepe cattle thereupon in the winter: and that no swine shall be kept upon the premises at any time, neither shall be any otherwise improved to the trespasse or prejudice of Uncas." Five months later, Uncas granted to Haughton "for some considerations to me knowne," the "neck of land that is called Massapeage, with all the privilidges thereto belonging." Also in August, Uncas granted to James Rogers of New London "a parsell of ground at Mohegon the name of the ground called Pamechak, the one side of it lyes by the great river of the west side of the river with a Coave at the end of the other side of the maine land." Both grants involved lands close to the Mohegan heartland, and he executed them during his short residence at Niantick.[31]

Some Englishmen sought to sidestep Uncas's authority by purchasing lands he claimed from his tributaries. In the spring of 1659, for instance, Indians named Haguntas and Allumps sold to John Endicott, John Winthrop Jr., and others from the Massachusetts Bay Colony 450 square miles at Quinebaug. Uncas challenged the sale. Haguntas and Allumps, he said, had come "from Narragansett uppon the Occasion of a fight or Quarrel" and sought his protection. Uncas gave the sachems permission to live at a location called Egunk, near present-day Stirling, but he did not give them any title to the lands or any right to sell them to the Bay Colony. If Uncas's reluctant tributaries could be persuaded to part with lands he claimed, then Mohegan land tenure rested upon extremely shaky foundations.[32]

In June 1659, with his sons Owaneco and Attawanhood, Uncas granted a nine-mile-square tract to the first settlers of Norwich, among them Major John Mason, "with all ponds, Rivers, Woods, Quarries, Mines, with all Royalties, priviledges, and appurtenances thereunto belonging." The number of English settlers in the region, now living both to the north and south of Shantok along the Thames and on the northern banks of the Yantic River, increased steadily, and by 1660 the Mohegans found their lands encircled by colonial settlements.[33]

In this environment of steadily mounting pressure on Mohegan lands, Uncas looked to establish closer ties with his old friend John Mason. The River Colony's military leader had always defended Uncas before colonial authorities; now, Uncas hoped, Mason would help him protect Mohegan lands from aggressive frontier settlers. In 1659 Uncas entrusted all the Mohegans' lands not actually planted or improved to Mason. A subsequent agreement, in 1665, guaranteed Mason and his heirs half of the profit from the sale of Mohegan lands, none of which could be sold without the consent of Uncas or his heirs.

Mason's price may have been high, but the agreement brought Uncas certain advantages. These deeds were put in writing. Historians of early New England too often have drawn a harsh dichotomy between nonliterate Indians and literate Englishmen, but the reality was more complicated. Uncas recognized the importance of written records when he inscribed his mark upon a page, even if he could not compose these documents independently. Mason provided him with entry into an English world of writing where deeds and documents, land titles and letters really mattered and could make the difference between dispossession and a measure of autonomy. Furthermore, though Mason granted legal jurisdiction over the Mohegan lands to Connecticut early in 1661, the magistrates left the right to sell the lands in "the hands of Major Mason," who insisted always that Uncas maintained a "native right" in the soil until he freely chose to sell. As trustee for Uncas, Mason had an interest in upholding Mohegan claims to as large a territory as possible, and over as many tributary peoples as possible. Mason and Uncas agreed, moreover, to set aside in the future a permanent tract for the Mohegans bounded on the east by the Thames, on the south by New London's as yet undetermined northern boundary, and on the north by the mouth of Trading Cove Brook.[34]

Uncas's cession of Mohegan hunting grounds at Wepowaug to Jonathan Brewster's son-in-law John Pickett, in December 1660, showed that the relationship with Mason, unique among Anglo-Indian relationships in seventeenth-century New England, could work to protect Mohegan interests. The cession took place "with the consent and allowance of Major John Mason," who secured for the Mohegans their liberty "to hunt with guns" upon the ceded lands, and "to catch Bever & fish within the limits aforesd." The only constraint upon Mohegan hunting was a prohibition against laying traps that could snare careless Englishmen and their livestock. Uncas's relationship with John Mason shows that the Mohegan leader recognized that his ability to protect his lands from encroachment by Englishmen had declined. He had, in fact, few other options. He could fight English settlers or organize Indians throughout the region against them, but history taught him the impossibility of succeeding with these strategies. Instead, Uncas entrusted Mohegan affairs to an English sachem who protected his interests in a relationship that had an English name—guardianship—but that must have looked familiar to Uncas in terms of the traditional relationship between lesser and greater sachems. The Mohegans continued to hold their lands in traditional ways, with distribution and allocation controlled by the sachem. After the cession to Pickett, and another to John Tinker in the spring of 1661, few other deeds to Mohegan lands were executed during Mason's lifetime.[35]

John Winthrop Jr., who likely saw a threat to his newly acquired interests at Quinebaug, contested Uncas's and Mason's understanding of guardianship. According to Winthrop, Mason had obtained the deed from Uncas in 1659 as an agent of the colony and, as a result, the cession extinguished Mohegan title to the soil. Uncas's lands, the governor argued, now belonged to Connecticut. Mason argued vociferously against Winthrop's interpretation, and the matter remained unresolved, but contested, well into the next century, long after Mason, Uncas, and the younger Winthrop had died. Nonetheless, Winthrop's challenge served as a salutary reminder to Uncas that he could not rely solely on Mason for protection. He would have to watch closely as well the functioning of the colony's government to prevent the further alienation of Mohegan land. Danger could come from many quarters.[36]

Mason, for example, could do little to help Uncas solve the problem of delineating the northern boundary of New London. Only the colonial government had the power to do that. Mason's permanent grant to the Mohegans would remain undefined until the line was drawn, and the settlers claimed lands that Uncas considered his own. In 1661, in response to Uncas's complaints, the magistrates appointed the first of a number of committees "to try the bounds of N. London, and to make report what is the extent of the bounds from the Sea northward into the Countrey." This committee, in October 1663, indeed found that the town of New London had taken Mohegan land without compensation. They called upon the town to pay Uncas £15. The New London men, however, felt little sympathy for Uncas and, encouraged by Governor Winthrop, they refused to raise the funds necessary to pay the Mohegans for their lands.[37]

There matters stood until 1666, when the issue came before the Connecticut General Court. The committee members, William Leete, Samuel Wyllys, Robert Chapman, and William Wadsworth, once again found that the New Londoners had encroached upon Uncas's land. Supported by the magistrates, the committee ordered the town this time to pay Uncas £20 "for the establishment of a clearer title, preservation of peace and preventing further trouble and charge to themselves or the Country." Furthermore, to preserve the Mohegans' remaining lands between New London's northern line and the southern boundary of Norwich, the committee, with Uncas's consent, ordered that "hee nor his heirs shall nott sell any partt" of their remaining lands "to any person or persons whatsoever but unto New London and not to them neither without the consent of his people reserving a competent portion to plant upon so to provide for him, his heirs, [and] his people and their successors for ever for their subsistence."[38]

Still the town would not yield. Finally, in 1669, at a gathering held in New London, Uncas and Owaneco executed a deed settling their boundary with the town. The northern boundary began, in the frustratingly vague language of seventeenth-century land transactions, "with a rock that lieth in Mohegan River, a little below a parcel of meadow, Comonly knowne & called by the name of Baylys meadow, and to runn from the afforesayde rock upon a westerly line to a marked tree in the woods marked with the Letter L." Everything below the line Uncas and Owaneco deeded to the New Londoners for ever, "with all the privileges and appurtenances to it belonging and appertaining, without any lett, molestation, or hindrance from us." Uncas and Owaneco reserved the right to continue to hunt, fish, and fowl below the line, and they could continue to work their fields within the town bounds until they were worn out.[39]

Uncas's eight-year struggle to resolve his boundary dispute with New London reveals much about the nature of his relationship with the growing numbers of Englishmen in the Thames River Valley. Uncas sought to resist the relentless pressure these colonists placed upon Mohegan lands. Despite his recent fall in favor, he could still appeal to his three decades of friendship with the River Colony and, at least with some of its leaders, make a convincing case for assistance. Through these English allies, Uncas managed to resist further as-

saults upon his lands, guarantee the right of his people to practice traditional subsistence activities, and preserve the critical core of the
Mohegans' traditional homeland.

•

The growing numbers of English settlers in the Thames River Valley
produced significant and unprecedented change for the Mohegans.
The decision of the English colonies to demonetize wampum in 1663
and 1664, following a return to political stability in England and an
influx of English currency, weakened the position of the Mohegans
and their Algonquian neighbors in the colonial economy. As long as
the colonists relied on wampum as a medium of exchange, ties of interest bound the colonies to those Indians who manufactured the
shell beads. Thereafter, the Mohegans found that the demand for
wampum fell precipitously, increasing their isolation from colonial
networks of exchange, upon which they had come to rely for the
acquisition of English trade goods. Some tried to stay afloat by per-
forming odd jobs, making baskets, catching stray hogs, and extermi-
nating the wolves that Puritans feared would prey upon their cattle.
Others entered into the English economy as servants, like the Mohegan gunned down by the Narragansetts at Mrs. Brewster's feet. Increasingly, Indians in southern New England found that they had
only one commodity remaining that they could exchange for colonial products—their land.[40]

It was a vicious cycle, and Uncas's success in preserving for the Mohegans the core of their ancestral homeland and the right to engage
in traditional subsistence activities in the recently ceded lands allowed his people to avoid the worst of the devastation neighboring
English settlements could produce. Still, the adjustments made by
the Mohegans were significant. As early as 1649, Uncas complained
to colonial authorities about damage done in Mohegan fields by English livestock. "A great company of hoggs," Connecticut's governor
John Haynes reported to John Winthrop Jr. in May of that year, had
"destroyed many parcels of their corne." The Mohegans, Haynes continued, were "certeine they come from your Towne." Despite good-
faith efforts to remedy the situation by colonial authorities, the

problems caused by English livestock would not go away. In October 1671, Uncas complained to colonial officials that "he had received great damage in his corn, by some horses belonging to New London or Norwich, and hath received no sattisfaction for the same." The animals could do a lot of harm. As they roamed the countryside, feeding on Mohegan crops, they also consumed forage that had sustained deer and other game animals. Protecting their fields from foraging English livestock became a fact of Mohegan life.[41]

The raising of crops itself became more difficult for the Mohegans as the number of settlers in the region grew. Surrounded by colonists, the Mohegans could no longer abandon worn-out fields as they traditionally had done. As the fertility of their fields declined, so too did the yield per acre. Uncas recognized that this problem could confront his people with a subsistence crisis, and that is why he and Mason insisted upon their right to carry on traditional subsistence activities on the lands he had recently sold to English settlers. Uncas also likely encouraged his people to begin raising hogs on their own as a source of food to replace increasingly scarce deer. By approximately 1700, the archaeological evidence from Shantok suggests, the Mohegans relied upon domesticated animals for over half of the meat they consumed.[42]

The Mohegans also found themselves increasingly subject to a foreign colonial legal system. English authorities, through their legislation, defined Indians as outsiders, living within the jurisdiction of the province but without full membership in the commonwealth. The colonists' readings of race and culture conspired to render Indians as foreigners, outsiders, objects of distrust and suspicion. In 1660 the River Colony magistrates ordered that those Indians who had bound themselves to the English as servants, as well as African slaves, would not be "required to traine, watch, or ward" in the colony. Three years later, "being sensible of the great inconveniency that may com to the members of this Colony by Indians" who entered English towns looking for alcohol, and who implicitly were *not* members of the colony, the magistrates ordered that any Indians they apprehended would pay a fine of twenty shillings. Indians and African slaves occupied a space within colonial society too far beyond the pale to be trusted with guns in their hands, even in a community where militia duty was an obligation imposed upon all able-bodied men. Indians, who came from without to buy English liquor in the night, brought disorder to the community and had to be excluded.[43]

Colonial authorities regularly tried to limit the flow of alcohol into Indian village communities. Initially the magistrates tried to punish colonists, like John Bissel, for "tradeing liquors to the Indians." Bissel paid a heavy fine of £40 for his offense, but attempts to control the trade by punishing dealers failed. There was simply too much money to be made through the illegal trade, so colonial authorities shifted their attention from English suppliers to Indian consumers. The New London County Court early in the 1660s, for instance, fined two Indians, possibly Mohegans, named Honory and Statugunk, "for being drunk and fighting" with a colonist named Hugh Mould. They would pay a fine in wampum to Mould or "be whipt" by the sheriff. It did not matter who provided them with alcohol.[44]

Mohegans also could expect to face punishment if found guilty of "labor or play on the Sabbath within the English limits & and on the English lands." Only certain colonists could sell Indians powder and shot, and no Indian could purchase from the English "any horse or mare, nor any boate or boate riginge, upon the penalty of five for one for any such default." Indians could not war upon their enemies within the English limits, and "strange Indians" could not enter into English towns.[45]

Colonial legislation unquestionably rendered Indians second-class subjects of the River Colony. To counter this disturbing trend Uncas learned well how to steer clear of colonial courts and how to navigate in this world of limited freedom. In 1660 the magistrates had to intervene to force him to pay a fine he owed a colonist named Quince Smith. A decade later, the New London County Court brought Uncas "under a bond of £100 for appearance of his son, Foxen, and two Indians, Jumpe and Towtukhag, and 8 Indians more for breaking open a warehouse. He was fined 50 bushels of Indian corn for his son, 5 pound in wampum to Mr. Samuel Clarke [the keeper of the warehouse] and 20 pound in wampum to the County treasury."

Beyond these widely scattered incidents, it is remarkable how few references to Uncas and his people appear in the court records of the towns of Norwich and New London. Perhaps a wall of separation, buttressed by the contempt and racism of frontier whites, limited Indian-white contact. Perhaps Uncas realized that he could accomplish little in the town meetings, and chose to take his complaints to the colonial government, where he still had a few friends. Perhaps the Mohegans chose to isolate themselves from their Puritan neighbors. In any case, more than other native leaders in southern New England, Uncas had succeeded in insulating his people from the operation of colonial legal systems. On those few occasions when they were called upon, he and his sons treaded carefully before colonial authorities. Otherwise they stayed away, unless they felt vital Mohegan interests were at stake.[46]

These colonial authorities remained suspicious of their Indian neighbors. In May 1669, for instance, Robin Cassacinamon petitioned the Connecticut Court, to relate his side of an event that had occurred in his village several months before. Cassacinamon told the magistrates "that this winter that Unckas and Ninycraft and a great Many other Indians mett together" at the Pequots' village "to make a Dance after the Indian fashion, intending no hurt at all to the Inglish." Wequash Cook attended the gathering, as well as Indians from Long Island and Block Island and from among the Nipmucks. So large an assemblage of Indians, many of whom had fought each other in the recent past, had alarmed Thomas Stanton. The impetuous Englishman led a group of soldiers into the gathering, convinced that Ninigret, once again, had organized a massive Indian conspiracy against the English. Stanton had demanded that Cassacinamon, the "governor" of the Pequots, help him seize Ninigret for questioning. Cassacinamon hesitated. "I was much afraid," he told the magistrates, "that some men would be kild because I then saw Ninicrafts men, almost one hundred of them have guns in their hands and the Inglish men layd their hands upoon their swords redy to draw." Cassacinamon negotiated a peaceful end to the stand-off by paying Stanton twenty fathoms of wampum to leave the village. But he worried that if Stanton had refused and tried to take Ninigret, the Niantic leader and his allies "might have fyred Inglishmens houses and that a great dell of hurt might have com of it."[47]

Stanton left, but he reported what he saw to colonial authorities. He "wondered to see Uncas and Ninigret together at Robin's dance, they who durst not looke each uppon the other this 20 yeares, but at the mussel of a gun or at the pille of an arrow." Cassacinamon had hoped to allay the suspicions of the magistrates, but by July, two months after the Pequot governor petitioned the General Court, other reports began to arrive to support Stanton's fears. John Mulford and Thomas James from Long Island told John Mason about the "designs of Nenecraft" to rise against the English, and "vent their malice & hatred against us." Francis Lovelace, the governor of New York, informed the other colonial governors that Ninigret was plotting against the colonists. Mason believed that Ninigret's latest conspiracy was real, and "as great a hazard as ever New England yet saw." Though he thought the Mohawks and Mohegans were still friendly, no one was above suspicion and, at Mason's urging, Owaneco surrendered some of the Mohegans' guns to the English. Mason believed that the French were supporting and encouraging Ninigret "speedily to cut off the English."[48]

Ninigret lived on lands claimed by Rhode Island, and the Rhode Islanders requested that the Connecticut men not attempt to capture him for questioning. The Niantics, John Crandall and Tobias Saunders argued, lived within Rhode Island's jurisdiction, and Ninigret would be called to account "befor the government under whom his majesty have put him." The Rhode Islanders referred to the work of royal commissioners, sent by the king five years earlier in 1664 to conquer New Netherland and rein in the independence of the Puritan colonies. The royal commissioners—Samuel Maverick, Richard Nicolls, Sir Robert Carr, and George Cartwright—confirmed and formally recognized that in 1644 Pessicus and Canonicus had submitted "themselves, people, and country into his Royall Majesties protection." (The turmoil of civil war, along with eleven years of Puritan rule in England under Oliver Cromwell, had prevented royal recognition at an earlier date.) Furthermore, the commissioners ordered that the Narragansetts' lands shall "hence forward be called the King's Province." Finally, because the "pretending" Atherton purchasers "knew that the said country was submitted to his Majestie, as well by witnesses, as by the said submission being . . . printed," the royal commissioners declared the Atherton claims null and void, and ordered the purchasers to "quit & goe of the said pretended purchased lands." The commissioners placed the power to govern the King's Province in Rhode Island's hands.[49]

Ninigret appeared before the Rhode Island authorities on July 28.

He asked who accused him. The Rhode Island council told him it was "an Indian from Long Island." Ninigret knew the informant, an Indian named Nonaconapoonog who, he said, had been "forsaken of all his kindred, and is in a very sad condition, laying his hand over his face; and the said Nonaconapoonog's friends say unto him, it is justly befallen him for the lyes he hath made, and for his disturbing the country." Ninigret dismissed English worries about the gathering at Cassacinamon's village. The colonists, he said, knew that dances were "noe unusuall thing for us soe to doe." He based the remainder of his defense firmly on the Narragansett submission to crown rule. He

> wondered that there should bee any such report raised, considering his own innocency, and that ever since himselfe heard the words by the [Royal] Commissioners, spoken as from King Charles his mouth, and hath since laid it up in his heart that the King did looke upon himselfe and [Pessicus] and their Indians as his subjects, together with the English; and he understood that the English of this Colony were to help them, if any should be too mighty for them, and they to doe the like to the English, if any should invade or make warr upon the Colony.

The crown's acceptance of the Narragansetts as subjects, Ninigret suggested, insulated him and his people from the workings of Puritan justice.[50]

The Rhode Islanders had few reasons to challenge the crown, which had protected the colony from the claims of the Atherton Company, and they listened closely to Ninigret's defense. They concluded that Ninigret was the victim of "his malicious enemies amongst the Indians," who "have took occasion to raise such horrible lyes against him." Part of Ninigret's problem, they pointed out, was that he had met with "seaven of Phillip the Sachems ancient men ... for nine or ten days." When questioned about this conference earlier in July, Ninigret "gave noe satisfactory answear to that point, but put it off with a laugh, and very slight returne which gives us some further cause of suspicion."[51]

Philip, the sachem of the Wampanoags, who lived to the east of the Narragansetts in Plymouth Colony, posed perhaps the most serious challenge to English control of the southern New England frontier. As early as 1662, the Plymouth magistrates had summoned Philip before them because they had heard "lately many rumers gon too and frow of danger of the rising of the Indians against the English." Philip pledged his desire to continue in "amitie and friendship" with the colonists, and "particularly that hee will not att any time needlessly or unjustly provoake or raise warr with any other of the natives, nor att any time give, sell or any way dispose of any lands . . . without our privity, consent, or appointment."[52]

After reviewing the agreement with Plymouth's governor, Thomas Prence, Philip concluded that the arrangement freed him from pressure to sell land for seven years. Whatever the intent of Philip and Prence, Plymouth settlers, desperate to eke a living out of New England's rocky soil, had other ideas. The Wampanoags continually complained to Plymouth authorities of damage done to their crops by ranging English livestock. In May 1667 reports that Philip was conspiring against the English surfaced once again. The Plymouth magistrates investigated but could find no supporting evidence. They fined Philip £40 for their trouble. By 1671 the Wampanoags clearly had reached a crisis in their relations with the Plymouth colonists. Destruction of Indian fields by English livestock had become so great that the colony's court appointed men in each settlement "to view the damage done to the Indians by the Horses and Hoggs of the English." In March of that year, the magistrates learned that Philip and his warriors "were generally employed in making of bows and arrows and half-pikes, and fixing up of guns," and that they had threatened some of the outlying settlements in the vicinity of the Mount Hope Peninsula.[53]

While the attention of English authorities remained fixed upon Ninigret and Philip, Uncas managed to remain largely above suspicion. In 1668, Massachusetts governor Richard Bellingham informed John Winthrop. Jr. "that Uncas doth secretly assist and hould Correspondence with the Mawhauks, and that some of his people are at present with them." They had joined together, Bellingham believed, to prey upon the Praying Indians settled in central Massachusetts, whom both the Mohawks and the Mohegans despised. The Connecticut men found no evidence to support Bellingham's claim, and the matter dropped.[54]

Pressure on Mohegan lands continued, however, both in the form of livestock doing damage in Indian fields, and in the English clamor to purchase additional acreage from Uncas and his sons. The Mohegans may have felt pinched, for in March 1670 Uncas's son Owaneco asked the town of Norwich to grant him a three hundred–acre parcel of land along the Shetucket River. The town's leaders did so, but they required that Owaneco agree to certain conditions. The town reserved its right of preemption over the lands, and would take no responsibility for damage done by English animals within the bounds of the grant. They expected Owaneco to fence his fields. Further, the town sought to protect itself from damage done to English crops by the growing quantity of Mohegan livestock. As pressure on their lands increased, Indians in southern New England adopted some English subsistence practices, including the raising of animals. The evidentiary record gives us little information on how the Mohegans may have felt about this considerable cultural transformation, or how Mohegan men saw themselves as they made the gradual shift from hunting to hog raising. With no distinct division between the world of human and other-than-human beings in the native cosmos, raising English domestic animals must have created some conceptual problems for the Mohegans. It is obvious, however, that with livestock and the damage animals could do in corn fields a constant irritant in Indian-white relations, the Mohegans could not count on fair and equitable enforcement of animal trespass laws. Owaneco, the town's leaders decided, had "no liberty to keepe hoggs but what they do keepe in theire owne lands, but no liberty to goe uppon the lands common to the English." Finally, Owaneco agreed

> that if any of his subjects, his Indians, do any wrong to the towne of Norwich, or any of the inhabitants of the said Towne by killing theire cattle or trespassing uppon them in any such way . . . the said Owaneco doth ingadge [himself to provide] legall satisfaction if there be legall proofe of the said wronge, and that if uppon sufficient evidence its manifest that the said Owaneco willnot be responsible . . . but [if] he or his men doe continue refractory & will not reforme such notorious disorderly practice specified and make satisfaction for the said damages & wrongs Owaneco shall then forfeite the same lands.[55]

In 1670 Uncas and Owaneco, with Mason's support, sold some of these lands to the Norwich settler Christopher Huntington, but more of their energy was devoted to preserving the Mohegan core area. Uncas, Owaneco, and Attawanhood renewed in May 1671 their earlier covenant with John Mason and his heirs. In return, Mason did "entail and bind over unto the said Uncas, Owaneco, and Attawanhood a certain parcel of lands at Mushantackuck." The tract, according to Mason, was bounded on the southeast "upon the River of Moheag ... upon New London bounds," and then ran westward "to the uttermost extent of London bound and from thence Northerly to the uttermost End of the Western bounds of Norwich, and from thence Eastwardly to the mouth of Trading Cove." The importance of the grant is clear in the wording Mason used to define its terms. He granted the land to Uncas, Owaneco, and Attawanhood forever, and stipulated "that neither they, their heirs, or successors shall at any time make sale or any otherwayes dispose of the Premises, or any part or parcel thereof." Both Mason and Uncas were old men, in their seventies, and Mason had only a year left to live. With their own mortality firmly in mind, they tried to secure the heart of the Mohegan country for subsequent generations, fulfilling the terms of the grants of 1659 and 1665. "If any person or persons," Mason wrote, "shall at any time procure any grants from the aforesaid Sachems or their successors" to these lands, "the same shall be of no value or effect."[56]

At the same time that the Mohegans struggled to resist English pressure on their lands, they also confronted Puritan attempts to Christianize them. As early as 1652, English missionaries had viewed Uncas as an obstacle to the progress of the Gospel. In a letter he sent that year to the New England Company, the Puritan organization established in England during the Interregnum to finance missionary endeavors, John Eliot, "the apostle to the Indians," reported that "there be two Great Sachems in the Country that are open & professed enemies against praying to God, namely Unkas and [Ninigret], & when ever the Lord removeth them, there will be a dore open for the preaching of the Gospell in those parts."[57]

The Lord showed little interest in cooperating with the Puritans in this instance, and Ninigret and Uncas remained objects of missionary concern. In the fall of 1654 the River Colony magistrates, aware of their obligation "to promoate and further what lyes in them a worke of that nature, wherein the glory of God & the everlasting welfare of those poore, lost, naked sonnes of Adam is so deepely concerned," ordered that the son of Thomas Minor be educated as a translator and assistant for future missionaries. Little came of this effort. Three years later the Commissioners of the United Colonies appointed William Thomson to minister to the Mohegans. Thomson was a failure. Faced with Uncas's opposition, he did not preach, and his stipend was revoked in 1661.[58]

Despite the slender harvest, the River Colony encouraged those willing to preach to the Indians, whenever and wherever they appeared. John Winthrop Jr. told the directors of the Corporation for the Propagation of the Gospel (the Restoration-era successor to the New England Company) that the Christianization of Connecticut's Indians would have significant economic benefits, for Christianized Indians would necessarily be civilized Indians. In the vicinity of New London, he gushed, there lived "many thousands" of Indians who "would willingly wear English apparel if they knew how to purchase it." Indians would consume English wares once they had converted, and diligently produce hemp, flax, pitch, tar, wheat, and "prarie grass" for the English and colonial market. Make an Indian a Christian, Winthrop seemed to suggest, and you can sell him a wool coat. Some years later, in 1669, a "Mr. John Blackleach" asked the magistrates to support his efforts "to make known to the Indians (in the best way he can) something of the knowledg of God according as he shall have opportunety." That opportunity seems not to have knocked. Dreamy economic ideas and good intentions were not enough to make any progress. The Gospel made little headway among the Mohegans and their neighbors in Connecticut.[59]

The reason for this lack of progress must rest at least in part on the shoulders of the erstwhile missionaries themselves. Few of them, it seems, really tried to approach Uncas. They were intimidated by the sachem. The Reverend James Fitch was different. The pastor at Norwich since settling there in 1660, Fitch had gained some familiarity with the Mohegans' Algonquin dialect. In 1671 the Connecticut magistrates asked Uncas and Owaneco if they would allow Fitch to preach at Mohegan. They later would send gifts to "incourage" Uncas "to attend on the ministry of the gospel by mr. ffitch." The Mohegan sachems offered no objection, causing the River Colony men to declare that Fitch's efforts "to convey something of the knowledge of God and the light of the Gospell to these poore heathen that have so long satt in darkness and the shadow of death, is gratefully accepted by this Court, who shall be ready to encourage Mr. Fitch in the worke." They knew enough not to trust Uncas entirely, however, for the magistrates also announced that they would "looke with an unpleasinge countenance upon those that shall any wayes interrupt or hinder them in their due attendance to what God shall be made knowne to them." Fitch hoped to reach Mohegan commoners, with or without Uncas's assistance.[60]

Uncas likely saw Fitch as an ally who could help him continue to protect Mohegan lands. After Mason's death in 1672, Uncas began to cultivate Fitch as a guardian. As a respected leader in Norwich, related to Mason by marriage, and capable of communicating with the Mohegan sachem, Fitch seems to have been viewed by Uncas as a logical successor to Mason. And to develop this relationship, Uncas was willing to allow Fitch access to his followers. For their relationship to be based upon reciprocity and balance, Uncas knew that he had to give a little. In 1673 he agreed to "attend upon Mr. James Fitch Minister of Norwich, at all such seasons as he shall appoint for preaching to and praying with the Indains" at Pamechaug, where Uncas was then living, or elsewhere in the Mohegan territory. Further, Uncas promised that he would

> command all my people to attend the same, in a constant way and solemn manner at all such times as shall be sett by the sayd Mr. James Fitch minister, alsoe I promis that I will not by any wayes or meanes whatsoever, either privately or openly use any plots or contrivances by words or actions to affright or discourage any of my people or others, from attending the good work aforesaid, upon suffering the most grievous punishments that can be inflicted upon me.

Uncas, who Fitch feared would intimidate prospective converts, also agreed to encourage the Mohegans to observe "such directions and instructions as shall be presented" to them by Fitch.[61]

The Norwich minister as a result began his missions among the Mohegans with a sense of optimism. Uncas, the inveterate opponent of the Gospel, would give Fitch a chance to carry the Bible to his followers. Fitch's hope that the word of God would work upon the hearts of Uncas's people, however, soon gave way to frequent expressions of frustration. By 1674 Uncas and his sons began directly to interfere with and obstruct Puritan preaching to the Mohegans and their tributaries. First, Eliot and his associates began to preach at Wabquissit, a Nipmuck town of 150, just north of the boundary between Massachusetts and Connecticut. Eliot and his fellow ministers met with "divers of the principle people" of the town, and "spent a good part of the night in prayer, singing psalms, and exhortations." One Indian, Eliot reported, sat aloof, watching the gathering in silence. At last he spoke. He represented Uncas, who claimed the people of Wabquissit as subjects. Uncas, the messenger told Eliot, "is not well pleased that the English should pass over Mohegon River, to call his Indians to pray to God."[62]

Eliot told Uncas's emissary to back off. Wabquissit, Eliot said, "was within the jurisdiction of Massachusetts," whatever Uncas claimed, "and that the government of that people did belong to them." Then, seemingly unaware of the contradiction, Eliot said that Uncas need not worry about Puritan missionary activity, for the English did not intend "to abridge the Indian sachems of their just and ancient right over the Indians, in respect of paying tribute or any other dues." The Puritans, moreover, "had taken no tribute from them, nor taxed them with any thing of that kind." They only hoped "to bring them to the good knowledge of God in Christ Jesus; and to suppress among them those sins of drunkenness, idolatry, powwowing or witchcraft, whoredom, murder, and like sins."[63]

In November Fitch himself found that Uncas had withdrawn his support for Christian missions among the Mohegans. Uncas saw the threat posed by missionaries as fundamentally political in nature. According to Fitch, when Uncas learned "that religion would not consist with a mere receiving of the word; and that practical religion will throw down their heathenish idols, and the sachems tyrannical monarchy," he and his sons "drew off their people, some by flatteries, and others by threatenings, and they would not suffer them to give so much as an outward attendance to the ministry of the word of God." Daniel Gookin, the publicist of Fitch's efforts, could only conclude that Uncas was "an old and wicked, willful man, a drunkard and otherwise very vitious, who hath always been an opposer and underminer of Praying to God."[64]

Uncas had watched some thirty of his followers, men and women, in addition to their children, embrace Fitch's message. He made life difficult for these converts. The Christian Mohegans, Fitch reported, "suffer much . . . that it is to wonderment that they are not utterly discouraged." Uncas and his followers "do the utmost what they can, by reproaches, revilings, and threatenings, especially in a clandestine manner, to dismay them." It is difficult to say for certain what drew these Indians toward the Gospel. Some received material benefits. Fitch allowed them to farm some of his excess lands; Uncas's son Attawanhood, who took the name Joshua, was given liberty by the General Court to purchase two horses, "the one for himselfe and the other for his interpreter, that they may be the better capacitated to attend their meetings with Mr. Fitch." Further, conversion may have brought freedom from tributary obligations to "tyrannical" sachems like Uncas. Finally, conversion to a new faith provided Indians with an intellectual tool for coping with a world thrown radically out of balance by European colonization.[65]

Thirty Mohegans, still, was a relatively small number. And though Uncas certainly was correct to see a threat to his political authority in the words and deeds of Puritan ministers, and as well an explicit threat to Mohegan traditional beliefs and culture, he proved to be a greater source of frustration to the preachers than they were to him. Uncas's opposition to their efforts, and his steadfast attempts to insulate the Mohegans from neighboring English colonists, largely account for the meager harvest of native souls in Connecticut. Though the two decades that followed Ninigret's defeat in 1654 witnessed increasing limits on Mohegan autonomy, English territorial aggression upon Mohegan lands, Puritan assaults upon Mohegan culture and religion, and a growing sense of doubt among Puritan authorities that Uncas could help them establish English dominion over the Anglo-American frontier, Uncas managed more successfully than other native New Englanders to confront these very significant threats to the Mohegans and their world, securing a foundation for his people's survival in the coming years of danger.

CHAPTER 7

Uncas, the Mohegans, and King Philip's War

Connecticut managed to avoid the horrors of war with its Indian neighbors for nearly four decades after Anglo-Mohegan forces destroyed the Pequots in 1637, despite periodic tumults, rumors of revolt, and continuous intercultural conflict among Algonquian village communities. Still, fighting among the Mohegans and their rivals destabilized the southern New England frontier in Puritan eyes, and caused colonial authorities in the River Colony to consider Uncas a nuisance whose freedom to act in his own behalf must be circumscribed. Especially after 1654, the English along the river were less willing to tolerate Indian behavior that they viewed as inconsistent with their plans for an orderly, peaceful, and ultimately *English* New England. The outbreak of a massive Algonquian uprising against the English in the summer of 1675 reversed this trend, at least in the short term, because it forced colonial officials once again to rely upon their Indian friends to secure the safety of English settlements along the Connecticut frontier. Uncas and his sons responded immediately to English appeals for assistance, but as they did so they used the war to pursue the interests of their people in a world of declining options and mounting hostility toward Indians.

•

The Algonquian uprising of 1675, commonly known as "King Philip's War," found its origins in Plymouth Plantation. The colony had done nothing to address the fundamental sources of Philip's disaffection, and the Wampanoags continued to complain of injuries done them by the frontier population. These appeals for redress became so numerous and such a burden to the colony's legal system that, beginning in 1673, Plymouth at times banned Indians from town when the court was in session. Instead of responding to the growing volume of Indian complaints and curbing the aggressiveness of the frontier population, the Pilgrims, in effect, covered their ears against the sounds of Wampanoag anger. In January 1675, the level of tension between Philip's followers and the Plymouth men reached dangerous proportions when the body of John Sassamon was found stuffed under the ice in a nearby pond. Sassamon was a Christian Indian who had betrayed Philip, spread rumors of his hostility toward the English, and attempted to defraud him of much of his land. The English tried and convicted three of Philip's followers for the murder early in June 1675.[1]

The Plymouth magistrates knew that the prosecution of Sassamon's killers angered Wampanoag warriors, who gave the colonists "frequent alarums by drums and guns in the night." Philip, too, was angry. In the middle of June, following the execution of his men for killing Sassamon, he told Rhode Island's Quaker lieutenant governor, John Easton, that the settlers made the Indians drunk "and then Cheted them in Bargens." They used coercive and deceptive means to acquire Indian land that the Wampanoags had no intention of selling. No matter the distance between native and newcomer, Philip continued, his followers "could not kepe their Coren from being spoyled" by English livestock. In 1675 it already was a very old story, and it would be repeated on many subsequent frontiers. Desperate Indians had killed aggressive English settlers for far less. Easton knew this, but he hoped, still, to avoid war. He offered to help Philip settle his differences with the English through arbitration, but Philip had little reason to place his faith in colonial remedies. "All English agred against" his people, he told Easton, so there could be little hope in looking to them for justice. Many Wampanoag warriors felt the same way. Appearing in war paint, weapons in hand, they traveled through Algonquian village communities to discuss their options. Some may have traveled to Mohegan. For them, war seemed the last best choice.[2]

The fighting started late in June, when two Plymouth settlers killed an Indian they caught rifling an abandoned house on the outskirts of Swansea. The next day, June 24, the Wampanoags killed these two colonists, and seven others, in retaliation. The neighbors of these Englishmen found their mutilated bodies at the scene of the massacre.³ It was the small beginning to a very large war, the most deadly conflict per capita in American history. After Philip's forces hit Swansea, they fell upon the neighboring villages of Rehoboth and Taunton. On July 9 they attacked Middleborough, burning most of the houses there. They then struck Dartmouth; in the southern part of Plymouth, burning thirty houses and killing "many people after a most barbarous manner; as skinning them all alive, some only their heads, cutting off their hands and feet." A week later, Nipmuck warriors in central Massachusetts attacked the town of Mendon. The number of Indian groups taking part in attacks increased with each native success, and the colonists' own offensives against the Algonquians proved little more than ill-led and poorly executed exercises in futility that killed needlessly large numbers of Englishmen.⁴

Philip's warriors must have recognized that the English colonists simply lacked the military means to defend isolated agricultural settlements scattered along three hundred miles of frontier. Colonial forces had not engaged them effectively. Colonial militia men, still trained in the formal standards of European warfare, Philip found easy prey. The amateur English soldiers stumbled into ambush after bloody Algonquian ambush, staged by determined Indians armed with flintlock muskets nearly identical to those that the colonists carried. Frustrated, Englishmen like Connecticut's lieutenant governor William Leete concluded that it was "hardly feasible to extirpate [the Indians] in an ordinary way, they being so cunning in a skulking, ambuscadoe maner, to take advantage of the woods, & so accurate markes men, abouve our men, to doe execution, whereby more of ours are like to fall, rather then of theirs, unlesse the Lord, by speciall providences, doe deliver them into our handes."⁵

The English could not counter the hostile Algonquians' "skulking way of war," but Leete and many of his associates thought that Connecticut's old Indian allies might be enlisted to defend the frontiers of the province and to carry the war into the homeland of their enemies. Why not, as one colonial poet put it, "imploy a wily roag to cach a thefe?"⁶ Indians, Leete reminded his countrymen, could fight in ways that colonists could not. But before Leete could employ Indians in the colony's defense, he had to overcome the mounting distrust his countrymen felt toward their native neighbors, and counter the growing body of evidence that more and more Algonquians had joined with Philip in attacks against English settlements. Massachusetts and Plymouth had already managed to ensure themselves the hatred of the Algonquian village communities in their colonies. The Mohegans came under suspicion too, and some colonial leaders believed that Uncas supported Philip's uprising. One New London settler, for instance, told John Winthrop Jr. that he feared a "universall combination of the Indians." Philip, the worried frontiersman wrote, "is very near us and expects further assistance from Uncas." Roger Williams, in Rhode Island, received numerous reports from the Narragansetts of Uncas's suspicious activity. The Mohegan sachem, Williams heard, had killed some Connecticut Indians and sent the heads and hands to the Mohawks, the powerful eastern-most of the Five Nations of the Iroquois, whose very name terrified English colonists. Uncas's son Owaneco had killed a lesser Narragansett sachem. The Mohegans continued to pursue their own interests, violently if necessary. Williams performed his usual duty, trying to keep the peace, but he feared the consequences of the impending war. He firmly believed that Philip would not have attacked Plymouth "had he not been assured to have bene seconded and assisted by the Monhiggins and Nahigonsicks."[7]

In this atmosphere of fear and suspicion, Uncas recognized the need to demonstrate his fidelity to the English once again. Shortly after the fighting started, he and a large number of his followers traveled along the "Great Indian Trail" to meet with the Commissioners of the United Colonies and the Massachusetts Bay Colony General Court at Boston. There Uncas pledged his assistance to the English and staked his sons on that promise. Owaneco, with fifty warriors, would join English forces from the Bay Colony and Plymouth in their efforts to capture Philip. Uncas left two of his youngest sons as well, Attawanhood and Ben, as hostages. He turned over to the Commissioners of the United Colonies a number of weapons, though of what sort and variety we never will know. The Bay Colony men and the commissioners were pleased. They accepted Uncas's offers with genuine appreciation and provided him with an armed escort, ensuring his safe return to the Mohegan heartland.

Several days later, on July 10, Uncas arrived in Norwich to solidify his relations with the River Colony. He addressed James Fitch with "a longe narrative of his acts of friendship in former dayes to the English, & professed that he will now in the time of hazarde be the same." The

Mohegan sachem knew that he could not simply sit upon his laurels. Uncas suggested that Connecticut needed his assistance to secure its eastern frontier and to serve as its eyes and ears there, on the watch always for potential threats. He provided Fitch with intelligence that he knew the English would find useful: Pessicus, the Narragansett sachem, "hath taken Philip's women & children & hath undertaken to keepe them safe while he goes about destroying the English." The Mohegans' old rivals, Uncas said, had assisted the colonists' enemies, and he was in the best position to monitor their activity.[8]

Fitch acknowledged Uncas's past contributions to the safety of the colony, and he appreciated the intelligence about the Narragansetts. The crisis the colony now faced, however, was of a higher order than earlier troubles, and Fitch conceded that "some did doubt what he [Uncas] would doe." Fitch and the Connecticut men expected that Uncas would leave additional hostages in Hartford and that when the time came "to the triall who are friends and who are foes," he "would indeed shewe his friendship" by following the orders of Connecticut's Council of War. Uncas accepted Fitch's conditions. He had little real choice. The meeting in Norwich must have left him with a bitter taste in his mouth, for the standard for proving oneself a friend to the English seemed to rise each year. For the first time, Connecticut officials required hostages of him. Two members of his immediate family remained in Massachusetts, and now the Connecticut men expected two more. Uncas offered his people's assistance to the English, but not out of unyielding loyalty to the colonists. Experience had taught him that risings against the English could not succeed, and that neutrality was not respected by the English, whose biblical belief was "those who are not for us are against us." The Mohegans entered the war in the summer of 1675, but not without conditions. Uncas, indeed, must have mentioned to Fitch that the commissioners had demanded that he leave many of his firearms in Massachusetts. Connecticut, if it wanted the Mohegans to help, needed to supply him with additional arms and ammunition for his warriors.[9]

•

Governor John Winthrop Jr.'s son Wait Winthrop argued early in July that Connecticut must act with energy to "prevent the Narrogansets from Joyning with Philip." A small English force, he suggested, "with sum of the Moheges and Pequots which seme redy to attend us," should visit Ninigret and the Narragansett sachems to determine their true intentions. Ninigret would meet with the colonists only if they did not bring "any of Uncas his men with us, for reasons which he will tell us when we speake with him." Wait Winthrop gave no indication as to why Ninigret, who had been at peace with Uncas for the past several years, would not want to meet with the Mohegans, but it seems likely that the Algonquian uprising both reawakened long-simmering resentments and distrust and provided an opportunity for Indians to settle old scores. Ninigret may have remembered how Uncas had used previous episodes of Anglo-Indian hostility to advance his own interests. This was no time for Ninigret to trust the Mohegans. Three weeks after the meeting, one of Ninigret's followers arrived in New London with a present to demonstrate his friendship to the English: "one of Phillip's mens heads." Ninigret hoped, the messenger said, that "the English will take notice of his fidelity," and allow him to stay out of harm's way.[10]

Ninigret broke with the Narragansetts during the war, so Governor Winthrop and his sons had one less thing to worry about. Other Narragansetts, colonial leaders sensed, would not be so helpful. The Connecticut Council of War ordered Captain Thomas Bull on July 16 to march from his post at Saybrook to New London or Norwich "to secure the borders" of the colony "if any trouble should arise by the Narragansetts." Once there, Bull would also meet with Uncas "respecting how many Indians he can raise and how ready fitted, and upon what warneing to march." He should obtain information on how much it would cost the colony to supply and equip Uncas's warriors with arms and ammunition. Fearing an attack from the east, the Council of War viewed the Mohegans as a vital component in the colony's overall defense.[11]

Connecticut's strategy was primarily defensive, but the colony's English neighbors had quickly launched offensives against Philip's followers. They too received assistance from the Mohegans. Owaneco and his fifty warriors accompanied the English force that left the Bay Colony late in July to pursue Philip. On August 1 the Mohegans overtook Philip's party near Rehoboth at a location called Nipsachuck. They killed thirty of Philip's men; another fifty-five surrendered. The

Mohegans stopped their pursuit after the battle, and the English would not proceed without them. Had the English pursued Philip, the Puritan divine Increase Mather wrote, the colonists and their Indian guides "might easily have overtaken the Women and Children that were with Philip, yea and himself also, and so have put an end to these tumults." God, Mather concluded, "saw it not good for us as yet" to triumph. The Saints learned that their Indian allies fought on their own terms, and that these allies would decide for themselves whether or not to pursue the enemy. Philip escaped into the Nipmuck territory, "kindling the flame of war in all the western plantations of the Massachusetts Colony wherever he came."[12]

The Mohegans' service was limited, but it did have the salutary effect of allaying the suspicions of the River Colony's military leaders. They "condescended to Uncass his request" to have his grandson, one of the Hartford hostages, transferred to Norwich. There the boy would live under the supervision of the Reverend Fitch, who apparently allowed him to return to his village with a promise not to leave the area without the councilors' permission. Attawanhood, released by the Commissioners of the United Colonies, returned to Connecticut and asked the Council of War "that his guns be delivered up to him." The Council of War found Attawanhood "very ready to be ordered by the English" and as a result judged "it convenient that his guns be delivered up to him." In a New England where nearly all Indians had become objects of fear and suspicion, where selling Indians weapons was in places a capital crime, the Connecticut men, responding to the actions of their Mohegan allies, placed guns in their hands.[13]

On August 5, Fitch and Lieutenants John Mason Jr. and James Avery encouraged the Mohegans and Pequots to pursue Philip's forces in the Nipmuck and Narragansett territory. Under the command of Lieutenant John Browne, eighty Pequots and nearly one hundred Mohegans moved out to war with a small number of Englishmen. On the 8th, two of the Mohegans arrived in Hartford, "with sundry heads or scalps, two whereof they bestowed upon the English." Meanwhile, the council sent Attawanhood with thirty men northward to help defend Springfield, in Massachusetts's part of the valley. Attawanhood's warriors had reached the town of Hadley by the 9th.[14]

The warfare brought benefits to the Mohegans in the form of

adoptees and additional population. On August 17 Reverend Fitch informed the Council of War that "120 of the Nipmuck Indians were coming to resign up themselves to Uncass with their familys." The council ordered that Uncas disarm these Indians, and that if any of them had "embrued their hands in English blood," he must turn them over. Fitch investigated. He found that the "Wabawquassock" Indians, Mohegan tributaries, had taken about 111 of Philip's men, women, and children, and that these Lieutenant Mason took "with strength both of English and Indians" for shipment to Boston and, ultimately, sale into West Indian slavery. Uncas, too, Fitch believed, provided shelter to Indians guilty of killing Englishmen. Uncas, however, refused to relinquish the Nipmuck surrenderers, who willingly accepted incorporation into Mohegan village communities as an alternative to summary execution or a short, but brutal, lifetime in slavery. Uncas, through these means, increased the strength and number of potential Mohegan warriors.[15]

Despite his advanced age, Uncas led some war parties himself into the Nipmuck country, where, with English support, he attempted to subjugate Algonquian communities that had slipped from his control over the preceding years. Colonial officials welcomed Uncas's assistance, but they believed that the elderly sachem could do even more for them. John Pynchon, writing from his exposed outpost at Springfield, suggested that Uncas conduct raids in the Connecticut River Valley because he was one "who hath of old had a grudge against the Upriver Indians." Pynchon believed that Uncas might be persuaded to attack the Saints' northernmost Indian enemies owing to the history of hostility that he had with them. After more than one hundred Englishmen died on the march to Hadley, the need for Uncas's assistance became even more urgent. Wait Winthrop and Lieutenant John Mason Jr. hastily led a force to garrison "those plantations up the River, to prosecute, persue, and destroy all such Indians as have risen up and are in hostility against the English." They had a crisis on their hands in the valley, and they needed the Mohegans to help.[16]

That the Mohegans did, and their presence in the valley prevented a number of English military disasters from turning out worse than they did. On September 18, for example, Captain Thomas Lathrop, with eighty English colonists, marched out of Hadley to escort the settlers at Deerfield to a more secure location downriver. Five miles south of the town, Wampanoag, Nipmuck, Pocumtuck, and Norwootuck warriors attacked. They caught Lathrop's men entirely by surprise. Some of the English soldiers had been "so foolish and secure" as to put their weapons in the empty carts that would haul the settlers' baggage. Others left the trail to gather grapes, which, Increase Mather wrote, "proved dear and deadly grapes to them." Lathrop fell immediately. The Indians knew to shoot the leaders first. Sixty men more, the "flower of the County of Essex," were gunned down as well. Samuel Mosely, a vicious Jamaican privateer known for feeding Indian captives to his war dogs, hurried from Deerfield to try to rescue Lathrop. Quickly he, too, found himself overrun, with the enemy pressing in "upon them with great numbers, so to knock them down with their Hatchets." Mosely must have feared that he would face, at last, some of the violence he had meted out upon his Indian opponents. At the last possible second, however, "threescore of Unkas his Indians" along with a force of one hundred Englishmen under Major Robert Treat, arrived "in the nick of time" to rescue Mosely. They turned the tide of the battle and drove off Philip's forces. Night fell before the combined Anglo-Mohegan force could pursue.[17]

English forces continued to patrol the Connecticut River Valley in Massachusetts, but the Mohegans had returned home by the twenty-fourth. Uncas promised the Council of War that they would "attend when there should be farther occasion," but he did not view his warriors as Connecticut's frontier irregulars. When James Fitch left Norwich on September 28 to "procure the Pequot and Moheag Indians to com up, to go forth with our army," Uncas refused. The River Colony, he said, expected too much from the Mohegans. Indians along the Connecticut, he said, who had demonstrated "their unwillingness to joyne with them in this war," should do more fighting. Uncas wanted his men to remain closer to home. He was more interested in the security of his own villages and the subjugation of his tributaries. The scattered English outposts along the river were not his problem.[18]

Though the Connecticut Council of War commissioned Attawanhood to patrol the hills on the east side of the Connecticut River in Massachusetts, Uncas concentrated the bulk of his activity in and around the Mohegan heartland. Combined English-Pequot and Anglo-Mohegan forces patrolled New London County, effectively securing the colony's eastern frontier. Uncas knew this service was valuable to the colony for, he believed, it could free the English to strike decisively at Philip's forces. He advised Connecticut's Council of War early in October "to stir up all their strength, to make war their work and trade, for endeavouring to suppresse these enemyes, before they grow too much for us." Uncas would secure "the frontier townes adjacent to the enemyes." The English, he suggested, must in the meantime carry the war into Philip's territory. The colonists must attack with energy, so that "the enemyes hearts wilbe weakened or dampened."[19]

The network of cooperation that existed between the Mohegans, the Pequots, and the River Colony spared Connecticut the worst of the slaughter that came with the war, but on other fronts the struggle was not going well for the Puritans. Provincial forces had neither successfully nor decisively engaged Philip's forces in battle, and they had failed to prevent Algonquian communities in Rhode Island and Massachusetts from joining him. This produced a level of frustration and fear outside Connecticut that manifested itself in increasingly vicious treatment of Indians, whether friendly or not. Little wonder that Uncas hesitated before leaving Connecticut Colony.

Massachusetts and Plymouth sold captured Indians into slavery in the West Indies. Others they "condemned unto perpetuall servitude . . . for and to the use of the collonie," or they executed on the spot. Puritan officials forced the Praying Indians, or "Preying Indians" as one suspiciously hostile colonist described them, into concentration camps on the windswept islands near Boston Harbor. Mobs in Boston roughed up Englishmen sympathetic to Indians. The Plymouth Court ordered that anyone who fired a gun in the colony for any reason, "except att an Indian or a woolfe," must pay a fine of five shillings, a telling suggestion of the shade English attitudes toward native neighbors had taken.[20]

Puritan ministers in the Bay Colony attributed colonial military failures to the wrath of God. The minister and historian William Hubbard feared that "God hath a controversie with New England, so now that the rod of affliction hath not only budded and blossomed, but brought forth its fruit." Colonial magistrates appointed days of fasting and humiliation, and called for the moral regeneration of their people. They understood the war in biblical terms. Nathaniel Saltonstall, for example, thought "the Dispensation we lay under was very Cloudy and Affrighting, Fresh Messengers (like Job's Servants) howrly arriving to bring Doleful Tidings of New Massacres, slaughters, and Devastations committed by the Brutish Heathens."[21]

That the "Brutish Heathens" did less damage in Connecticut than elsewhere did not go unnoticed by Puritan preachers. "It was prudently done" by the River Colony men, Increase Mather noted, "not to make the Indians who lived amongst them their enemies, and the Lord hath made them to be as a wall to them, and also made use of them to do great service against the common Enemies of the English." Mather saw God's hand in everything. Indians became friend or foe of the English only as instruments of divine justice. Mather could not recognize that peace in the River Colony resulted from the shrewd and calculated decisions made by English and Native American leaders who each saw in a peaceful and orderly frontier the best interests of their people.[22]

The River Colony did have its draconian laws, severely punishing illegal arms sales to Indians, but much of the time Connecticut actively cultivated its Indian allies and appealed to their interests. James Fitch Jr., the minister's son, supplied the Mohegans and Pequots with powder and shot. The colony's Council of War allowed Owaneco to govern the "Wangum or Nayeag" Indians as he saw fit and to "dispose" of some of Philip's men "by sale or other wayes as he shall find most advantageous to himselfe" if they would not willingly submit to his authority.[23]

Uncas and Owaneco responded favorably to Puritan calls for assistance when doing so allowed them to attack old enemies. During the two decades that preceded King Philip's uprising, the English had attempted to limit the Mohegans' efforts to make war, closing off the traditional path young Mohegans had taken to achieve manhood and status within their village communities. War always had been a central element in Eastern Algonquian culture. Now the Mohegans found themselves equipped by the River Colony men with guns and ammunition. They were encouraged to attack their old rivals.

Uncas sent Mohegan warriors under the command of Owaneco to participate in the bloodiest campaign of King Philip's war, a combined Anglo-Indian raid into the heart of the Narragansett country. Catapazet, a son of the Pequot sachem Hermon Garrett, led a small force of Pequots as well. The Commissioners of the United Colonies, on the basis of evidence they had received from Uncas and others, suspected that the Narragansetts had provided shelter and assistance to Philip's forces. In October 1675, they had obtained a pledge from the Narragansett sachems to hand over all Wampanoags settled among them, but by November 2, the deadline, the Narragansetts still had not complied. The commissioners thus concluded that "the Narragansett Indians are deeply accessory in the present bloody outrages," and "in open hostillitie with the English." The commissioners called for an army of one thousand men to invade the Narragansett territory. On the 22nd the Connecticut Council of War agreed to raise its quota of 315 men. Six days later the council sent ambassadors to line up assistance from the Mohegans and Pequots.[24]

Little is known about the Mohegan and Pequot role in the ensuing campaign. The English troops began to assemble in Rhode Island in December during a brutal winter. The majority of them came from the Bay Colony. Plymouth sent a contingent of 159 soldiers. Major Robert Treat commanded Connecticut's forces, which included the 150 Mohegans and Pequots under Owaneco and Catapazet. Josiah Winslow of Massachusetts took the reins as commander-in-chief of the combined English force.

Before dawn on December 19, the English forces, following the lead of a captured Narragansett informant, advanced across the frozen swamp near West Kingston, Rhode Island, toward the Narragansetts' fortification, a hidden complex complete with breastworks and palisades, located upon "a Piece of firm Land, about three or four acres of Ground." The fighting was fierce. The Narragansetts directed their fire at those Englishmen barking out orders, hoping to spread confusion among the inexperienced soldiers. Samuel Mosely claimed that he saw fifty warriors aim at him at once. According to Joseph Dudley, the defenders "entertained us with a fierce fight, and many thousands shot, for about an hour." Nearly seventy Englishmen died in the assault, including "six brave captains." The Narragansetts wounded 150 more before the English broke through the palisades, drove off the defenders, and set fire to the fortress. The English killed ninety-seven warriors and wounded forty-eight, not counting many more who perished "by the burning of the houses." Hundreds of Narragansetts must have died in the Great Swamp Fight.[25]

Owaneco's forces likely scouted for the English and served as flankers on their march to the fort, protecting the Puritans from the threat of Narragansett ambush, though we can never know for sure. There is conflicting testimony on the Mohegans' role in the actual assault on the Narragansett fortress. One eighteenth-century historian of Connecticut believed that the Mohegans and Pequots suffered heavy casualties attacking the palisades. Fifty-one Mohegans died and eighty-two received wounds, out of a total force of no more than 150 warriors. A casualty rate of almost 87 percent seems too high to have escaped comment by the English. But other sources, suggesting Mohegan treachery during the battle, seem equally unbelievable. The prisoner Joshua Tefft, an Englishman who lived, fought, and identified with the Narragansetts, told Roger Williams a month after the battle that "if the Monhiggins & Pequts had been true, they might have destroyed most of the Nihaggonsiks; but the Nahigonsiks parleyed with them in the beginning of the fight, so that they promised to shoot high, which they did, & killed not one Nahigonsik man, except against their wills." The Bay Colony's James Oliver, similarly, had heard that the "Monhegins and Pequods proved very false, fired into the air, and sent word before they came they would do so, but got much plunder, guns and kettles," but he may have merely repeated Tefft's story. The Mohegans would have little to gain through such deception. The story originates, moreover, with sources hostile to them: a condemned English traitor and adopted Narragansett, and a magistrate from the Bay Colony, where distrust of the Mohegans had a long history.[26]

The truth, as it does so often, probably lies somewhere in the middle. The Mohegans would have joined in the assault, and they would have suffered some casualties, though not as many as the highest estimates suggest. Unfamiliar with attacking fortified positions, they may have fought poorly, lending some credence to rumors that they had leagued with the Narragansetts. Yet there is no reason to believe that Owaneco would show such mercy to the Narragansetts and risk bringing down upon his father's people the wrath of the colonists. Neither the Mohegans nor the English knew the location of the fort before it was revealed to them by their captured Narragansett guide. At no point in their history had the Mohegans given breath to a cornered enemy, and here there would have been nothing to gain by altering this practice. The Connecticut men, especially battered in the assault, said nothing of Mohegan treachery, and certainly would have had they witnessed it. They called upon the Mohegans to join with them in battle on numerous occasions after the Swamp Fight, and they would not have done so if they suspected the Mohegans were unfaithful. After the fight they had no more stomach for pursuing the fleeing Narragansetts than did Owaneco's warriors. The Mohegans joined their English neighbors in limping home.

That the River Colony men and their Mohegan and Pequot allies returned home angered the leaders of the Massachusetts Bay Colony. The Bay Colony maintained a garrison in the Narragansett country after the Swamp Fight, and its troops suffered terribly from the cold. Connecticut redeemed itself in January. The Council of War raised a three hundred-man force and placed it under the command once again of Major Treat. The council ordered Treat, "if the Moheags and Pequots doe still proffer their service," to see that they "be duely encouraged, treated, and improved to best advantage." The Indian allies should be armed, equipped, and given "a signal marke to distinguish [them] from other Indians." The council knew that Indian-hating was on the rise. Two Indian prisoners had just been gunned down in a New London jail "by two wounded soldiers it is said." The town's leaders chose not to investigate, but the council took precautions to protect their allies from an increasingly anti-Indian frontier population.[27]

Seeking revenge for their losses in the Swamp Fight, a large number of Mohegans and Pequots responded to the council's call for assistance. Uncas, one member of the expedition reported, "is gon forth in person," seeking vengeance. Treat's soldiers and Uncas's warriors left New London on January 26, passing through Stonington, on their way into the Narragansett country. They rendezvoused with a Bay Colony force and set off in pursuit of the enemy. No Indians would stand and fight, and Connecticut's contingent returned to New London by February 7 without capturing their prey. They failed to land a decisive blow, but the Council of War appreciated their efforts in any case. They voted to "return thanks to Uncas, Owanecoe, Mawmawho and Robbin for their good service in the last expedition."[28]

Several days after the Mohegans returned home, Uncas sent word to the Reverend Fitch that a group of hostile Indians had assembled in the Wabequassit territory. Mohegan tributaries, these Wabequassits saw in King Philip's War an opportunity not only to strike at the English but to throw off their subjection to Uncas as well. They were playing a game with which Uncas was very familiar. Fitch relayed Uncas's intelligence to the Council of War at Hartford, who quickly ordered Thomas Avery and George Denison to press into service "60 or 80 men" from Norwich, New London, and Stonington, "taking with them the Mohegan and Pequot Indians." Once again, Uncas had secured English military support for Mohegan objectives. The combined Anglo-Indian force drove off the hostile Wabequassits and asserted Mohegan control over the area. Uncas had effectively sent them a message: remain faithful, or be driven from your homelands.[29]

The Narragansetts remained the principal object of Connecticut's concern. The River Colony men knew that they had inflicted significant damage upon the tribe at the Great Swamp Fight, but they knew as well that they had not defeated the Narragansetts. The Swamp Fight, as one nineteenth-century historian put it, "had enraged the Indians and made them desperate, and the English plantations, after that, were in greater danger than before." Connecticut forces, aided by Uncas and Mohegan warriors, remained on the offensive. They burned Pomham's town near Warwick, Rhode Island, captured and killed important Narragansett sachems, and destroyed a large quantity of their winter provisions. Ashpoet, a lesser Mohegan sachem, launched a series of raids against the Narragansetts "to distresse the enemie" and "to seiz them and what provisions they could find." Mohegan war parties brought a stream of Indian captives into New London through March and into April.[30]

Yet the Council of War still needed a knockout blow. In the spring of 1676 it began to lay plans for a campaign to destroy the Narragansetts. Once again, the Mohegans and Pequots played a central role in the plans. Robert Treat would march out with the colony's Indian allies "to attaque and destroy the enemye, and such provision and estate as you can come at." The council empowered Treat "to doe what in you lyeth for the public good, either by destroying or treating the enemie as you shall seem best." To encourage volunteers to join the expedition, the Council of War promised Indians and Englishmen that they "shall have all such plunder as they shall seize, both of persons and corn or other estate, to be disspossed by them in way of sale, so as they may best advantage themselves, provided Authority have had the first tender of theire dispose of captives, alloweing them the market price; to be divided amongst them."[31]

Events late in March 1676 underscored the urgency of launching a campaign against the Narragansetts. On the 26th, Narragansett warriors attacked and destroyed the village of Simsbury in eastern Connecticut. On the same day, another Narragansett force ambushed a group of Plymouth soldiers near the present-day town of Central Falls, Rhode Island. Only a handful of Englishmen survived. Two days later, led by their sachem Canonchet, Narragansetts destroyed Rehoboth in Plymouth Colony, and, on the 29th they sacked Providence. Among the more than one hundred buildings burned was Roger Williams's house.[32]

The combined Anglo-Indian force left Connecticut early in April in pursuit of the Narragansetts. On the 11th, a detachment of forty-seven Englishmen and eighty Mohegans and Pequots captured Canonchet in a swamp near Seaconk, Rhode Island, after a brief firefight. The English immediately executed most of the Narragansetts they had taken captive, but they carried Canonchet to Stonington. The Narragansett sachem knew his fate. When told he would be killed, Canonchet reportedly told his captors that "it is well. I shall die before my heart is soft." The English consented to their Indian allies' request to carry out the execution. Cassacinamon shot the Narragansett sachem; Owaneco, representing the Mohegans, beheaded and quartered him, and other Pequots kindled a fire and burned the body. The head they presented to the English as a trophy.[33]

The success of this foray into the heart of the Narragansett country encouraged the Connecticut Council of War to send out George Denison on other occasions with combined forces of River Colony men, Pequots, and Mohegans. In July Owaneco captured one Narragansett warrior who boasted of all the Mohegans he had killed. Owaneco asked if his men could put their enemy to death. Denison agreed. He understood that for the Mohegans, King Philip's War held different meanings than it did for the English. They had their own scores to settle, for their own reasons. The Mohegans formed a circle with the captive at its center, William Hubbard wrote, "that all their eyes might at the same time, be pleased with the utmost revenge upon him." Denison told his men not to interfere. He may have told them not to watch; some were shocked to tears by the violence they witnessed. The Mohegans approached the prisoner, and

> they cut one of his fingers round the joint, and at the Trunck of his hand, with a sharp knife, and then broke it off, as men used to do with a slaughtered beast, before they uncase him; then they cut off another and another, till they had dismembered one hand of all its digits, the blood sometimes spirting out in streams a yard from his hand . . . Yet did not the Sufferer ever relent, or shew any sign of anguish, for being asked of his tormentors, how he liked the War? . . . this unsensible and hard-hearted monster answered, he liked it very well, and found it as sweet, as English men do their sugar. In this frame he continued, till his executioners had dealt with the toes of his feet, as they had done with the Fingers of his Hands, all the while making him dance round the Circle, and sing, till he had wearied both himself and them. At last they brake the Bones of his Legs, after which he was forced to sit down, which, 'tis said he silently did, till they knocked out his brains.

The Mohegans had avenged their fallen kin.[34]

•

The July raid against the Narragansetts marked one of the final occasions when the Mohegans actively assisted the English war effort. The death of Attawanhood, or Joshua, Uncas's third son, in May 1676, may have influenced the Mohegans' decision to limit their participation in the conflict. The colonists said nothing about the cause of Attawanhood's death, though in the will recorded three months before he died it is clear that he suffered from a long illness. Attawanhood bequeathed thousands of acres of land along the Connecticut River to English friends and patrons. He left to his two sons "all that tract of land lying between Nippamug Path and the lands given to the people of Saybrook." His children were still young, and if they died before they reached the age of twenty, Attawanhood wanted the lands to go to Uncas and his successors. Whoever ultimately received these lands, Attawanhood stated that all Indians living upon them "should live under my father Uncas." Though he wanted his children equipped to confront a world increasingly dominated by the colonists by having them taught English, Attawanhood expressed a desire to preserve intact the Mohegans' lands in Connecticut. The Mohegans grieved for Attawanhood so much, according to the River Colony's Major John Talcott, that they sat out much of the remainder of the war. Talcott reported to the Council of War that the Mohegans, "much sadened" by Attawanhood's death, "will not goe with us with such a number as otherwise might have been expected."[35]

By the spring of 1676, King Philip's War was increasingly taking on the appearance of a mop-up operation in any case. Philip's forces remained on the run. The decisive blow came not in Connecticut, nor anywhere in southern New England, but at a site called Hoosick, fifty miles east of Albany, where Mohawk warriors had attacked and killed a large number of Philip's followers in January. Armed and assisted by the imperialist governor of New York, Sir Edmund Andros, who worried that Algonquian rage might spill across the Hudson River into his jurisdiction, the Mohawks broke the back of Philip's uprising. The Mohawk attack succeeded in cutting off the flow of weapons to Philip from the French in Canada, in demoralizing his forces, and in driving his followers eastward where they confronted New England militias that had finally developed an ability to fight "Indian-style."[36] A combined force of colonists and Christian Indians led by Plymouth's Benjamin Church tracked down Philip and his desperate forces, ravaged by disease and hunger, on the Mount Hope Peninsula, where the war had begun a year before. Philip died there on August 12, gunned down by a Praying Indian named Alderman. Church hacked off Philip's head, quartered his body, and hung the pieces from four trees. Meanwhile, only a small number of Mohegans joined in Connecticut's final action in the war. Uncas told James Fitch that "his soldiers are so wearie at present that they are not willing to move so soone as is propounded." Perhaps Owaneco and he still mourned for Attawanhood. They were apparently unwilling to lead any Mohegan warriors, and "Ashpoet, his chief captain," was sick. Epidemic diseases still affected southern New England Algonquians. Thus few Indian allies were present then when Major John Talcott's troops devastated a group of natives fleeing westward near present-day Great Barrington, Massachusetts, on August 15. Talcott and his men captured twenty of the desperate refugees and killed three dozen more. The war, for the River Colony men, had come to a close, and Talcott's troops returned home to Connecticut on August 18, 1676.[37]

•

King Philip's War brought significant change to the Mohegan heartland, reversing, for a brief period of time, the two-decade-old trend tending toward the marginalization of Uncas's people in Connecticut. The arms and ammunition provided by the Connecticut Council of War allowed the Mohegans to defend themselves from their native neighbors. Without this assistance, Owaneco told John Mason Jr. in April 1676, Uncas's people were "in very great hazard if the enemy should Asault them," for "they have not the wherewithe to defend themselves." Mason reminded the council of the Mohegans' "readiness and helpfulness," and urged them to grant Owaneco the weapons he desired.[38]

The Mohegans used this ammunition to good effect, against the Indian enemies of the English, and for themselves. When the Council of War agreed to pay its Indian allies "for every man, woman, and child they receive, two coates a peice, except for sucking children, and for them, they to pay one coat a peice, upon the delivery of the said Indians," they sanctioned the traditional raiding and captive-taking that long had characterized warfare in the Eastern Woodlands. Payment in duffels, in knives and kettles and copper pots, and in firearms and ammunition offered the Mohegans access to highly valued English manufactured goods that the collapse of the wampum economy had made increasingly difficult for them to obtain. King Philip's War, and the colonists' reliance on their Indian allies, in many ways brought profitable hunting back to Connecticut. The taking of captives and incorporation of outsiders into Mohegan village communities allowed Uncas and Owaneco to resume the activity they had begun after the Pequot War, and that had made the Mohegans a regional power.[39]

Yet in most ways there was no going back, for the Mohegans or other Indians, and the new postwar world required of Uncas continued creative adaptation as he confronted rapid change. The English victory in King Philip's War, though achieved only with the assistance of the Mohawks and the Puritans' Indian allies, was complete. Algonquian resistance to English settlement was shattered and English power, in Indian eyes, seemed immense. More Mohegans, in this environment, began to question the efficacy of their cultural practices. They saw themselves losing power, and even Uncas began to experiment with English rituals to regain it.[40]

In August, the same month that Philip died, a drought so severe that "the Trees began to languish, and the Indians to despair of an Harvest," gripped the River Colony. Uncas, who the Puritan historian Increase Mather said was "a friend to the English, yet he and all his men continue Pagans still, sent his Powaws on work to see if they could by powwowing (i.e. conjuring) procure rain." Mohegan ritual, however, failed to break the drought. Uncas then summoned a "noted Powaw" from somewhere in the west "to try his skill, but neither could that Wizzard by all his hideous and diabolical howlings obtain showers." The Mohegan sachem then asked the Reverend Fitch for help.[41]

To Mather, Fitch was "the Faithfull and able Teacher of the Church in Norwich." To Uncas and the Mohegans he was its chief practitioner of ritual. Uncas asked Fitch to pray to the English god for rain. The English minister may have sensed the Mohegans' desperation. Certainly he sensed an opportunity to lecture the Indians on the power of the English. Fitch agreed to ask his God for help, but only if Uncas assured him that he "would not attribute it to their Pawawes." Fitch wanted credit for his god. Uncas admitted to Fitch that his people's rituals had failed. Here Fitch felt that he had Uncas. He told Uncas that "if you will declare it before all these Indians, you shall see what God will do for us; for although this year he hath shewen his anger against the English, and not only against the Indians, yet he hath begun to save us; and I have found by experience twice in the like case, when we sought him by Fasting and Prayer, he hath given us rain, and never denied us."[42] Uncas did as Fitch requested. In "a great speech to the Indians," Uncas "confessed" that "if God should then send rain, it could not be ascribed to their Pawawing, but must be acknowledged to be an answer of our Prayers." Clouds began to gather, William Hubbard noted, "and the next day there was such a plenty of rain" that the Thames River "rose more than two feet in height."[43]

Englishmen like Hubbard and Mather looked during the dark days after Philip's War for signs that God was with them again, that the days of his anger had passed. Uncas's encounter with Fitch demonstrated for them the power of their religion over that of the heathens. It was a sign, however small, that New England had passed through its time of trial. Had Mather and Hubbard had a greater understanding of Algonquian spirituality, however, they might have recognized that Uncas and his people still lived their lives in a world governed by the power of ritual, and that Uncas had used the English god as he had used English guns: as a means to pursue Mohegan ends. Indeed, during the war, Uncas watched as the Council of War in Connecticut denounced the sins of the Jeremiad, called for the moral regeneration of Puritan New England, and outlawed drunkenness, "the sin of uncleannesse," excess in apparel, Sabbath-breaking, and disrespect for parents. The Puritan response, fundamentally a call for a return to ritual, would have made perfect sense to Uncas. When his own spiritual advisers could not effectively counter the force of the drought that gripped the region that summer, Uncas simply turned to other sources of ritual to appease Hobbomok. Doing so entailed no abandonment of his commitment to Mohegan beliefs, and Uncas's experimentation with English rituals did not last long. Fitch, in fact, in the spring of 1678 once again denounced Uncas and complained that he was "so reproachful to vilifie our rulers, our lawes and religion, and is the greate opponent of any meanes of soul's good & concernment to his people." He and his followers, Fitch continued, had participated "more in dancing & in all maner of Heathenish impieties since the warrs and vilifying what hath been done by the English,and attributed the victorie to theire Indean helps." The spiritual world of the Mohegans survived intact both King Philip's War and the drought that followed it.[44]

In addition to frustrating the hopes of those Saints who sought the Christianization of the Mohegans, Uncas and his people proved remarkably difficult for the Puritans to control in other ways as well. Fitch would complain of "one strange accident after another" in his colony's relations with Uncas. He and other Connecticut leaders knew that the Mohegan sachem provided shelter to the Algonquian refugees created by King Philip's War, but they never succeeded entirely in developing a policy that brought Uncas under colonial control. In April 1676 the Council of War prohibited colonists from "buying" Indian captives without an official license, and they allowed Uncas to extend his authority over those refugees who had settled in Mohegan village communities. In August, three months later, however, the council summoned Uncas to Hartford. They told him "that the warr was the Englishe's, and the successe belongs to them." The colonists, as such, would dispose of Indian refugees as they saw fit. Whatever Uncas thought of this the old sachem "did freely owne the war to be the Englishe's and the dispose of all the said persons to belong to them, and did cheerfully leave the same to the Councill so to be done." Uncas knew what the members of the Council of War wanted to hear: that the surrendering Indians would pose no threat to the colony's security. Satisfied, the council allowed "about sixty-five of the enemie, fighting men, besides their retennue of old men, women and children," to remain with the Mohegans, provided that Uncas "shall not suffer any of them for future to beare armes nor to travill from Mowheag without speciall lycennses" from the colonial government. Many of the surrenderers, apparently, were "Wabaquassogs," former Mohegan tributaries, who had broken away during the war, but Wampanoags, Nipmucks, Narragansetts, and their respective tributaries had settled in villages under Uncas's protection as well. There they confronted a simple, stark choice: become Mohegan or die; join with us, or face sale into West Indian slavery and a certain death far from home.[45]

Fitch was uncomfortable with this arrangement. He conceded that Uncas had been helpful during the war but he always held in the back of his mind a belief that Uncas "was conjunct with Philip in his bloody complottment." Fitch complained constantly of the Mohegan sachem's "falseness and vileness." In the story Uncas provided colonial leaders, Algonquian refugees sought shelter in Mohegan village communities. Uncas did not seek them out. More and more of them trickled in each day. Uncas merely welcomed them. Fitch thought this was nonsense, and he was convinced that Uncas had used the chaos spawned by the war to extend his power over the remnants of so many shattered Algonquian communities. Some evidence existed to support Fitch's suspicions. First, despite Uncas's claims to desire peace, there came complaints from Ninigret that late in 1676 Mohegan warriors had stolen his wampum and roughed up some of his kin. Next, Roger Williams learned that a sachem called Aswaysewaukit, a Mohegan tributary who lived at a village called Mittabauscutt along a branch of the Pawtuxet River, had provided Uncas with captives in exchange for a gift of wampum.[46]

Fitch made a lot of noise and, after the end of the war, the Connecticut magistrates took a closer look at the fate of Philip's surviving followers. In October the magistrates codified a list of rules to determine the status of surrendering Indians. Those who had killed English soldiers and settlers could be executed or sold into West Indian slavery. Those who had not murdered Englishmen and women, the magistrates ruled, "shall have theire lives and shall not be sould out of the Country for slaves." They would be "well-used" in service by the English for a period of ten years, after which they were free to live in English towns under English laws. In November the colonial government appointed commissioners to meet with the Mohegans, Pequots, and Niantic and Narragansett followers of Ninigret at Norwich. The commissioners would assemble a list "of all captives and the surrendering Indians" and secure something "more than words to binde them to fidelity," they having "forfeited their lives by warring against us." They would impose a yearly tribute for each adult male and then "take off all young and single persons of all sorts to be put into English famalys (as pledges for theyr fidelity) and to be apprentices for ten yeares; after which terme they may be returned to their parents, upon the proofe of the fidelity of both children and parents; otherwise to be forfeited to slavery."[47]

The surviving records shed no light on how the commissioners' December meeting with the Indians went, though it must have involved a large gathering of native peoples and Englishmen. Although Fitch remained convinced that Uncas was secretly thumbing his nose at the English, the Mohegan sachem was allowed to extend his authority over a growing number of tributaries and effectively to increase Mohegan strength. When Fitch took into custody from the Mohegans several Indians who had played an important role in the uprising, including "Phillip's Captaine" and "Phillip's sister," the magistrates ordered them released and permitted them to remain with Uncas. The colonial court prohibited "all persons whatsoever from seizing, interrupting, or molesting the said surrenderers ... they demeaning themselves inoffensively and carrying orderly towards the English." The magistrates felt confident that Uncas would not allow the surrenderers to cross to the eastern side of the Thames, and that neither would he allow them to travel any farther than four miles to the west of the river. When some surrenderers did leave Mohegan territory, the General Court seemed satisfied with Uncas's pledge to be more careful in the future.[48]

By the following spring, Fitch was livid. From Norwich he could watch Uncas more closely than could the colonial magistrates at Hartford. Fitch felt that he knew the *real* Uncas, and his frustration showed in two blistering letters that he wrote in May 1678 to the Connecticut General Court and to John Allyn, a member of that body. Fitch, at heart, believed that many of the Indian surrenderers wanted to be free "from under the yoake of Uncus his monarchy." They had settled in Mohegan village communities out of fear. If Connecticut could protect these Indians, Fitch argued, the River Colony leaders could finally shatter the network of tributaries and subject people Uncas had assembled since the Pequot War. Fitch offered the example of Kockanampauit, who at first settled under the Mohegan sachem but later led a group of refugees away from Uncas to settle at Shetucket. Shortly thereafter, Kockanampauit's brother was found dead. Fitch suspected that Uncas had arranged the murder.[49]

The night before Kockanampauit's brother was killed, Fitch pointed out, Uncas had warned the Shetucket Indians that he had seen Mohawk warriors scouting in the woods. Many other Indians that day had been about, Fitch argued, and none of them had seen any sign of Iroquois raiders. The Mohawks, therefore, could not have killed Kockanampauit's brother. It had to have been Uncas who ordered the killing, Fitch concluded, because it was "well knowen that his owne men dare not act contrarye to his pleasure, and his enemies are more afraid to come neere to him then to all other Indeans in these parts of the country, because of his strength." Uncas, Fitch warned, possessed dangerous power in eastern Connecticut, and he must be brought under control.[50]

Fitch's tone became increasingly hysterical as he reminded Allyn of Pabweegannuck, whose case he felt raised disturbing questions about the relationship between the Mohegans, the Mohawks, the colony of New York, and the defeated remnants of Philip's Algonquian followers. Governor Andros in New York had long despised the Puritan commonwealths to his east. A loyal servant of King Charles II and his brother, James, duke of York, Andros believed that the crown, and not narrow-minded provincials, must direct relations between Indians and the English. The Puritans, Andros believed, had provoked King Philip's War through poor frontier management, and Andros hoped after the war to eliminate the conditions which led to its outbreak. To prevent the Puritan colonies from making individual treaties with defeated Algonquian communities, Andros declared "that all Indyans, who will come in & submitt, shall be received to live under the protection of the Government" of the duke of York, New York's proprietor.[51]

Pinched between the Mohawks, who did not make fine distinctions between Philip's people and the other New England Algonquians they disliked, and vengeful Puritans, large numbers of Connecticut Algonquians accepted Andros's offer and settled at the Mahican village of Schagticoke, near Philip's camp at Hoosick. The group of Indians that Talcott had caught in August was heading in this direction. At Schagticoke, these Indians escaped the enslavement, summary execution, and dispossession that characterized the New Englanders' postwar "justice."[52]

Fitch believed that Pabweegannuck, a lesser Mohegan sachem, or a Mohegan tributary, had joined the movement of Algonquians westward at the urging of Uncas. The Mohegans, he suggested, intended to leave Connecticut and settle among the Mohawks, raising the prospect in Fitch's mind of a powerful combined force of Indians who intensely disliked the Puritans. There were reasons why the Mohegans would consider moving. The pressure placed upon Indian lands by English settlers was much less in New York than in Connecticut. Andros kept order in the duke's province and kept the small frontier population under control. New York, under Andros, was at peace. Uncas, however, denied Fitch's accusation, arguing that he had been at Saybrook when Pabweegannuck departed and that he had no knowledge of it. Fitch did not believe him and said, of Uncas's alibi, "that this covert is worne so threadbare & thin, that every one amongst us doe see through it." Uncas's "falsness," Fitch concluded, was "so notorious that if he be not restrained it will not be possible for the English to keepe any Indean servant."[53]

And here, it seems, Fitch let the cat out of the bag. Indians fled to New York, or assimilated into Mohegan communities, rather than face servitude in New England. Uncas, Fitch implied, upset the minister's emerging sense of the ideal order of things, a New England society where Englishmen were masters and Indians slaves. Fitch's postwar world had no room for powerful Indian sachems with hundreds of tributaries, including the shattered peoples many Puritans wanted to subject and enslave. If Uncas encouraged his followers to seek shelter with the Mohawks under the protection of Sir Edmund Andros, these Indians, too, would move beyond the reach of the English in Connecticut. The Mohegan sachem and the duke's governor of New York both thwarted Fitch's vision of the future, a vision colored by the racism of postwar New England.[54]

Before the Connecticut Council, Pabweegannuck acknowledged his "great crime & treachery against the English by drawing & conducting about 90 of the surrendering Indians from the state of their appointment to have gone out of the Collony," but he was not punished. The councilors accepted his promise of good behavior and honored a petition from Uncas, "who ought to have prevented all such Treacherie," to govern "the said Pabeweegonnitt & his kindred" more carefully in the future. Pabweegannuck, who likely was fleeing from Uncas, was placed by the council under the Mohegan sachem's authority.[55]

The councilors thus showed him their support, but Uncas still made a spirited response to Fitch's charges, petitioning the Connecticut General Court with the help of John Mason's heirs. Samuel Mason, the son of his old friend, felt that "Unkus is & hath been disadvantaged by various reports raysed and fostered upon him by disaffected persons." Uncas feared that the magistrates would, "by giving Credence to such ungrounded reports, swollow down prejudice into their hearts agaynst me an inocent man whoe can cheerful look the whole country in the face as my very good friends whome I allways loved and stood for." He admitted "tis true I aimed something at self-interest in the late war," but he emphasized his long-standing faithfulness to the colonists.

Uncas argued that his friendship with the English was the source of his current problems. Former enemies, embittered by the war, sought to discredit the colony's closest Indian ally, and they complained to Fitch. Uncas asked the magistrates to consider "whether my being active with the English ... may not bee one reason of my being soe sorely vexed and grieved with false clamours or whether merely because I am inocent and not at all nor any of my people gilty of sheding of English blood, as most others have been." He reminded the magistrates that he had always been willing to fight to defend the colony, and that he did so "not without the peril & hazard of my life, and of my people in the Englishes cause against any foraign or common enemy."[56]

He responded directly to Fitch's charge that he had encouraged his people to settle under the Mohawks in New York. When Andros's Iroquois allies attacked Philip's followers, Uncas pointed out, they fell upon the Mohegans as well. In the middle of June 1677, the Mohawks had captured Owaneco, whom they had "surprised and taken from the English." Other Mohegans had been killed in Mohawk raids. When Connecticut asked Uncas to visit the Mohawks and to deliver gifts so that the colony could gain access to Algonquian enemies who had settled under Iroquois protection, the Mohegan sachem had suggested at the time that it was a bad idea, that "afterward when the Enemy was fled out of the Country & had found favour with the Mohoks then I thought to send was too late." He was not helping the Indians escape from the Puritans; he was trying to explain to the Connecticut English that their Algonquian enemies were now, for all intents and purposes, Iroquois. Uncas was not friendly with the Mohawks, and he angrily denied that he "was accessory or principally instrumentall in sending Pabweegannuck to the Mohoks to the end that hee the said Pabweeganuk as a harvenger should make way for Unkas & his peoples acceptance with the Mohoks, declaring that doubtless Unkas & his people would follow after to the Mohoks." He did not control Pabweeganuk and could not prevent his departure. Though Andros and the Mohawks likely invited Owaneco to stay in New York, and Owaneco may have told them what he thought they wanted to hear, Uncas could not blame his son for using "deceipt with a deceiver." Uncas had, he said, no intention of settling his people under the Mohawks, and he did not need Andros's offer of protection. The Mohegans, Uncas suggested, still retained their power in southern New England. "I hope," he said, that "the English will not see me quite crusht by them." He had no intention of moving anywhere.[57]

Yet at the same time that Uncas reminded the magistrates of his long-enduring friendship with the colony and boasted of his continued strength and autonomy, his petition to the magistrates betrayed a sense that the world had indeed changed after King Philip's War. Charges of the sort made by Fitch, Uncas realized, posed a significant danger to the Mohegans, and he carefully raised the issue of his fears in the petition. "The serious consideration" of these charges, he said,

> has sometimes put me in minde of what the Enemy did sometimes to say to my men and the Pequits when wee were in pursuite after them, viz: that wee were very zealous in killing our Country folk, but sayd that it will be your own turns nixt, &c: therefore wee have feares upon us as you may have jealousies concerning us: which Incites mee earnestly to desier that all occasions of a distrustfull nature may bee removed, for I am now grown ould and my hearty desier is that frendship & love might be maintained and renewed between us & that I might leave the same as a legacy to settle my posteritie to walk in the straight path, to hould the like correspond with the English Nation all their days, which is the desier of him whoe hath been and is your ould friend.

The aged sachem, keenly feeling his own mortality, knew well that the Puritans had killed many Indians simply because they did not trust them. Relations with the colony must be set right and balance restored before he died.[58]

Several days later, on May 14, 1678, Uncas and Owaneco formally pledged their friendship to the colony. They promised that "we will not plott or contrive any mischiefe against the English, and that ourselves and those under our Government shall behave them selves in a friendly laudable and peaceable manner towards the English, not suffering any abuse to be offered to them in word or deed." They would inform colonial officials if they learned of any Indian conspiracies, and pledged their readiness "upon all occasions to defend the interest, estates and persons of the English when by them called thereunto, to the utmost of our power." The colony, in return, promised "that we will not allow or suffer any wrong or damage to be done to you by the English, you keeping your promises with the English as above sayd."[59]

•

Many of the River Colony's leaders probably intended to do Uncas and his people justice, at least as they understood it. The Mohegans, after all, shared a long history with Connecticut, and no reasoned observer could deny Uncas's contributions to the colony's growth and success over four decades. Yet King Philip's War produced in parts of New England an Indian-hating people who, in the wake of a terrifying and bloody conflict, wanted access to Algonquian lands. Uncas, in this atmosphere, found it increasingly difficult to defend his lands and his people from outside forces after the war.[60]

Uncas complained to the Connecticut magistrates, for instance, of the "abuse in words" he had received from a group of threatening frontier thugs. The court agreed that such behavior was unacceptable, but did nothing more. When the Mohegans "complained of damage done to their corn in their fields between Norwich and New London by horses and cattle," they were offered a small sum in damages and allowed to make pens to hold runaway livestock.[61] The magistrates provided some assistance, but they also exercised their power over the Mohegans. They ordered Uncas to pay one hundred acres of land as damages to Thomas Tracy after one of the sachem's sons killed several pigs belonging to the English planter. When an intoxicated Mohegan incarcerated in the New London jail accidentally set the building on fire, they ordered Uncas to pay to the county six hundred acres of land, an enormously disproportionate fine that caused the Mohegans to feel "that they were very harshly dealt with."[62]

These and other matters weighed heavily upon Uncas when he approached the Connecticut General Court in May 1680. He asked a special committee appointed by the magistrates "that the bownds of his lands may be setled before he dyeth: being now ould," Uncas said he knew "not how long he shall live and how soon he may dye, and is desireous to leave peace twixt his children & people and the English." It had been a hard winter for Uncas. He deferentially expressed "his desire to be guided" by the colony's leaders, "and in his old age if he should mistake himselfe through frailty, stands ready to be reduced by them."[63]

Uncas asked the committee members to provide him with powder and shot, items Indians had difficulty acquiring after the war, instead of corn as compensation for the damage done in Mohegan fields by English livestock. The committee, sensing Mohegan discontent, agreed to pay to Uncas £10 for the six hundred acres his people had been forced to deliver to New London County. They ordered the New London men once again to run and mark the boundary line between the town and the Mohegans' lands. Further, the court ordered that if any colonist purchased land within a town that had been laid out for an individual Indian, he would pay a fine three times the purchase price and the bargain would be null and void.[64]

One year later, in May 1681, Uncas again came before the colonial government in Hartford. He told the court that his son Owaneco would be handling more of the Mohegans' business with outsiders, something that had been obvious to all observers for some time. He asked the magistrates to firmly define Mohegan bounds and those of the neighboring English settlements. The Mohegans, Uncas complained, continued to suffer from English encroachments upon their lands, and the new town of Lyme had taken up lands that he claimed. Uncas asked that the Mohegans and the colony draw up a series of "Articles" placing their relationship on a firm foundation for posterity.[65]

Uncas promised "that I with my people will carry it as friends and allies to the said collony . . . and will doe no wrong nor injury nor damage to them or any of their people." He agreed to compensate the colonists for any damage done by his followers. He also confirmed all previous grants of land made to the colony and did "resigne up to the said collony of Conocticutt all my lands and territories hereby for myself my heires and successors binding myself and them that I will make no other disposal of them to any person or people whatsoever without their grant and allowance first had and obtained." As in his earlier arrangements with the Mason family, it appears that Uncas, in his view, had given up nothing more than a right to first purchase. The colonial magistrates saw things differently, but Uncas appears to have expected the agreement to relieve him from the pressure English settlers placed upon him to sell Mohegan lands. In effect he granted to Connecticut a right of preemption over Mohegan lands— something he had granted to the Mason family previously—in return for a promise from Leete that the Mohegans would receive equal justice under colonial law and the freedom to decide when and how to dispose of tribal land to the growing number of English towns that pressed upon the Mohegan heartland. Finally, Uncas pledged to continue defending the colony from its enemies, and to continue to serve as Connecticut's principal source of information along the southern New England frontier.[66]

Governor Leete in return promised Uncas that the colonial government would do the Mohegans "no wrong nor suffer any of our people to doe them wrong." The Mohegans, Leete continued, "shall have equall justice from us and our own people in all matters which they shall bring before us." Leete also promised that Connecticut's towns would "take care that sufficitiency of land for those Indians and their successours be still reserved for them to plant on and a just price be paide for the residue."[67]

Uncas sold some Mohegan lands after the war—100 acres here, 200 acres there—mostly west of the Mohegan heartland, to colonists described in the deeds as friends.[68] Owaneco, who had lands of his own to dispose, sold far more Mohegan land. Though Uncas had done much to secure the Mohegan land base, he had failed to transmit these values to his children. The son, in this instance, was not nearly so diligent a guardian of Mohegan lands as his father. In February 1679, for example, Owaneco sold to Charles Hill 200 acres adjoining the lands held by the Mason family, and another 200 acres "between the Sawmill Brooke and the head of Trading Cove Brooke on the Lower side of the path that goes from Norwich to Say Brooke." Six weeks later, he sold to Samuel Rogers 200 acres of "upland and meadow" on the east side of the Thames River. He sold 250 acres to Samuel Buell in June 1680 and 110 acres to Stephen Merick in July. And so it went: 200 acres to Samuel Foresdick in January 1682; 40 acres to the west of the Norwich line to Thomas and Jonathan Tracy.[69]

The Reverend Fitch benefited more than many from Owaneco's willingness to sell Mohegan lands. Uncas's son, by his own admission, had a problem with alcohol, and claimed that many of the deeds he signed resulted from Englishmen "taking advantage of me, when I am in drink." Owaneco's alcoholism seems to have been common knowledge in Norwich and New London, but Fitch's only efforts to protect the Mohegans from land jobbers were patently self-serving. In May 1680, for instance, Uncas deeded to his son all his lands along the Quinebaug River. Fitch persuaded Owaneco, in turn, to deed these lands to the minister for "him to dispose of unto such as shall see cause provided he dispose not of too big a quantity to one man." Large grants could upset the colonial government's plan for a Puritan utopia of small farmers working their individual farmsteads. Owaneco reserved "to my selfe one hundred acres to be for me and my heires" along the Quinebaug. Fitch, meanwhile, had accumulated thousands of acres of Mohegan land in a number of transactions.[70]

These were dark days in Mohegan history. Uncas in the 1680s no longer exercised the powerful leadership that had characterized much of his earlier career. According to one local historian, the sachem during the last years of his life could be found often "sitting by the door of his wigwam asleep, and that it was not easy to rouse his mind to activity." Tired, he had seen much, and no longer had the ability to guide his people through a tumultuous intercultural environment.[71]

•

On June 13, 1683, Uncas, along with Owaneco and Josiah, Owaneco's son, granted two hundred acres each to Samuel Chester and Ralph Parker, "where it can conveniently be spared out to the lands wee now posses."[72] In June 1684, Owaneco identified himself in yet another deed to James Fitch as "son of Uncas, deceased." At some point during the course of the year, Uncas had died.[73]

The English said nothing about his death. No entry appears in the Norwich or New London Town Records, and nothing in the records of the smaller English villages either. The colony's magistrates, meeting in Hartford, did not interrupt their business to reflect upon Uncas's passing. No aged Puritan or old comrade in arms paused to reminisce. While many of their descendants would visit the Uncas Monument in Norwich, completed a century and a half after Uncas's death, no party of colonial dignitaries attended his funeral or paid their respects at his grave. Uncas, who had played so fundamental a role in the history of southern New England, died, as he lived, a Mohegan sachem.

In this sense the silence of the surviving English accounts speaks volumes, for it shows the great distance that existed still between the Mohegan and English worlds. Even in the land deeds that whittled down the Mohegan estate, it is evident that the sachemship survived in its traditional form well into the eighteenth century. Englishmen who wanted to purchase Mohegan land, whether they intended to employ fair means or foul, knew that only Uncas and his heirs could determine the disposition of tribal property. Indians and Englishmen alike recognized Uncas as the leader of the Mohegans up until the time of his death.

Uncas was buried out of sight of the Englishmen with whom he had interacted since the middle of the 1630s, among his own people, on lands the Mohegans long had occupied and fought to preserve as their own. If he was buried in a manner consistent with what we know from archaeological research in southern New England, his head would have pointed to the southwest, toward Cautantouwwit's house. His grave would have been located near water, close to the realm of Hobbomok. Grave goods denoting his status as a great sachem, to serve as ritualized offerings and to help him in the after-life, would have been placed next to his body. Uncas was buried as a Mohegan, and the rituals and rites accompanying his death his followers chose not to share with outsiders.[74]

CONCLUSION

Uncas's Legacy

In May 1684 Governor Robert Treat and John Talcott made their report to the General Court of Connecticut on "the Moheagan Sachems native boundaries and royalties." It was the colony's response to Uncas's request, shortly before his death, to clarify one last time conflicting claims to the Mohegans' territories. Treat and Talcott examined the documents chronicling the Mohegans' loss of lands. They took testimony from Mohegan, Pequot, and Narragansett Indians. They made, they suggested, every effort to ascertain the true bounds of the Mohegans' lands. The report they composed, despite their hard work, is difficult to decipher, and even Treat conceded, nineteen years later, that neither he nor Talcott could "positvelye Assert or determine anything concerning the true bounds of the said country." Part of the problem was that their native witnesses described Mohegan boundaries "by strange names of places unknown to us." Treat and Talcott's report testifies to a geography of native New England that resisted the efforts of Englishmen to measure, mark off, and transform Indian lands into a colonial province.[1]

While much of the land that Treat and Talcott listed in their report the Mohegans already had granted away, the "entailed or Sequestered lands," the critical heart of the Mohegan country that Uncas long had fought to preserve, still remained in Owaneco's hands, a tract eight miles long and four miles broad between Norwich and New London. John Mason had confirmed the Mohegans' ownership of these lands in the deed to Uncas and his sons recorded in 1671. He had defined the core of the Mohegan homeland in the colony's official records. The Mohegans also still possessed "a small parcel of land which lies upon the North Township of Lyme, nine miles in length and two miles in breadth, the westerly end whereof lies upon Connecticut River." And then there were the "Mohegan Hunting Grounds," lying between the towns of Norwich, Haddam, Lyme, Lebanon, and Matabesett.[2] The rest was gone. Fearing that he would lose these remaining pieces of the Mohegan heartland, and fully aware that he might "be empaired by strong drink which som English endeavour & in drink dispos of the said lands," Owaneco, in February 1684, reestablished his father's old relationship with the Mason family. The sachem's followers, meanwhile, simply not trusting him with sole control over the Mohegans' remaining lands and in search of greater security than that afforded by an English "protector," insisted that Owaneco renounce any and all rights to sell the all-important "tract of land between New London Town Bounds and the Trading Cove Brook." Owaneco deeded these lands "unto the Mohegan Indians for their use, to plant," forever.[3]

In October 1692, Owaneco asked the Connecticut Court to approve his request that no Mohegan lands be sold by him or his son Mahomet, "without it be by the consent of Captain Samuel Mason and be acknowledged before him." The magistrates agreed to do so, but Mohegan lands continued to slip from the grasp of the tribe.[4] Owaneco deeded away land in large quantities (the low point came, perhaps, in 1704, when the intoxicated sachem fell out of a canoe and nearly drowned; he gave each of his English rescuers one hundred acres of Mohegan land).[5] And the colony, despite its 1692 agreement with Owaneco, began to grant to its own citizens Mohegan land without consulting him or the Mason family.[6]

Fitz-John Winthrop, the colony's governor, and Gurdon Saltonstall both received grants of Mohegan land in 1698 from the magistrates in appreciation for their leadership during the era of the Dominion of New England. In 1699 colonists founded the town of Colchester, the bounds of which included a portion of the Mohegan Hunting Grounds. The Colchester settlers were an unsavory lot, and Owaneco complained that the Mohegans had been "wronged by the Generall Court & particular persons in taking away our Lands and Liberties." The Mohegans, Owaneco continued, from "time to time" were "threatened by them of Colchester whoe are settled upon our land without our consent to be killed." The settlers had burned Mohegan wigwams and, Owaneco complained, his followers dared "not goe hunting upon our own Land for feare of being killed by them." His petitions fell upon deaf ears. The colony would not honor its earlier agreements with Uncas. In May 1703 the town of New London took control, with the assistance of the colonial assembly, of "a small tract of land lying on the west side" of the Thames, between New London's northern line "and the northeast bounds of the town of Lyme and by a strait line from the northeast corner of Lyme bounds to the southwest corner of Norwich south bounds," and then along a line eastward "to Trading Cove, and so by the said Cove to the said Great river," the Thames. The "sequestered lands," through this agreement, had been added to the town of New London without the Mohegans or their English protectors being consulted.[7]

Large numbers of Mohegans joined Connecticut's forces as the colony fought in King William's War and Queen Anne's War, the opening rounds of England's struggle with France for control of the North American continent. Such activity was, by the eighteenth century, the only permissible outlet for Mohegan men who aspired to become warriors. Yet despite their contribution to the empire, the colony of Connecticut no longer considered the Mohegans a vital component of the colony's defense. Philip's uprising was a distant memory, and an invasion of eastern Connecticut by the French and their Indian allies seemed a remote possibility at most. Settlers at Norwich and New London, unlike colonists in the upper Connecticut River Valley in Massachusetts, did not lose sleep out of fear that Catholics and savages would carry them away in the night. They did not need the Mohegans to stand guard, to alert them to approaching danger. And as the Mohegans became largely irrelevant to colonial security, the Indians also grew weaker. Some Mohegan men, certainly, died "in the queen's service." Others succumbed to disease while on campaign or died of illness in their communities, or moved to other locations in search of economic livelihood, or, in the parlance of New England's nineteenth-century antiquarians, simply "disappeared." With the English population of eastern Connecticut growing rapidly, the Mohegans became a small and surrounded minority. The colonists no longer needed to fear disaffected Mohegans.[8]

In 1703 John Mason's heirs asked the crown to create a court of royal commissioners to rule on the legality of Connecticut's appropriation of the Mohegans' remaining lands. Joseph Dudley, the governor of Massachusetts, and Thomas Hyde, Lord Cornbury, governor of New York, received appointments as judges, as did other supporters of strong royal oversight of colonial land and Indian policy. They would decide the first case in the "Mohegan Land Controversy," a series of proceedings that would continue in fits and starts until its final resolution in 1773.[9]

At heart, the Masons' case rested upon interpretations of Uncas's actions, beginning with his 1659 agreement with John Mason. The Mason family provided the commissioners with a map showing "the Mohegan Sachems Hereditary Country." The Mohegans, Samuel Mason argued, did not want all these lands restored to them, but they did want the three tracts they still held at the time of Uncas's death. Mason recounted the history of his family's relationship with Uncas and the Mohegans. Uncas, he argued, in 1659 and again in 1665, "did make over his lands" "to Major John Mason," who, in the year 1671, "the better to secure some of their lands to them and their posterity, reconveys, to Uncas and others, and their heirs, that tract of land between New London and Norwich, for their planting, with an express limitation on that deed, that neither they nor their heirs should ever alienate the same, which after that time passed commonly by the name of the 'sequestered lands.'" Connecticut, by ignoring these provisions and subsequent Mason-Mohegan agreements, had unlawfully and illegally seized Indian lands.[10]

The Connecticut colonial government complained of "the injustice of those complaints against" the colony and insisted that the royal commissioners had no legitimate authority to determine the legality of the Masons' and the Mohegans' claims. They protested the proceedings and vowed to appeal to the crown any decision adverse to the colony's interests.[11]

Nonetheless, the commissioners began hearing evidence in the summer of 1705. Mohegan witnesses, before the court and in depositions, emphasized their people's long-standing loyalty to the English and their many sacrifices in war. They then told the court of their dispossession at the hands of Connecticut and its frontier settlers. Ashnehunt said that "the English had turned them out of their houses in

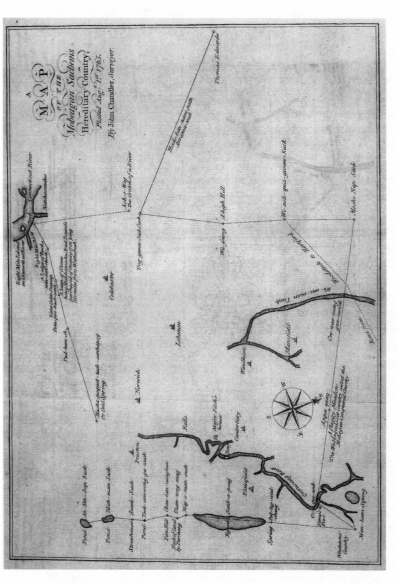

FIG. 6 "A Map of the Mohegan Sachems' Hereditary Country" (1705), showing the lands claimed by Uncas east of the Connecticut River at the greatest extent of his power. Reproduced by permission of The Huntington Library, San Marino, Calif.

the time of snow from Massapeage." Appagese, another Mohegan, told the commissioners that "from a boy their ground and he grew up together, and they have always been friends to the English." Why, he said, "our ground and we should be parted now, we know not." The Mohegans testified to their strong and continuing connection to their traditional lands along the Thames.[12]

English witnesses also testified to the Mohegans' losses. Nicholas Hallam, a friend of the Masons, recalled that in 1703 "he met with about thirty or forty Moheagan Indians, men, women, and children." It was, he remembered, a cold and snowy day, and the Indians he met were "in a very poor and naked condition, many of them crying lamentably." Hallam asked the Mohegans what troubled them. They said that "the governor had been up with them that day, and had drove them from their planting land, which they had enjoyed ever since the English came into the country."[13]

The commissioners made quick work of the proceedings. They accepted entirely the substance of the Masons' case. They ruled that "Owaneco Uncas and the Mohegan Indians, shall be immediately put into Possession" of all the lands that they owned at the time of Uncas's death, and that they had been "unjustly deprived and dispossessed of them, any act or order of the General Assembly of the Colony of Connecticut, or other Proceedings to the Contrary notwithstanding."[14]

The colony immediately appealed to the crown, and the queen, in 1706, granted a commission of review to consider further Connecticut's claims to Mohegan territory by right of conquest and by virtue of deeds from Uncas to the colony. The commission of review never met, however, and the 1705 decision remained unexecuted. Samuel Mason died that year, and neither his heirs nor the Mohegans protested this inaction until 1735 when Captain John Mason, Major Mason's grandson, reopened the proceedings. During the years that had passed in between, Owaneco had died, drunk and so poor, one source suggested, that his wife had no choice but to beg for food. As one anonymous poet put it,

> Oneco, king, his queen doth bring,
>   To beg a little food;
> As they go along his friends among
>   To try how kind, how good.

Some pork, some beef, for their relief,
   And if you can't spare bread,
She'll thank you for a pudding, as they go a gooding,
   And carry it on her head.[15]

After Owaneco's death, the sachemship passed through a number of hands. Caesar, Owaneco's only surviving son, led the Mohegans from 1715 until 1723. Upon his death, the rightful heir should have been Mahomet, Owaneco's grandson, and son of the first Mahomet. He was still young, however, and Ben Uncas, Uncas's youngest son, became sachem. He lasted three years, until his death in 1726, when he was replaced by his son, also named Ben. Most Mohegans, by the 1730s, came to believe that the second Ben Uncas was too close to the colonial leadership, and that he was not an effective guardian of Mohegan interests. Most favored and recognized Mahomet as their leader.[16]

In 1735 Mahomet and Captain John Mason traveled to England to present their case to the crown. Identifying himself as "Chief Sachem of the Moheagan Indians," Mahomet asked the king for protection "against the Injuries and Wrongs, which he and his people suffer from your Majesty's Subjects the Colony of Connecticut." Uncas, he wrote, had helped the English settle Connecticut and saved them from destruction during the Pequot War. The Mohegans had always maintained their friendship with the colonists, and the colony always had appreciated and recognized the tribe's importance to its defense. By the end of the seventeenth century, however, at last "a Generation arose in the Colony of Connecticut who knew not Unchas and his successors." This generation, Mahomet argued, "did, contrary to the faith of their Father's Leagues, their Publick Records, and the Terms of the Royal Charter, Encroach upon the Remainder of the Mohegan lands, which your Petitioners Ancestors had reserved to themselves and their People for their Hunting and Planting Grounds." The colonists, Mahomet suggested, had abandoned that relationship between Indians and Englishmen that had played so important a role in the security of the colony. Mahomet asked for the king's justice.[17]

Both Mahomet and Mason died during their stay in England, but Captain John's sons continued to pursue their family's case. The king granted another commission to review the case. It met in 1738 and

1739, but the judges so clearly favored the colony that the attorneys for the Mason family, William Shirley and William Bollan, left the proceedings in protest. Further appeals resulted in the appointment of yet another royal commission that met in Greenwich, and then in Norwich, in the spring of 1743.[18]

Bollan, who again represented the Mason family, argued a case which, as in 1705, rested upon interpretations of the nature of Uncas's historic relationship with the Connecticut colonists. Bollan wanted the decision of Dudley's Commission from 1705 affirmed, with remedy given to the Mohegans and the Mason family. The colony, represented by the prominent New York attorney William Smith, wanted the 1705 ruling set aside. Smith argued what was now a familiar case: Uncas had given his land to the colony on numerous occasions beginning in 1640. The land, quite simply, now belonged to the English. Smith presented Ben Uncas to the commissioners. Uncas's grandson testified that Smith's documents were authentic and that the colonists had always treated the Mohegans well. The Mohegans still retained more than a thousand acres of "good and valuable land," Ben Uncas told the commissioners, "which is more than sufficient for the habitation and improvement of me and my nation, and with which I am fully content." Smith added that many settlers had purchased these lands in good faith, improved them, and lived much of their lives there. Putting these lands back into the hands of the Mohegans, Smith argued, would ruin these colonists, "and tend to the demolishing of many Christian churches, and depopulating a considerable part of the colony, and turning it once again into a wilderness."[19]

Bollan, in his counterargument, came as close as any colonial Englishman to understanding the nature of Uncas's historical relationship with his English neighbors.

Bollan reminded the commissioners that the Mohegans had initially welcomed the English and entered into "a strict alliance" and a "firm and unshaken friendship towards them." At first they had allowed the newcomers to settle freely on Mohegan lands but, "after some years of Experience," they found the English "to be a people, some of whom were full of Craft and Guile, and others abounded with Wisdom and Probity." The Mohegans, Bollan argued, discovered that they "were not a Match for the wiles of the former, so for the protection of their estates against them, they fled to the latter." Uncas and his successors thus made use of Major John Mason and his family "as Instruments to prevent their being cheated by any fraudulent or unfair Purchase of their Lands." The Mason family's role as guardians of the Mohegans, Bollan continued, had been repeatedly recognized by the colonial government, and they had never consented to any cession of the Mohegans' land. Rather, Connecticut had illegally seized the tribe's holdings. The Dudley Commission's ruling should stand.[20]

The colony rested its case on the same documents Bollan pointed to, but argued that they meant less than they actually said. The recognition of Mohegan land rights, Smith maintained, was done to humor the Indians and soothe the egos of Mohegan sachems. Bollan disagreed entirely. The relevant documents, he said, repeatedly recognized Mohegan rights to the lands in question. Further, Bollan called for a reading of the evidence that accorded with the Indians' understanding of it. The Mohegans, he argued, "are a People unskilled in letters," and their adversaries in this case "have had the penning" of the relevant documents. Connecticut, Bollan argued, must have phrased these documents in a fashion that favored its own interests. The documents, in this sense, had become instruments of control, a means to dispossess the Indians. If the Mohegans could not understand them, "the most favorable construction for the said Indians, as they conceive, should be put upon these writings." Doing so, Bollan concluded, would lead the commissioners to affirm the decision of the Dudley court.[21]

Bollan convinced Daniel Horsmanden, the chief justice of the colony of New York, that the Mohegans were indeed "a separate and distinct people" from the colonists they lived amongst, and that "they have a polity of their own, and make peace and warr with any Nation of Indians when they think fit, without Controul from the English." This was a position that Uncas might have advanced, and Horsmanden concluded that the Dudley Commission's ruling should be affirmed and executed. His fellow commissioners, however, disagreed. The majority of the commission ruled that the findings of the Dudley Commission "and every part thereof, be revoked, replaced, and made void." They decided that Uncas had surrendered his lands to the colony of Connecticut on several occasions, and that the colony had presented a much stronger case.[22]

The decision of the commission in 1743 did not end the "Mohegan Land Controversy." The Masons would continue to appeal to the crown until 1773, when the case was finally decided in favor of the colony. But never again would so much attention and so much energy be devoted to it. In the summer of 1743 in Norwich, not far from where Uncas and Wawequa had put Miantonomi to death one century before, attorneys for the Mason family and for the colony of Connecticut presented competing visions of the colony's history. William Smith, for the River Colony, painted a picture of conquered Indians, "humored" by paternalistic Englishmen at ostentatious diplomatic gatherings, signing over their lands to their benevolent overlords. The commissioners accepted Smith's argument, but Bollan had made a much better historical case. Uncas had allied with the English and defended the infant settlement. In time, his people felt the pressure of increasing English population and unscrupulous frontier land barons. Uncas found in the Mason family allies to help him fend off the coming dispossession. Though he and they relinquished much of the land that Uncas claimed after the Pequot War, at the time of his death the Mohegan heartland was still secure.[23]

•

And so we return to Charles Frederick Chapin's question: "Who then, and what was Uncas?" Chapin's own answer, now a century old, contains, when one pares away from it the encrusted layers of belief that caused him to view Indians as a race doomed to decline in the face of "civilization," some important kernels of truth. When Uncas became sachem after the death of his father, the Mohegans may have consisted of little more than the Indians who lived in and around Shantok. If the Mohegan community was indeed larger than this before the arrival of Europeans in Connecticut, the effects of disease, which preceded settlement, along with the Pequots' aggressive drive to control wampum production along the coast of Long Island Sound, conspired to render the Mohegans a tributary people. Alliance with the English—John Mason and Jonathan Brewster, then the colonial governments, and then the Commissioners of the United Colonies—allowed Uncas to break free from the Pequots and to emerge at the head of a regional power. Backed by the threat of English military might, a potent force in itself after the Pequot War, Uncas extended his authority over tributaries of his own, incorporating and adopting them into Mohegan village communities. The Mohegan "tribe" that Uncas, in Chapin's words, "built up … out of nothing," consisted of Pequots, Narragansetts, Niantics, and Nipmucks to be sure, but also Massapeags, Shetuckets, Nayeags, Wangums, Wabequassits, and more.

Uncas's Mohegans, a polyglot people, were held together through his extraordinarily effective leadership. On the one hand, he established ties of kinship with his tributaries. On the other, he coerced his new subjects. He employed both force and persuasion, the threat of violence together with an offer of protection. Archaeological evidence from Shantok reveals the new Mohegan identity of Uncas's people in the design of their pottery. The evidence indicates that Uncas forged increasingly unified Mohegan communities out of a great diversity of native New Englanders.

Yet Uncas also had to interact with the English. That he did so effectively for so long at least in part explains his success as sachem. He quickly recognized the benefits he and his people could receive by assisting the newcomers. He recognized, as well, that he must bargain with the English from a position of strength. The Puritans would appreciate Mohegan friendship, Uncas believed, but they must also fear him. Uncas worked to maintain the allegiance of enough warriors, including on occasion those suspected of killing English colonists, to make him a credible threat to colonial security should he become disaffected.

This "consistent theory of conduct," as Chapin described it, Uncas pursued for as long as he could. He recognized that the promoters of English settlement in the region could achieve their colonial objectives more easily, and less expensively, with the assistance of Indian leaders like himself. In order to attain their goals—profit for their colonial organizations, the security of their dominions from enemies native and European, and the establishment of a society planted in accordance with God's law—the Puritan elite needed to control the frontier and the activities of those who lived there. They had to remain wary always of the Dutch settlements to their west and the Catholic French to their north. Most of all, they had to come to terms with the Indians among whom they settled. Uncas provided crucial assistance. In this sense, he became an ally of New England's founding fathers "whose faithfulness mingled with their enterprise and piety in the enduring foundations" of Connecticut. He balanced successfully for a time Mohegan and English interests.

But this relationship rested upon extremely shaky foundations. It could endure only so long as the two principal parties involved, the Mohegans and the Connecticut English, needed each other. And that situation eroded after the United Colonies disarmed Ninigret's conspiracy in 1654 and even faster after 1676, that critical year in the history of Anglo-America.[24] After King Philip's War, with its English population growing, and with its Indian population in decline and no longer a credible military threat, Connecticut could act with impunity in its relations with its Indian neighbors. If Uncas, or his heirs, grew angry after King Philip's War, it did not matter much. There were no enemies for him to join in an uprising against colonial authority. In pursuing the best interests of his own community, Uncas could still frustrate and exasperate colonial authorities but, after King Philip's War, the Mohegans could no longer harm the English. The colonists could work their small farms and prosper from New England's rocky soil; they could, after King Philip's War, rest secure that they need not fear the alarming prospect of Indian attack. And they could do these things with equal facility with or without the friendship of the Mohegans.

The decline in Mohegan power over the course of the seventeenth century was significant. It's a sad story. Connecticut was more than willing to dispossess Uncas's heirs when the colony's safety no longer relied on Indian allies. That Uncas's people became, by the early eighteenth century, the dispossessed whom Nicholas Hallam encountered along the Thames, "crying lamentably," in "a very poor and naked condition," however, should not obscure their importance in the history of English settlement in America. Early Connecticut, and early New England in general, was a world of villages, and the history of the Mohegan villages at Shantok and Niantic, if we are to understand the region in all its richness, must be set beside the story of the English river towns, of Saybrook and of Norwich, New London, and Lyme. It would be too easy to cast the story of Uncas and the Mohegans in terms of the inevitable decline of native peoples, of Indians resisting briefly and then disappearing. To do so, again, would be to commit a historical crime that has been committed too many times: to write Indians out of New England's past.

Uncas constructed the Mohegans out of the wreckage spawned by epidemic disease and warfare against the Pequots. He assembled a powerful Native American chiefdom that remained a significant power in southern New England through much of the seventeenth century. He lived a long life as Mohegan sachem, dying a peaceful death without converting to Christianity and abandoning his people's customary beliefs. In addition to acting in an Indian story, much of which took place beyond the view or the comprehension of English observers, Uncas walked on the same historical stage as Winthrop and Bradford, Williams and Mason, the Commissioners of the United Colonies and the members of the Connecticut General Court. Uncas and his people, and his native rivals and their followers, often set the agenda for meetings of the Puritan elite. He retained the initiative in Anglo-Indian relations through much of his life. He played as large a role in the history of this part of Anglo-America, a region shaped by its English settlers and by Indian natives, as any other individual. Though the English increasingly dominated and dictated the nature of the Anglo-Indian exchange, and though the Mohegans lost nearly all of their lands by the beginning of the eighteenth century, the Mohegans survived as a community along the Thames River, and along the margins of colonial society. Uncas's descendants still live along the Thames today. They owe him much.

Abbreviations Used in Notes

CA: Indians	Connecticut Archives, Indian Affairs, Series 1 and 2, Connecticut State Library, Hartford
CR	J. Hammond Trumbull, ed., *The Public Records of the Colony of Connecticut*, 15 vols. (Hartford, 1850)
MBR	Nathaniel B. Shurtleff, *Records of the Governor and Company of Massachusetts Bay in New England*, 5 vols. (Boston, 1853)
MHS Coll	*Collections of the Massachusetts Historical Society*
NEHGR	*New England Historical and Genealogical Register*
NHR	Charles J. Hoadly, ed., *Records of the Colony and Plantation of New Haven* (Hartford, 1857–1858)
NYCD	E. B. O'Callaghan, ed. *Documents Relative to the Colonial History of New York State*, 14 vols. (Albany, 1853–1887)
PCR	Nathaniel B. Shurtleff, ed., *Records of the Colony of New Plymouth in New England*, 12 vols. (Boston, 1853)
RICR	J. R. Bartlett, ed., *Records of the Colony of Rhode Island and Providence Plantations in New England, 1636–1792*, 10 vols. (Providence, 1856–1865)
RUC	*Records of the United Colonies of New England*, published as vols. 9 and 10 of *Records of the Colony of New Plymouth* (*PCR*)

RWC   Glenn W. La Fantasie, ed., *The Correspondence of Roger Williams*, 2 vols. (Hanover, N.H., 1988)

WP   Samuel Eliot Morison et al., eds., *Winthrop Papers*, 6 vols. (Boston, 1929–1992)

Notes

Introduction

1. Charles Frederick Chapin, "Uncas," *Papers and Addresses of the Society of Colonial Wars in the State of Connecticut* 1 (1903): 26, 41, 46–47.

2. Ibid., 46.

3. James Fenimore Cooper, *The Leatherstocking Tales* (New York, 1985), 1:877–878. For useful discussions of Cooper's work, see Richard Slotkin, *The Fatal Environment: The Myth of the Frontier in the Age of Industrialization, 1800–1890* (New York, 1985); Brian W. Dippie, *The Vanishing American: White Attitudes and U.S. Indian Policy* (Middletown, Conn., 1982), 21–25; and Martin Barkel and Roger Sabin, *The Lasting of the Mohicans: History of an American Myth* (Jackson, Miss., 1995).

4. Anonymous review in the *New York Review and Atheneum*, quoted in George Dekker and John P. McWilliams, *Fenimore Cooper: The Critical Heritage* (London, 1973), 94; Cass quoted in Marcel Clavel, *Fenimore Cooper and His Critics: American, British, and French Criticisms of the Novelist's Early Work* (Aix-en-Provence, 1938), 320.

5. Mohegan tribal historian Melissa Jayne Fawcett titled her first book *The Lasting of the Mohegans* (Uncasville, Conn., 1995). In the prologue to *Medicine Trail: The Life and Lessons of Gladys Tantaquidgeon* (Tempe, Ariz., 2000), xi, Fawcett begins by quoting the closing lines of Cooper's novel, though she misrepresents the conclusion to *The Last of the Mohicans* and errs in claiming that Uncas jumped "off a precipice to his death."

6. John McWilliams, *The Last of the Mohicans: Civil Savagery and Savage Civility* (New York, 1993).

7. *Norwich Courier*, 19 June 1833; Arthur L. Peale, *Memorials and Pilgrimages in the Mohegan Country* (Norwich, Conn., 1930), 8; Peale, *Uncas and the Mohegan-Pequot* (Boston, 1934), 167.

8. On the supposed inevitability of Indian decline, see Reginald Horsman, *Race and Manifest Destiny: The Origins of American Racial Anglo-Saxonism* (Cambridge, Mass., 1981); and Dippie, *Vanishing American*, 56–78.

9. Charles L. Lincoln to George L. Perkins, 17 August 1841 and 15 September 1841, and George L. Perkins to Noah Webster, 13 August 1841, Connecticut State Archives, Hartford. Other spellings that appear in the records are Uncus, Unckas, Unquas, Unkus, Woncas, Woncase, Okace, Onkus, Ocas, and Unchas.

10. *The Uncas Monument, Published Once in Three Hundred and Fifty Years* (Norwich, 1842), 1–8.

11. William Leete Stone, *Uncas and Miantonomoh: A Historical Discourse* (New York, 1842), vii, 28, 168–169.

12. Ibid., 171–172.

13. *Niles' Weekly Register*, 31 December 1842, 280.

14. George H. Martin, *The Grave of Uncas: A Ballad* (Boston, 1850).

15. Daniel Coit Gilman, *A Historical Discourse Delivered in Norwich, Connecticut, September 7, 1859, at the Bicentennial Celebration of the Settlement of the Town*, 2d ed. (Boston, 1859), 13–14. See also John W. Stedman, *The Norwich Jubilee: A Report on the Celebration at Norwich, Connecticut, on the Two Hundredth Anniversary of the Settlement of the Town* (Norwich, 1859).

16. *Norwich Bulletin*, 3 July 1907; Peale, *Memorials and Pilgrimages*, 27.

17. *Norwich Bulletin*, 3 July 1907.

18. Ibid., 4 July 1907.

19. Philip Deloria, *Playing Indian* (New Haven, Conn., 1998), 62–68.

20. Poem by Mazie V. Caruthers in Peale, *Uncas*, 49. For other materials mythologizing Uncas, see Gertrude Bell Browne, *Hot Suns and Great Whiteness* (Norwich, 1927); Lyman Gilman Hill, *The Rimes of Uncas* (New York, 1968), especially 11–12; Virginia Frances Voight, *Uncas, Sachem of the Wolf People: The Story of a Great Indian Chief* (New York, 1963); Albert Payson Terhune, *50 Famous American Indians: Clippings from Newspapers, June 28–November 1, 1909* (New York, 1909); "Poem by L.H.S. (1830)," in John Warner Barber, *Connecticut Historical Collections* (New Haven, Conn., 1836), 344; and "The Grave of Uncas, Last of the Mohegans," *Family Magazine* 6 (1839): 149–150.

21. Samuel Peters, *A General History of Connecticut, from its First Settlement under George Fenwick, Esq., to its Latest Period of Amity with Great Britain* (London, 1781), 22–23, 112–113.

22. John W. De Forest, *History of the Indians of Connecticut from the Earliest Known Period to 1850* (Hartford, 1851), 154, 297.

23. Herbert Milton Sylvester, *Indian Wars of New England*, 3 vols. (Cleveland, 1910), 1:246–247, 391; 2:616.

24. Alvin G. Weeks, *Massasoit of the Wampanoags, with a Brief Commentary on Indian Character; and Sketches of Other Great Chiefs, Tribes,*

and Nations (Norwood, Mass., 1919), 229, 233. On the Improved Order of Red Men, see Deloria, *Playing Indian*, 62–68.

25. John A. Sainsbury, "Miantonomo's Death and New England Politics," *Rhode Island History* 30 (1971): 116, 122; Francis Jennings, *The Invasion of America: Indians, Colonists, and the Cant of Conquest* (New York, 1975), 179, 227; Alfred P. Knapp, *Connecticut's Yesteryears: So Saith the Wind* (Old Saybrook, Conn., 1985). See also Laurie Weinstein-Farson, "Land Politics, and Power: The Mohegan Indians in the Seventeenth and Eighteenth Centuries," *Man in the Northeast* 42 (1991): 9.

26. Jack Campisi, "The Emergence of the Pequots," in *The Pequots in Southern New England: The Fall and Rise of an American Indian Nation*, ed. Laurence M. Hauptman and James D. Wherry (Norman, Okla., 1990), 117.

27. Several scholars have attempted to move beyond this harshly dichotomized view of Uncas. See P. Richard Metcalf, "Who Should Rule at Home? Native American Politics and Indian-White Relations," *Journal of American History* 61 (1974): 651–665; William Burton and Richard Lowenthal, "The First of the Mohegans," *American Ethnologist* 1 (1974): 589–599; Eric S. Johnson, "Uncas and the Politics of Contact," in *Northeastern Indian Lives, 1632–1816*, ed. Robert S. Grumet (Amherst, Mass., 1996), 29–47; and idem, "'Some by Flatteries and Others by Threatenings': Political Strategies among Native Americans of Seventeenth-Century Southern New England" (diss., University of Massachusetts–Amherst, 1993).

28. Calvin Martin, "The Metaphysics of Writing Indian-White History," in *The American Indian and the Problem of History* (New York, 1987), 31.

29. Michael Leroy Oberg, *Dominion and Civility: English Imperialism and Native America, 1585–1685* (Ithaca, N.Y., 1999).

30. I have borrowed this phrase from Peter A. Thomas's outstanding study, *In the Maelstrom of Change: The Indian Trade and Cultural Process in the Middle Connecticut Valley, 1635–1665* (New York, 1990).

Chapter 1. World in Balance

1. Gabriel Archer, "Account of Gosnold's Voyage," in *The English New England Voyages, 1602–1608*, ed. David B. Quinn and Alison M. Quinn (London, 1983), 124–125; Francis Higginson, "New England's Plantation," in *Chronicles of the First Planters of the Colony of Massachusetts Bay, from 1623–1636*, ed. Alexander Young (Boston, 1846), 246–247; Thomas Morton, *New English Canaan*, ed. Charles Francis Adams, *Publications of the Prince Society*, vol. 14 (Boston, 1883), 180; William Wood, *New England's Prospect*, ed. Alden T. Vaughan (Amherst, Mass., 1977), 36–38.

2. Roger Williams, *A Key into the Language of America*, ed. John J. Teunissen and Evelyn Hinz (Detroit, 1973), 84. For an examination of Roger Williams as an observer of Narragansett culture and society, see Patricia E. Rubertone, *Grave Undertakings: An Archaeology of Roger Williams and the Narragansett Indians* (Washington, D.C., 2001). On what "discovery" meant to the first European explorers, see Wilcomb F. Washburn, "The Meaning of *Discovery* in the Fifteenth and Sixteenth Centuries," *American Historical Review* 68 (1962): 1–21.

3. Dean Snow, *The Archaeology of New England* (New York, 1980), 331; Bert Salwen, "A Tentative 'In Situ' Solution to the Mohegan-Pequot Problem," in *The Connecticut Valley Indian: An Introduction to Their Archaeology and History*, ed. William R. Young (Springfield, Mass., 1969), 82; Laurie Weinstein-Farson, "Land Politics and Power: The Mohegan Indians in the 17th and 18th Centuries," *Man in the Northeast* 42 (1991): 10; Alfred A. Cave, "The Pequot Invasion of Southern New England: A Reassessment of the Evidence," *New England Quarterly* 62 (1989): 27–44. The current Mohegan tribal historian argues that her tribe moved into Connecticut from New York. See Melissa Jayne Fawcett, *The Lasting of the Mohegans*, part 1, *The Story of the Wolf People* (Uncasville, Conn., 1995), 8–10.

4. Robert S. Grumet, *Historic Contact: Indian Peoples and Colonists in Today's Northeastern United States in the 16th through 18th Centuries* (Norman, Okla., 1995), 143; Lorraine Elise Williams, "Ft. Shantok and Ft. Corchaug: A Comparative Study of Seventeenth-Century Culture Contact in the Long Island Sound Area" (diss., New York University, 1972), 12, 70–72; Frank G. Speck, "Notes on the Mohegan and Niantic Indians," *Anthropological Papers of the American Museum of Natural History* 3 (1909): 185; Bert Salwen, "European Trade Goods and the Chronology of the Fort Shantok Site," *Bulletin of the Archaeological Society of Connecticut* 34 (1966): 7; D. Hamilton Hurd, *History of New London County, Connecticut, with Biographical Sketches of Many of its Pioneers and Prominent Men* (Philadelphia, 1882), 250.

5. Carroll Alton Means, "Mohegan-Pequot Relationships, as Indicated by the Events Leading to the Pequot Massacre of 1637 and Subsequent Claims in the Mohegan Land Controversy," *Bulletin of the Archaeological Society of Connecticut* 18 (1945): 29, 31; Weinstein-Farson, "Land Politics," 12; "Pedigree of Uncas," *NEHGR* 10 (1856): 227–228. On marriage and family among southern New England Algonquians, see Ann Marie Plane, *Colonial Intimacies: Indian Marriage in Early New England* (Ithaca, N.Y., 2000).

6. Weinstein-Farson, "Land Politics," 14; Eric Spencer Johnson, "'Some by Flatteries and Others by Threatenings': Political Strategies among Na-

tive Americans of Seventeenth-Century Southern New England" (diss., University of Massachusetts–Amherst, 1993), 45; Kevin McBride, "The Historical Archaeology of the Mashantucket Pequots, 1637–1900," in *The Pequots in Southern New England: The Fall and Rise of an American Indian Nation*, ed. Laurence M. Hauptman and James D. Wherry (Norman, Okla., 1990), 99.

7. McBride, "Historical Archaeology," 97; Snow, *Archaeology*, 33; William A. Starna, "The Pequots in the Early Seventeenth Century," in *The Pequots in Southern New England*, 46; Grumet (*Historic Contact*, 139), says the figure could be as high as 30,000.

8. Grumet, *Historic Contact*, 153–154; Snow, *Archaeology*, 33.

9. John W. De Forest, *History of the Indians of Connecticut from the Earliest Known Period to 1850* (Hartford, 1851), 52–53; Grumet, *Historic Contact*, 153; Froelich G. Rainey, "A Compilation of Historical Data Contributing to the Ethnography of Connecticut and Southern New England Indians," *Bulletin of the Archaeological Society of Connecticut* 3 (1936): 7–8; Benjamin Trumbull, *A Complete History of Connecticut*, 2 vols. (New London, Conn., 1898), 1:22.

10. John Mason, "A Brief History of the Pequot War," *MHS Coll*, 2d ser., 8 (1826): 122–123; Grumet, *Historic Contact*, 129–130; Snow, *Archaeology*, 33; Neal Salisbury, *Manitou and Providence: Indians, Europeans, and the Making of New England, 1500–1643* (New York, 1986), 147–148.

11. Williams, *Key*, 167; William Cronon, *Changes in the Land: Indians, Colonists, and the Ecology of New England* (New York, 1983), 62, 65; Laurie Lee Weinstein, "The Dynamics of Seventeenth Century Wampanoag Land Relations: The Ethnohistorical Evidence for Locational Change," *Bulletin of the Massachusetts Archaeological Society* 46 (1985): 22; Kathleen J. Bragdon, *Native People of Southern New England, 1500–1650* (Norman, Okla., 1996), 136.

12. Bragdon, *Native People*, xvii.

13. Frank G. Speck, "Native Tribes and Dialects of Connecticut: A Mohegan-Pequot Diary," *Forty-Third Annual Report of the United States Bureau of Ethnology, 1925–1926* (Washington, D.C., 1928), 207; Williams, "Ft. Shantok," 14.

14. Higginson, "New England's Plantation," 256–257; Wood, *New England's Prospect*, 82, 84.

15. Wood, *New England's Prospect*, 83–85; Williams, *Key*, 185; Bragdon, *Native People*, 173.

16. Bert Salwen, "Indians of Southern New England and Long Island: Early Period," in *Handbook of North American Indians*, vol. 15, *Northeast*, ed. William C. Sturtevant (Washington, D.C., 1978), 166; Starna, "Pequots,"

43; Salisbury, *Manitou and Providence*, 41; Johnson, "Some by Flatteries," 41–42; Peter A. Thomas, "Bridging the Cultural Gap: Indian/White Relations," in *Early Settlement in the Connecticut Valley*, ed. Stephen Innes (Deerfield, Mass., 1984), 5; Paul Alden Robinson, "The Struggle Within: The Indian Debate in Seventeenth Century Narragansett Country" (diss., SUNY–Binghamton, 1990), 48–49.

17. Wood, *New England's Prospect*, 97–98.

18. Bragdon, *Native People*, 157–161.

19. Williams, *Key*, 202; Daniel Gookin, *Historical Collections of the Indians in New England* (1674; reprint, New York, 1970), 20.

20. Bragdon, *Native People*, 153–154; Johnson, "Some by Flatteries," 92–93.

21. William S. Simmons, *Spirit of the New England Tribes: Indian History and Folklore, 1620–1984* (Hanover, N.H., 1986), 12–13; Salwen, "Indians of Southern New England," 166; Bragdon, *Native People*, 91, 121, 146. See also Kenneth Feder, "Of Stone and Metal: Trade and Warfare in Southern New England," *New England Social Studies Bulletin* 44 (1986): 26–41.

22. Gookin, *Historical Collections*, 18; Edward Winslow's "Relation" in *Chronicles of the Pilgrim Fathers of the Colony of Plymouth, from 1602 to 1625*, ed. Alexander Young (Boston, 1841), 362. The collection of tribute was common in the Eastern Woodlands. See Bragdon, *Native People*; Stephen R. Potter, *Commoners, Tribute, and Chiefs: The Development of Algonquian Culture in the Potomac Valley* (Charlottesville, Va., 1993), 149–174; and Timothy K. Earle, "Chiefdoms in Archaeological and Ethnohistorical Perspective," *Annual Review of Anthropology* 16 (1987): 279–308.

23. Bragdon, *Native People*, 147–148.

24. Simmons, *Spirit*, 236; Speck, "Native Tribes and Dialects." Fidelia Fielding, Speck's Mohegan informant, was the last speaker of the Mohegan-Pequot dialect. With the assistance of Gladys Tantaquidgeon, Speck began to transcribe these stories early in the twentieth century, along with bits and pieces of the Mohegan-Pequot language. Fielding reportedly did not teach the language to younger Mohegans for fear that they would be punished for speaking it. Tantaquidgeon, Fielding's niece, investigated many of these stories further and became a repository of Mohegan oral tradition. Her story is told in Melissa Jayne Fawcett, *Medicine Trail: The Life and Lessons of Gladys Tantaquidgeon* (Tucson, 2000).

25. Bragdon, *Native People*, 131.

26. Williams, *Key*, 203; Salisbury, *Manitou and Providence*, 187; Bragdon, *Native People*, 145.

27. Williams, *Key*, 104; Salisbury, *Manitou and Providence*, 42.

28. Speck, "Native Tribes and Dialects," 272.

29. Lynn Ceci, "Watchers of the Pleiades: Ethnoastronomy among Native Cultivators in Northeastern North America," *Ethnohistory* 25 (1978): 301–317.

30. Speck, "Native Tribes and Dialects," 270–271; Howard S. Russell, *Indian New England before the Mayflower* (Hanover, N.H., 1980), 165–166.

31. Christopher Vecsey, "American Indian Environmental Religions," in *American Indian Environments: Ecological Issues in Native American History*, ed. Christopher Vecsey and Robert W. Venables (Syracuse, N.Y., 1980), 8, 12–13, 23; Ake Hultkrantz, "Feelings for Nature among North American Indians," in *Belief and Worship in Native North America*, ed. Christopher Vecsey (Syracuse, N.Y., 1981), 123.

32. Bragdon, *Native People*, 31–36; Michael Heckenberger, James B. Petersen, and Nancy Asch Sidell, "Early Evidence of Maize Agriculture in the Connecticut River Valley of Vermont," *Archaeology of Eastern North America* 20 (1992): 141.

33. Lynn Ceci, "Method and Theory in Coastal New York Archaeology: Paradigms of Settlement Patterns," *North American Archaeologist* 3 (1982): 8.

34. Kevin A. McBride and Robert E. Dewar, "Agriculture and Cultural Evolution: Causes and Effects in the Lower Connecticut River Valley," in *Emergent Horticultural Economies in the Eastern Woodlands*, ed. William F. Keegan (Carbondale, Ill., 1987), 324; Bragdon, *Native People*, 35–36, 90, 100.

35. Bragdon, *Native People*, 74–77. See also David J. Bernstein, "Prehistoric Seasonality Studies in Coastal Southern New England," *American Archaeologist* 92 (1991): 126–127.

36. Jeffrey C. M. Bendremer, Elizabeth A. Kellogg, and Tonya Baroody Largy, "A Grass-Lined Maize Storage Pit and Early Maize Horticulture in Central Connecticut," *North American Archaeologist* 12 (1991): 314; McBride and Dewar, "Agriculture," 310; Bragdon, *Native People*, 90.

37. Heckenberger, Petersen, and Sidell, "Early Evidence," 144.

38. Salwen, "Indians of Southern New England," 163; Rainey, "Historical Data," 10; Eva L. Butler, "Algonkian Culture and the Use of Maize in Southern New England," *Bulletin of the Archaeological Society of Connecticut* 22 (1948): 34; Pynchon quoted in Peter A. Thomas, *In the Maelstrom of Change: The Indian Trade and Cultural Process in the Middle Connecticut Valley, 1635–1665* (New York, 1990), 96.

39. Williams, *Key*, 163.

40. Heckenberger, Petersen, and Sidell, "Early Evidence," 139; Kevin A. McBride and Nicholas F. Bellantoni, "The Utility of Ethnohistorical Models for Understanding Late Woodland Contact Change in Southern New

England," *Bulletin of the Archaeological Society of Connecticut* 45 (1982): 52–53; Peter A. Thomas, "Contrastive Subsistence Strategies and Land Use as Factors for Understanding Indian-White Relations in New England," *Ethnohistory* 23 (1976): 10.

41. Morton, *New English Canaan*, 20; McBride and Bellantoni, "Utility," 53.

42. Williams, *Key*, 182; Williams, "Ft. Shantok," 72; Starna, "Pequots," 35–36; Jeffrey Cap Millen Bendremer, "Late Woodland Settlement and Subsistence in Eastern Connecticut" (diss., University of Connecticut, 1993), 29.

43. Williams, *Key*, 170; Morton, *New English Canaan*, 30; Cronon, *Changes in the Land*, 44.

44. Cronon, *Changes in the Land*, 46; Thomas, "Contrastive Subsistence Strategies," 10.

45. Wood, *New England's Prospect*, 106; Thomas, "Contrastive Subsistence Strategies," 10; Salwen, "Indians of Southern New England," 161–162; Williams, *Key*, 128, Williams, "Ft. Shantok," 152.

46. Thomas, "Contrastive Subsistence Strategies," 10.

47. Wood, *New England's Prospect*, 113.

48. The sexual division of labor was reflected in the distribution of grave goods in native graveyards. Indians in southern New England buried their dead with items appropriate to the life they had just lived. See William S. Simmons, *Cautantowwit's House: An Indian Burial Ground on the Island of Conanicut in Narragansett Bay* (Providence, 1970), 45; and Rubertone, *Grave Undertakings*, 132–164.

49. See the discussion in Gregory Evans Dowd, *A Spirited Resistance: The North American Indian Struggle for Unity, 1745–1815* (Baltimore, 1992), 3–8; Bragdon, *Native People*, 197; Winslow, "Relation," 364; Williams, *Key*, 117; and Rubertone, *Grave Undertakings*, 156.

50. Williams, *Key*, 190; Simmons, *Spirit*, 40; Bragdon, *Native People*, 193–196.

51. Simmons, *Spirit*, 130; William S. Simmons, "Frank Speck and 'The Old Mohegan Stone Cutter,'" *Ethnohistory* 32 (1985): 155–163.

52. Frank G. Speck, "A Pequot-Mohegan Witchcraft Tale," *Journal of American Folklore* 16 (1903): 104–106; idem, "Notes on the Mohegans," 195; idem, "Native Tribes and Dialects," 270. Fidelia Fielding told Speck this story in 1902. Current Mohegan tribal historian Melissa Jayne Fawcett has found additional significance in the tale of Chahnameed. The woman in the tale used her mortar and pestle in the magic that aided her escape. For Fawcett, the mortars and pestles in the story "invoke individual magic and solidify tribal identity." Mohegan mortars, Fawcett argued,

were often inscribed with cup-shaped carvings that symbolized "the life-giving powers of Mohegan womanhood" (Fawcett, *Medicine Trail*, 50).

53. Higginson, "New England's Plantation," 257; Morton, *New English Canaan*, 35; Wood, *New England's Prospect*, 100–101.

54. Williams, *Key*, 164, 86, 199; Paul A. Robinson, Marc A. Kelley, and Patricia E. Rubertone, "Preliminary Biocultural Interpretations from a Seventeenth-Century Narragansett Indian Cemetary in Rhode Island," in *Cultures in Contact: The Impact of European Contacts on Native American Cultural Institutions*, ed. Wiliam W. Fitzhugh (Washington, D.C., 1985), 114–115.

55. John Josselyn, *An Account of Two Voyages to New England* (Boston, 1865), 103; Winslow, "Relation," 356.

56. Williams, *Key*, 191.

57. Josselyn, *Two Voyages*, 104; Winslow, "Relation," 357–358; Bragdon, *Native People*, 201.

58. Simmons, *Cautantowwit's House*, 53; Wood, *New England's Prospect*, 101.

59. Dowd, *Spirited Resistance*, ch. 1.

60. Williams, *Key*, 191, 225, 132; Dowd, *Spirited Resistance*, 4–6; Constance A. Crosby, "The Algonkian Spiritual Landscape," in *Algonkians of New England: Past and Present*, ed. Peter Benes (Boston, 1993), 36. On Indian-animal relationships, see Calvin Luther Martin, *Keepers of the Game: Indian-Animal Relationships and the Fur Trade* (Berkeley, Calif., 1978), but also *Indians, Animals, and the Fur Trade: A Critique of 'Keepers of the Game,'* ed. J. Shepard Krech III (Athens, Ga., 1981) and J. Shepard Krech III, *The Ecological Indian: Myth and History* (New York, 2000). For Martin's latest statement on Indian-animal relationships, see *The Way of the Human Being* (New Haven, Conn., 1999), especially 67–68.

Chapter 2. The Mohegans' New World

1. Melissa Jayne Fawcett, *The Lasting of the Mohegans*, part 1, *The Story of the Wolf People* (Uncasville, Conn., 1995), 10. Fawcett learned of the story from Gladys Tantaquidgeon, Mohegan elder, protégée of the anthropologist Frank Speck, and conservator of the tribe's oral tradition. Tantaquidgeon told the story in a radio address commemorating the founding of the Campfire Girls organization in 1938. See Melissa Jayne Fawcett, *Medicine Trail: The Life and Lessons of Gladys Tantaquidgeon* (Tucson, 2000), 124.

2. Robert Steven Grumet, *Historic Contact: Indian People and Colonists in Today's Northeastern United States in the Sixteenth through Eighteenth Centuries* (Norman, Okla., 1995), 10. The title to this chapter is inspired by

James H. Merrell's important book *The Indians' New World: Catawbas and Their Neighbors from European Contact through the Era of Removal* (Chapel Hill, N.C., 1989).

3. Constance A. Crosby, "From Myth to History, Or, Why King Philip's Ghost Walks Abroad," in *The Recovery of Meaning: Historical Archaeology in the Eastern United States*, ed. Mark P. Leone and Parker Potter (Washington, D.C., 1988), 184–185; George R. Hamell, "Mythical Realities and European Contact in the Northeast during the Sixteenth and Seventeenth Centuries," *Man in the Northeast* 33 (1987): 71–72; James Axtell, *The Invasion Within: The Contest of Cultures in Colonial North America* (New York, 1985), 10–11. Similar processes seem to have been at work elsewhere in early America. See Hamell and Christopher L. Miller, "A New Perspective on Indian-White Contact: Cultural Symbols and Colonial Trade," *Journal of American History* 73 (1986): 311–328; Bruce M. White, "Encounters with Spirits: Ojibwa and Dakota Theories about the French and Their Merchandise," *Ethnohistory* 41 (1994): 378; Bruce G. Trigger, *The Children of Aataentsic: A History of the Huron People to 1660* (Montreal, 1976), 429–431, 566; James W. Bradley, *Evolution of the Onondaga Iroquois: Accommodating Change, 1500–1655* (New York, 1985) and Michael Leroy Oberg, "Gods and Men: The Meeting of Indian and White Worlds on the Carolina Outer Banks, 1584–1586," *North Carolina Historical Review* 76 (1999): 374–381.

4. Rosier quoted in *The English New England Voyages, 1602–1608*, ed. David B. Quinn and Alison M. Quinn (London, 1983), 274; William Wood, *New England's Prospect*, ed. Alden T. Vaughan (Amherst, Mass., 1977), 96. On Rosier, see David Beers Quinn, *North America from Earliest Discovery to First Settlements: The Norse Voyages to 1612* (New York, 1975), 400–401.

5. Thomas Morton, *The New English Canaan*, ed. Charles Francis Adams, *Publications of the Prince Society*, vol. 14 (Boston, 1883), 132–133. On the epidemic of 1616–1619, see Arthur E. Speiss and Bruce D. Weiss, "New England Pandemic of 1616–1622: Cause and Archaeological Implication," *Man in the Northeast* 34 (1987): 71–72. Speiss and Weiss suggest that the epidemic resulted from an outbreak of hepatitis, but see also Alfred Crosby, "Virgin Soil Epidemics as a Factor in Aboriginal Depopulation in America," *William and Mary Quarterly* 33 (1976): 300; Sherburne F. Cook, "The Significance of Disease in the Extinction of the New England Indians," *Human Biology* 45 (1973): 499; and William Cronon, *Changes in the Land: Indians, Colonists, and the Ecology of New England* (New York, 1983), 87, who suggests that the epidemic might have been chicken pox.

6. J. Franklin Jameson, ed., *Narratives of New Netherland, 1609–1664* (New York, 1909), 43.

7. Ibid., 86–87; Lynn Ceci, *The Effect of European Contact and Trade on the Settlement Patterns of Indians in Coastal New York, 1525–1665* (New York, 1990), 193; Paul Alden Robinson, "The Struggle Within: The Indian Debate in Seventeenth Century Narragansett Country" (diss., SUNY–Binghamton, 1990), 92. For general discussions of Dutch trading activities, see Paul Andrew Otto, "New Netherland Frontier: Europeans and Native Americans along the Lower Hudson Valley, 1524–1664" (diss., Indiana University, 1995), 76–167, though Otto does not deal directly with Dutch activity in southern New England, and Kevin A. McBride, "Source and Mother of the Fur Trade: Native-Dutch Relations in Eastern New Netherland," in *Enduring Traditions: The Native Peoples of New England*, ed. Laurie Lee Weinstein (Westport, Conn., 1994).

8. Benjamin Trumbull, *A Complete History of Connecticut*, 2 vols. (New London, Conn., 1898), 1:18; D. W. Mulholland, "Dutch Yankees and English Patroons," *De Halve Maen* 58 (1984): 1.

9. Frank G. Speck, "The Functions of Wampum among the Eastern Algonkin," *Memoirs of the American Anthropological Association* 6 (1919): 56; Elizabeth Shapiro Peña, "Wampum Production in New Netherland and Colonial New York: The Historical and Archaeological Context" (diss., Boston University, 1990), 21–23. See also T. S. Slotkin and Karl Schmitt, "Studies of Wampum," *American Anthropologist* 51 (1949): 123–236; and Marshall Joseph Becker, "Wampum: The Development of an Early American Currency," *Bulletin of the Archaeological Society of New Jersey* 36 (1980): 1–11.

10. Robinson, "Struggle," 82–83; Alfred A. Cave, *The Pequot War* (Amherst, Mass., 1996), 50; William Bradford, *Of Plymouth Plantation*, ed. Samuel Eliot Morison (New York, 1952), 203–204. Neal Salisbury coined the phrase "wampum revolution." See his *Manitou and Providence: Indians, Europeans, and the Making of New England, 1500–1643* (New York, 1982), 147–152.

11. Bradford, *Plymouth Plantation*, 203; Cronon, *Changes in the Land*, 101–102; Ceci, *Effect*, 135–283; Bert Salwen, "European Trade Goods and the Chronology of the Fort Shantok Site," *Bulletin of the Archaeological Society of Connecticut* 34 (1966): 34.

12. Lorraine Elise Williams, "Ft. Shantok and Ft. Corchaug: A Comparative Study of Seventeenth Century Culture Contact in the Long Island Sound Area" (diss., New York University, 1972), 20, 49, 96, 133, 179–180; Eric Spencer Johnson, "'Some by Flatteries and Others by Threatenings': Political Strategies among Native Americans of Seventeenth-Century Southern New England" (diss., University of Massachusetts–Amherst, 1993), 223.

13. "Pedigree of Uncas," *NEHGR* 10 (1856): 228; *Connecticut Archives: Town and Lands*, Connecticut State Library, Hartford, 1st ser., 1:67; Salisbury, *Manitou and Providence*, 150.

14. *Connecticut Archives: Town and Lands*, Connecticut State Library, Hartford, 1st ser., 1:67; Simon Bradstreet to the Commissioners of the United Colonies, 19 September 1662, in Eva L. Butler, ed., "Indian Related Materials" (typescript housed in Connecticut State Library, Hartford); John W. De Forest, *History of the Indians of Connecticut from the Earliest Known Period to 1850* (Hartford, 1851), 86.

15. Ceci, *Effect*, 209; Shepard's "Memoir" in *Chronicles of the First Planters of the Colony of Massachusetts Bay, From 1623–1636*, ed. Alexander Young (Boston, 1846), 548–549; Daniel Gookin, *Historical Collections of the Indians of New England* (1674; reprint, New York, 1970), 7; Salisbury, *Manitou and Providence*, 147.

16. Salisbury, *Manitou and Providence*, 204–205.

17. *The Journal of John Winthrop, 1630–1649*, ed. Richard S. Dunn, James Savage, and Laetitia Yeandle (Cambridge, Mass., 1996), 49–50.

18. Bradford, *Plymouth Plantation*, 258; Winthrop, *Journal*, 49–50, 65; Salisbury, *Manitou and Providence*, 205.

19. John Winthrop, "Modell of Christian Charity," in *WP*, 2:282–295; Michael Leroy Oberg, *Dominion and Civility: English Imperialism and Native America, 1585–1685* (Ithaca, N.Y., 1999), 82–83.

20. Oberg, *Dominion and Civility*, 98.

21. Bradford, *Plymouth Plantation*, 202–203.

22. Oberg, *Dominion and Civility*, 98.

23. Allen W. Trelease, *Indian Affairs in Colonial New York: The Seventeenth Century* (Ithaca, N.Y., 1960), 55; Trumbull, *Connecticut*, 1:17; De Forest, *Indians*, 71.

24. Bradford, *Plymouth Plantation*, 259.

25. Ibid.; Oberg, *Dominion and Civility*, 99.

26. Trelease, *Indian Affairs*, 55–56; Francis Jennings, *The Invasion of America: Indians, Colonists, and the Cant of Conquest* (Chapel Hill, N.C., 1975), 189.

27. Winthrop, *Journal*, 108, 118; Bradford, *Plymouth Plantation*, 269–270.

28. Bradford, *Plymouth Plantation*, 270; Winthrop, *Journal*, 133–134.

29. John Winthrop to John Winthrop Jr., 12 December 1634, *WP*, 3:177; Winthrop, *Journal*, 133–134; Salisbury, *Manitou and Providence*, 209–212; Alfred A. Cave, "Who Killed John Stone? A Note on the Origins of the Pequot War," *William and Mary Quarterly* 49 (1992): 514.

30. Winthrop, *Journal*, 133–134; Henry A. Baker, *History of Montville*,

Connecticut, formerly the North Parish of New London, from 1640–1896 (Hartford, 1896), 6.

31. Winthrop, *Journal*, 134–135; Bradford, *Plymouth Plantation*, 271; Cave, *Pequot War*, 59–63.

32. Winthrop, *Journal*, 105–106, 108–110; John Winthrop to Sir Nathaniel Rich, 22 May 1634, *WP*, 3:167; Bradford, *Plymouth Plantation*, 270–271.

33. Brenda J. Baker, "Pilgrim's Progress and Praying Indians: The Biocultural Consequences of Contact in Southern New England," in *In the Wake of Contact: Biological Responses to Conquest*, ed. Clark Spencer Larsen and George R. Milner (New York, 1994), 36.

34. Cronon, *Changes in the Land*, 88–89; William A. Starna, "The Pequots in the Early Seventeenth-Century," in *The Pequots in Southern New England: The Fall and Rise of an American Indian Nation*, ed. Laurence M. Hauptman and James D. Wherry (Norman, Okla., 1990), 47; Peter A. Thomas, *In the Maelstrom of Change: The Indian Trade and Cultural Process in the Middle Connecticut River Valley, 1635–1665* (New York, 1990), 55.

35. Winthrop, *Journal*, 126; On the "Great Migration," see David Cressy, *Coming Over: Migration and Communication between England and New England in the Seventeenth Century* (Cambridge, 1987), 63.

36. Oberg, *Dominion and Civility*, 100–101.

37. Bradford, *Plymouth Plantation*, 280–284; *MBR*, 6 May 1635, 1:46; 3 March 1636, 1:170–171.

38. *CR*, 1:1–4.

39. Jonathan Brewster to William Bradford, 6 July 1635, in Bradford, *Plymouth Plantation*, 280–281; Peter A. Thomas, "Contrastive Subsistence Strategies and Land Use as Factors for Understanding Indian-White Relations in New England," *Ethnohistory* 23 (1976): 4–14; Thomas, *Maelstrom*, 89–120.

40. Thomas, "Contrastive Subsistence Strategies," 14; idem, *Maelstrom*, 118–119.

41. De Forest, *Indians*, 83–85.

42. Roger Williams to John Winthrop, 25 August 1636, in *RWC*, 1:57; Cave, *Pequot War*, 66; Eric S. Johnson, "Uncas and the Politics of Contact," in *Northeastern Indian Lives, 1632–1816*, ed. Robert S. Grumet (Amherst, Mass., 1996), 34; P. Richard Metcalf, "Who Should Rule at Home? Native American Politics and Indian-White Relations," *Journal of American History* 61 (1974): 653. Karen Ordahl Kupperman, *Indians and English: Facing Off in Early America* (Ithaca, N.Y., 2000), 219–220.

43. Kathleen J. Bragdon, *Native People of Southern New England, 1500–*

1650 (Norman, Okla., 1996), 151; *CR*, 3:479–480; Salisbury, *Manitou and Providence*, 205–206.

44. Johnson, "Some by Flatteries," 54–55; Salisbury, *Manitou and Providence*, 215.

45. Roger Williams to John Winthrop, 9 September 1637, *WP*, 3:495; Johnson, "Some by Flatteries," 54–55, 192.

46. Johnson, "Some by Flatteries," 55.

47. Herbert Milton Sylvester, *Indian Wars of New England*, 3 vols. (Cleveland, 1910), 1:246–247n.

48. Greg Dening, "Histories of Self," in *Through a Glass Darkly: Reflections on Personal Identity in Early America*, ed. Ronald Hoffman, Fredrika Teute, and Mechal Sobel (Chapel Hill, N.C., 1997), 9.

49. William Burton and Richard Lowenthal, "The First of the Mohegans," *American Ethnologist* 1 (1974): 593; Metcalf, "Who Should Rule at Home?" 657; Johnson, "Some by Flatteries," 33. A number of works recently have explored the experiences of Indians who became "go-betweens," or who in other ways worked with both Indian and non-Indian power structures and communities. Uncas's story contains many parallels to the Indians described in this exciting body of scholarship. See James H. Merrell, *Into the American Woods: Negotiators on the Pennsylvania Frontier* (New York, 1999); idem, "'Minding the Business of the Nation': Hagler as Catawba Leader," *Ethnohistory* 33 (1986), 55–70; Colin G. Calloway, "Wanalancent and Kancagamus: Indian Strategy and Leadership on the New Hampshire Frontier," *Historical New Hampshire* 43 (1988): 264–290; and Kevin A. McBride, "The Legacy of Robin Cassacinamon: Mashantucket Pequot Leadership in the Historic Period," in *Northeastern Indian Lives*, ed. Grumet, 74–92.

50. John Mason, *A Brief History of the Pequot War* (Boston, 1736), iii; Louis P. Benezet, "John Mason," in *Founders and Leaders of Connecticut, 1633–1783*, ed. Edward Perry (Boston, 1934), 90; Louis Bond Mason, *The Life and Times of Major John Mason of Connecticut, 1600–1672* (New York, 1935), 48. On cross-cultural communication, see James Axtell, "Babel of Tongues: Communication with the Indians," in *Natives and Newcomers: The Cultural Origins of North America* (New York, 2000), 56, 60–61. Also useful are Ives Goddard, "Some Early Examples of American Indian Pidgin English from New England," *International Journal of American Linguistics* 43 (1977): 37–41; and Lois Feister, "Linguistic Communication between the Dutch and Indians in New Netherland, 1609–1664," *Ethnohistory* 20 (1973): 25–38.

51. Benezet, "Mason," 90.

52. *NEHGR*, 53 (1899): 112; Harral Ayres, *The Great Trail of New England* (Boston, 1940), 126–127.
53. Jonathan Brewster to John Winthrop Jr., 18 June 1636, *WP*, 3:270.
54. Ibid., 270–271.
55. Ibid.
56. Ibid.
57. Cave, *Pequot War*, 98–99; Sir Henry Vane to John Winthrop Jr., 1 July 1636, *WP*, 3:282; Vane and John Winthrop to John Winthrop Jr., 4 July 1636, *MHS Coll*, 3d ser., 3 (1833): 130–131.
58. Sir Henry Vane and John Winthrop to John Winthrop Jr., 4 July 1636, *MHS Coll*, 3d ser., 3 (1833): 133.
59. Winthrop, *Journal*, 181.
60. Ibid., 182–183; Cave, *Pequot War*, 107.
61. John Underhill, "Newes from America," *MHS Coll*, 3d ser., 6 (1837): 4; Winthrop, *Journal*, 183.
62. Underhill, "Newes," 6–7.
63. "Lieft Lion Gardener his Relation of the Pequot Warres," *MHS Coll*, 3d. ser., 3 (1833): 140.
64. Roger Williams to John Winthrop, ca. August–September 1636, *WP*, 3:298; Underhill, "Newes," 7–8.
65. Underhill, "Newes," 8–11; Gardener, "Relation," 141; Adam J. Hirsch, "The Collision of Military Cultures in Seventeenth-Century New England," *Journal of American History* 74 (1988): 1197.
66. Winthrop, *Journal*, 185–186; Alden T. Vaughan, *New England Frontier: Puritans and Indians, 1620–1675* (Boston, 1965), 137; Mason, *History*, ix; De Forest, *Indians*, 99.
67. Nathaniel Morton, *New England's Memoriall: Or, a Brief Relation of the Most Memorable and Remarkable Passages of the Providence of God* (Cambridge, Mass., 1669), 100.
68. Winthrop, *Journal*, 190–192; Vaughan, *New England Frontier*, 132.
69. Gardener, "Relation," 142–143; Lyon Gardener to John Winthrop Jr., 7 November 1636, *WP*, 3:321.
70. Gardener, "Relation," 145–146.
71. Underhill, "Newes," 12; Winthrop, *Journal*, 212–213.
72. Underhill, "Newes," 12; Philip Vincent, "A True Relation of the late Batell Fought in New England between the English and the Pequot Savages," *MHS Coll*, 3d. ser., 6 (1837): 35; John Higginson to John Winthrop, May 1637, *WP*, 3:405–406.
73. Roger Williams to Henry Vane and John Winthrop, 13 May 1637, *RWC*, 1:78; Thomas Hooker to John Winthrop, May 1637, *WP*, 3:407.

74. On the first point, see Jennings, *Invasion*. On the second, see Vaughan, *New England Frontier*.

75. Underhill, "Newes," 15–16; De Forest, *Indians*, 119–120; Charles Frederick Chapin, "Uncas," *Papers and Addresses of the Society of Colonial Wars in the State of Connecticut* 1 (1903): 29.

76. *CR*, 1:9–10.

77. Edward Winslow to John Winthrop, 17 April 1637, *WP*, 3:391–392.

78. Mason, *History*, 1.

79. Ibid.

80. *MBR*, 1:192–193.

81. Roger Williams to John Winthrop and Sir Henry Vane, 1 May 1637, *RWC*, 1:72–74.

82. Gardener, "Relation," 149.

83. Underhill, "Newes," 16–17.

84. Gardener, "Relation," 149; Sylvester, *Indian Wars*, 1:252.

85. Vincent, "True Relation," 36; Gardener, "Relation," 149; Trumbull, *Connecticut*, 1:56–57.

86. John Leete Stone, *Uncas and Miantunomoh: A Historical Discourse* (New York, 1842), 50; Trumbull, *Connecticut*, 1:56–57; Winthrop, *Journal*, 218; Jennings, *Invasion*, 218.

87. My understanding of these issues has been informed by Gregory Evans Dowd, *A Spirited Resistance: The North American Indian Struggle for Unity, 1745–1815* (Baltimore, 1992), 13–16.

Chapter 3. The Rise of the Mohegans

1. John Mason, *A Brief History of the Pequot War* (Boston, 1736), 2. Much of the following is drawn from Mason's account, published a century after the war by his descendants, who then were engaged in a legal battle with the colony of Connecticut over the ownership of Mohegan lands (I discuss this in the conclusion). While there is no way of knowing whether Mason's heirs altered the document to fit the needs of the 1730s, there is no doubt that his *History* demonstrated the close relationship between Uncas and Mason that his heirs, and later colonial officials, interpreted in drastically different ways.

2. Ibid., 2–3; John Underhill, "Newes from America," *MHS Coll*, 3d ser., 6 (1837): 16–17.

3. Mason, *History*, 4.

4. Ibid., 4, 2.

5. Ibid., 4–5.

6. Ibid., 6.

7. Ibid., 5–6.

8. Ibid., 6–7; Philip Vincent, "A True Relation of the late Batell Fought in New England between the English and the Pequot Savages," *MHS Coll*, 3d ser., 6 (1837): 38–39. The number of warriors in the Mystic fortress has proven a source of contention among historians of the Pequot War. Francis Jennings, in *The Invasion of America: Indians, Colonists, and the Cant of Conquest* (Chapel Hill, N.C., 1975), 220–222, argues that Mason attacked Mystic to avoid the large number of warriors at Weinshauks. Fewer warriors, he argued, were at Mystic, and those there were not as well armed. There is no evidence to support Jennings's claim. The surviving evidence does not allow us to reconstruct with any accuracy the disposition of Pequot forces, and all the English sources agree that the Mystic fort, a well-constructed defensive position, was guarded by armed Pequots. See Alfred Cave, *The Pequot War* (Amherst, Mass., 1996), 209–210.

9. Mason, *History*, 8–9; Vincent, "True Relation," 39.

10. Underhill, "Newes," 24–25.

11. Ibid., 27; William Bradford did not witness the Puritan assault. See Bradford, *Of Plymouth Plantation*, ed. Samuel Eliot Morison (New York, 1952), 296. The word "naught" in the seventeenth century meant "evil."

12. Underhill, "Newes," 25, 27.

13. *The Journal of John Winthrop*, ed. Richard S. Dunn, James Savage, and Laetitia Yeandle (Cambridge, Mass., 1996), 220; Roger Williams to John Winthrop, 2 June 1637, *RWC*, 1:83–84; Alden T. Vaughan, *New England Frontier: Puritans and Indians, 1620–1675* (Boston, 1965), 145.

14. Mason, *History*, 10–12.

15. William Burton and Richard Lowenthal, "The First of the Mohegans," *American Ethnologist* 1 (1974), passim.

16. Underhill, "Newes," 26. On the importance of keeping casualties in warfare to a minimum, see Daniel K. Richter, "War and Culture: The Iroquois Experience," *William and Mary Quarterly* 40 (1983): 528–559.

17. Paul Alden Robinson, "The Struggle Within: The Indian Debate in Seventeenth Century Narragansett Country" (diss., SUNY–Binghamton, 1990), 111. On English violence at Mystic and its consequences, see Adam J. Hirsch, "The Collision of Military Cultures in Seventeenth-Century New England," *Journal of American History* 74 (1988): 1187–1212; Ronald Dale Karr, "'Why Should You Be So Furious?' The Violence of the Pequot War," *Journal of American History* 85 (1998): 876–909; Harold E. Selesky, *War and Society in Colonial Connecticut* (New Haven, Conn., 1990), 9; and Patrick M. Malone, *The Skulking Way of War: Technology and Tactics among the New England Indians* (Baltimore, 1991), 103, 105.

18. Roger Williams to John Williams, 21 June 1637, *RWC*, 1:86; Mason, *History*, 14; Cave, *Pequot War*, 157.

19. Mason, *History*, 17; Roger Williams to John Winthrop, 21 July 1637, *RWC*, 1:107; "Lieft Lion Gardener his Relation of the Pequot Warres," *MHS Coll*, 3d ser., 3 (1833): 150; Vincent, "True Relation," 39.

20. *CR*, 1:10; Winthrop, *Journal*, 225–227; Mason, *History*, 15; Cave, *Pequot War*, 159; Herbert Milton Sylvester, *Indian Wars of New England*, 3 vols. (Cleveland, 1910), 1:301–302.

21. Mason, *History*, 15–17; Winthrop, *Journal*, 227; Benjamin Trumbull, *A Compendium of the Indians Wars in New England*, ed. Frederic Berg Hartranft (Hartford, 1926), 28.

22. John Winthrop to William Bradford, 28 July 1637, *WP*, 3:457; Winthrop, *Journal*, 227; Kevin A. McBride, "The Legacy of Robin Cassacinamon: Mashantucket Pequot Leadership in the Historic Period," in *Northeastern Indian Lives, 1632–1816*, ed. Robert Steven Grumet (Amherst, Mass., 1996), 74. The enormous loss of life at Mystic has generated a debate over the extent to which the Pequot War can be considered a genocidal conflict. See Michael Freeman, "Puritans and Pequots: The Question of Genocide," *New England Quarterly* 68 (1995): 278–293; Steven T. Katz, "The Pequot War Reconsidered," *New England Quarterly* 64 (1991): 206–224; and idem, "Pequots and the Question of Genocide: A Reply to Michael Freeman," *New England Quarterly* 68 (1995): 641–649.

23. Richard Davenport to John Winthrop, August 1637, *Trumbull Papers*, Connecticut State Library, Hartford, part 1, p. 2; Roger Williams to John Winthrop, 21 June 1637, *RWC*, 1:86–87.

24. *MBR* 1:196–197, 209; *CR*, 1:14–17, 19–20.

25. Thomas Hooker to John Winthrop, December 1638, *WP*, 4:76; *MBR*, 1:216; *CR*, 1:10; Roger Williams to John Winthrop, 21 June 1637, *RWC*, 1:86–87.

26. Eric Spencer Johnson, "'Some by Flatteries and Others by Threatenings': Political Strategies among Native Americans in Seventeenth-Century Southern New England" (diss., University of Massachusetts–Amherst, 1993), 56–58, 99, 120.

27. Roger Williams to John Winthrop, 26 October 1637, *RWC*, 1:127; Robinson, "Struggle," 133–134.

28. Roger Ludlow to John Winthrop, 3 July 1638, *WP*, 4:43–44.

29. Ibid., 45; Roger Williams to John Winthrop, 1 August 1638, *RWC*, 1:170, and 14 August 1638, *WP*, 4:52; Timothy J. Sehr, "Ninigret's Tactics of Accommodation: Indian Diplomacy in New England, 1637–1675," *Rhode Island History* 36 (1977): 44.

30. Roger Williams to John Winthrop, 21 June 1637, *RWC*, 1:86–87, and 10 July 1637, *RWC*, 1:110; Paul Alden Robinson, "Lost Opportunities: Miantonomi and the English in the Seventeenth-Century Narragansett

Country," *Northeastern Indian Lives*, ed. Grumet, 14. On Pequot captives, see Israel Stoughton to John Winthrop, 28 June 1637, *WP*, 3:435; Roger Williams to John Winthrop, 30 June 1637, *WP*, 3:436, and 12 August 1637, *RWC*, 1:110; and Michael F. Fickes, "'They Could Not Endure That Yoke': The Captivity of Pequot Women and Children after the War of 1637," *New England Quarterly* 73 (2000): 58–81.

31. Roger Williams to John Winthrop, 28 February 1637/8, *RWC*, 1:146, and 10 July 1637, *RWC*, 1:97.

32. Israel Stoughton to John Winthrop, 6 July 1637, *WP*, 3:441–442; Roger Williams to John Winthrop, 30 June 1637, *RWC*, 1:88.

33. Israel Stoughton to John Winthrop, 6 July 1637, *WP*, 3:442; Robinson, "Struggle," 118–119.

34. Roger Williams to John Winthrop, 15 July 1637, *RWC*, 1:101, and 10 November 1637, *RWC*, 1:131.

35. Winthrop, *Journal*, 1:238; Jennings, *Invasion*, 258.

36. Roger Williams to John Winthrop, 14 August 1638, *RWC*, 1:176; Robinson, "Struggle," 128.

37. Roger Williams to John Winthrop, 9 September 1637, *RWC*, 1:119.

38. Roger Williams to John Winthrop, 10 February 1638, *WP*, 4:6–7.

39. Roger Williams to John Winthrop, 23 October 1637, *RWC*, 1:126; 10 February 1638, *WP*, 4:7; 28 February 1638, *RWC* 1:145; and 22 May 1638, *RWC*, 1:155.

40. Roger Williams to John Winthrop, 14 June 1638, *WP*, 4:40; Winthrop, *Journal*, 258.

41. Winthrop, *Journal*, 258.

42. Ibid.

43. Roger Williams to John Winthrop, 14 June 1638, *RWC*, 1:163–164, and 10 September 1638, *RWC*, 1:179–180.

44. Roger Williams to John Winthrop, 14 June 1638, *RWC*, 1:163–164.

45. Richard Davenport to John Winthrop, ca. 23 August 1637, *WP*, 3:491; Roger Williams to John Winthrop, 9 September 1637, *WP*, 3:494, and 23 July 1638, *WP*, 4:46–47; Johnson, "Some by Flatteries," 207.

46. Roger Williams to John Winthrop, 10 September 1638, *RWC*, 1:180.

47. Roger Williams to John Winthrop, 28 February 1638, *RWC*, 1:146; Johnson, "Some by Flatteries," 40; McBride, "Robin Cassacinamon," 76.

48. Johnson, "Some by Flatteries," 273–274, 277–278, 283.

49. Roger Williams to John Winthrop, 10 September 1638, *RWC*, 1:180.

50. Roger Williams to John Winthrop, 27 May 1638, *RWC*, 1:157, and 14 August 1638, *RWC*, 1:176; Thomas Hooker to John Winthrop, *WP*, 4:78–79; Roger Williams to John Winthrop, 21 September 1638, *RWC*, 1:182; Jennings, *Invasion*, 258–259.

51. Roger Williams to John Winthrop, 21 September 1638, *RWC*, 1:182.

52. Ibid., 183.

53. Ibid., 183–184.

54. "The Hartford Treaty with the Narragansetts and the Fenwick Letters," *NEHGR* 46 (1982): 355–356.

55. Bradford, *Plymouth Plantation*, 338; Roger Williams to John Winthrop, 21 July 1640, *RWC*, 1:203.

56. The quotation comes from Melissa Jayne Fawcett, *Medicine Trail: The Life and Lessons of Gladys Tantaquidgeon* (Tucson, 2000), xii.

Chapter 4. Killing Miantonomi

1. Frederick Jackson Turner, "The Significance of the Frontier in American History," in *Frontier and Section: Selected Essays of Frederick Jackson Turner*, ed. Ray Allen Billington (Englewood Cliffs, N.J., 1961), 38. Turner, principally interested in the effects of the frontier experience upon American character and institutions, saw the Anglo-Indian encounter primarily in terms of conflict, as Indians resisted an expanding line of white settlements. More recently, historians have begun to take a more sophisticated look at the European-Indian frontier. They have explored the complicated processes of accommodation, adaptation, and coexistence that developed during the early stages of the encounter. They have also analyzed the complex ways through which Indians and Europeans arrived at understandings of each other. For a sampling of some of the best works in this vast and growing literature, see: Matthew Dennis, *Cultivating a Landscape of Peace: Iroquois-European Encounters in Seventeenth-Century America* (Ithaca, N.Y., 1993), 3–4; Richard White, *The Middle Ground: Indians, Empires, and Republics in the Great Lakes Region* (Cambridge, 1991), 52; James H. Merrell, *The Indians' New World: The Catawbas and Their Neighbors from European Contact through the Era of Removal* (Chapel Hill, N.C., 1989), 47; and Karen Ordahl Kupperman, *Indians and English: Facing Off in Early America* (Ithaca, N.Y., 2000). These middle grounds always remained tenuous, and collapsed once European settlers began moving into a region and clearing the land. See Michael Leroy Oberg, *Dominion and Civility: English Imperialism and Native America, 1585–1685* (Ithaca, N.Y., 1999), chaps. 2–5; Daniel H. Usner Jr., *Indians, Settlers, and Slaves in a Frontier Exchange Economy: The Lower Mississippi Valley before 1783* (Chapel Hill, N.C., 1992), 112–113; Eric Hinderaker, *Elusive Empires: Constructing Colonialism in the Ohio Valley* (New York, 1997); and Peter C. Mancall, *Valley of Opportunity: Economic Culture along the Upper Susquehanna, 1700–1800* (Ithaca, N.Y., 1991).

2. *CR*, 1:46–47, 49, 52, 58, 61, 79; Lynn Ceci, "Native Wampum as a Peripheral Resource in the Seventeenth-Century World System," in *The Pequots in Southern New England: The Fall and Rise of an American Indian Nation*, ed. Laurence M. Hauptman and James D. Wherry (Norman, Okla., 1990), 50. On Puritan attempts to govern the Anglo-American frontier, see Oberg, *Dominion and Civility*, chaps. 3 and 4.

3. Arthur L. Peale, *Uncas and the Mohegan-Pequot* (Boston, 1934), 105; *The Journal of John Winthrop*, ed. Richard S. Dunn, James S. Savage and Laetitia Yeandle (Cambridge, Mass., 1996), 401.

4. Winthrop, *Journal*, 401.

5. Paul Alden Robinson, "The Struggle Within: The Indian Debate in Seventeenth-Century Narragansett Country" (diss., SUNY–Binghamton, 1990), 135; Eric Spencer Johnson, "'Some by Flatteries and Others by Threatenings': Political Strategies among Native Americans in Seventeenth-Century New England" (diss., University of Massachusetts–Amherst, 1993), 206.

6. On the limited contact between Mohegans and colonists in the 1630s, see Lorraine Elise Williams, "Ft. Shantok and Ft. Corchaug: A Comparative Study of Seventeenth-Century Culture Contact in the Long Island Sound Area" (diss., New York University, 1972), 46.

7. Roger Williams to John Winthrop, 21 July 1640, *WP*, 4:269; Johnson, "Some by Flatteries," 180.

8. The deed is reprinted in Henry A. Baker, *History of Montville, Connecticut, formerly the North Parish of New London, from 1640–1896* (Hartford, 1896), 11. For Algonquian place-names in southern New England, see R. A. Douglas-Lithgow, *Dictionary of American Indian Place and Proper Names in New England* (Salem, Mass., 1909).

9. Baker, *Montville*, 11. For the "deed game," see Francis Jennings, *The Invasion of America: Indians, Colonists, and the Cant of Conquest* (Chapel Hill, N.C., 1975), chap. 8.

10. Eric S. Johnson, "Uncas and the Politics of Contact," *Northeastern Indian Lives, 1632–1816*, ed. Robert Steven Grumet (Amherst, Mass., 1996), 37; idem, "Some by Flatteries," 108; Harold E. Selesky, *War and Society in Colonial Connecticut* (New Haven, Conn., 1990), 11–12. For a discussion of English settlers confronting similar problems elsewhere, see James H. Merrell, *Into the American Woods: Negotiators on the Pennsylvania Frontier* (New York, 1999), chaps. 1–2.

11. Herbert Milton Sylvester, *Indian Wars of New England*, 3 vols. (Cleveland, 1910), 1:360; Benjamin Trumbull, *A Complete History of Connecticut*, 2 vols. (New London, Conn., 1898), 1:85–86.

12. *CR*, 1:32; Trumbull, *Connecticut*, 1:85.

13. Trumbull, *Connecticut*, 1:85–86.

14. John Mason, *A Brief History of the Pequot War* (Boston, 1736); Sylvester, *Indian Wars*, 1:362.

15. Roger Williams to John Winthrop, 7 August 1640, *RWC*, 1:206.

16. William Coddington to John Winthrop, 25 August 1640, *WP*, 4:278; Timothy J. Sehr, "Ninigret's Tactics of Accommodation: Indian Diplomacy in New England, 1637–1675," *Rhode Island History* 36 (1977): 44.

17. Roger Williams to John Winthrop, 21 July 1640, *WP*, 4:269.

18. Ibid.

19. Roger Williams to John Winthrop, 7 August 1640, *WP*, 4:273.

20. Winthrop, *Journal*, 328–329; William Bradford to John Winthrop, 29 June 1640, *WP*, 4:258–259.

21. William Bradford to John Winthrop, 16 August 1640, *WP*, 4:275.

22. For a detailed discussion of this dynamic in Early America, see James H. Merrell, "'The Customes of Our Countrey': Indians and Colonists in Early America," in *"Strangers within the Realm": Cultural Margins of the First British Empire*, ed. Bernard Bailyn and Philip D. Morgan (Chapel Hill, N.C., 1991). For a discussion of the concept of a "middle ground," see White, *Middle Ground*, chap. 2.

23. Winthrop, *Journal*, 336–337; Paul Alden Robinson, "Lost Opportunities: Miantonomi and the English in the Seventeenth-Century Narragansett Country," in *Northeastern Indian Lives*, ed. Grumet, 26.

24. "Journal of New Netherland," *NYCD*, 1:183.

25. "Relation of the Plott," *MHS Coll*, 3d ser., 3 (1833): 161–164; "Lieft Lion Gardener his Relation of the Pequot Warres," *MHS Coll*, 3d ser., 3 (1833): 153.

26. Gardener, "Relation," 153–154; Winthrop, *Journal*, 406.

27. Gardener, "Relation," 154; On Waiandance, see John A. Strong, "The Imposition of Colonial Jurisdiction over the Montauk Indians of Long Island," *Ethnohistory* 41 (1994): 562. On Kieft's War, see Oberg, *Dominion and Civility*, 139–141. Miantonomi's call for a united Indian resistance to Anglo-Dutch colonization on Long Island and in the Hudson and Connecticut River Valleys bears a resemblance to what the historian Gregory Evans Dowd has described as "a Spirited Resistance," in which Indians, believing that the misfortunes which had befallen them stemmed from an inattention to religious ritual and a toleration of the European presence, unified to drive out the intruders. See Dowd, *A Spirited Resistance: The North American Indian Struggle for Unity, 1745–1815* (Baltimore, 1992), introduction. It is worth remembering that Canonicus, in 1637, had blamed the English for "sending the plague amongst them," according to Roger Williams (Williams to John Winthrop and Sir Henry Vane, 1 May

1637, *RWC*, 1:72–74). For other discussions of Indian "revitalization movements," see James Mooney, "The Ghost Dance Religion and the Sioux Outbreak of 1890," in *Fourteenth Annual Report of the Bureau of American Ethnology*, pt. 2. (Washington, D.C., 1896); Anthony F. C. Wallace, *The Death and Rebirth of the Senecas* (New York, 1969); R. David Edmunds, *The Shawnee Prophet* (Lincoln, Nebr., 1983); and William G. McLoughlin, "The Cherokee Ghost Dance Movement," in *The Cherokee Ghost Dance: Essays on the Southeastern Indians, 1785–1861* (Macon, Ga., 1984).

28. John Winthrop, *A Declaration of Former Passages and Proceedings Betwixt the English and the Narrowgansets, with their Confederates, Wherein the Grounds and Justice of the Ensuing Warr Are Opened and Cleared* (Boston, 1645), 2; Winthrop, *Journal*, 406.

29. Richard I. Melvoin, *New England Outpost: War and Society in Colonial Deerfield* (New York, 1989), 41; Johnson, "Some by Flatteries," 111; Neal Salisbury, "Toward the Covenant Chain: Iroquois and Southern New England Algonquians, 1637–1684," in *Beyond the Covenant Chain: The Iroquois and Their Neighbors*, ed. James Merrell and Daniel K. Richter (Syracuse, N.Y., 1987), 64–65; *CR*, 1:73–74; Winthrop, *Journal*, 408–409; *MBR*, 2:23–28; *PCR*, 2:46.

30. Winthrop, *Journal*, 409–410.

31. Ibid., 410–412; Johnson, "Some by Flatteries," 111–112.

32. Salisbury, "Toward the Covenant Chain," 63; Johnson, "Some by Flatteries," 111–112.

33. Howard M. Chapin, *Sachems of the Narragansetts* (Providence, 1931), 44; Winthrop, *Declaration*, 3.

34. Winthrop, *Declaration*, 3; Chapin, *Sachems*, 45.

35. Winthrop, *Declaration*, 3; Sylvester, *Indian Wars*, 1: 388; Trumbull, *Connecticut*, 1: 101–102.

36. Winthrop, *Journal*, 468.

37. Ibid., 458–462, 468; Oberg, *Dominion and Civility*, 119.

38. Winthrop, *Declaration*, 2–3.

39. *RUC*, 1:3–4, 6; Oberg, *Dominion and Civility*, 119. The Colony of New Haven was founded in 1638.

40. Sylvester, *Indian Wars*, 1:391–392; Baker, *Montville*, 15.

41. The account comes from a letter written by the Reverend Richard Hyde to Benjamin Trumbull in October 1769, included in Daniel Coit Gilman, *A Historical Discourse Delivered in Norwich, Connecticut, September 7th, 1859, at the Bicentennial Celebration of the Settlement of the Town*, 2d ed. (Boston, 1859), 82–84. According to Gilman, Hyde heard this story "from some of the ancient Fathers of this Town who were Contemporary with Uncas."

42. Sylvester, *Indian Wars*, 1:391–392; Baker, *Montville*, 17; Arthur L. Peale, *Memorials and Pilgrimages in the Mohegan Country* (Norwich, Conn., 1930), 11.

43. Baker, *Montville*, 17.

44. Trumbull, *Connecticut*, 1:102–103; Chapin, *Sachems*, 47; Winthrop, *Journal*, 471.

45. Neal Salisbury, *Manitou and Providence: Indians, Europeans, and the Making of New England, 1500–1643* (New York, 1982), 232–233; Baker, *Montville*, 18; Oberg, *Dominion and Civility*, 139–140; Allen W. Trelease, *Indian Affairs in Colonial New York: The Seventeenth Century* (Ithaca, N.Y., 1960), 64–85; Paul Andrew Otto, "New Netherland Frontier: Europeans and Native Americans along the Lower Hudson River, 1524–1664," (diss., Indiana University, 1993), ch. 4.

46. John Haynes to John Winthrop, 17 February 1643/4, *WP*, 4:507.

47. Winthrop, *Journal*, 472–473; *RUC*, 1:10–12.

48. *RUC*, 1:11–12; Winthrop, *Journal*, 473.

49. Frances Manwaring Caulkins, *History of Norwich, Connecticut: From Its Possession by the Indians to the Year 1866* (1866; reprint, Chester, Conn., 1976), 39. For more recent criticisms, see John A. Sainsbury, "Miantonomo's Death and New England Politics," *Rhode Island History* 30 (1971): 116, 122; Jennings, *Invasion*; and Salisbury, *Manitou and Providence*, 234–235.

50. "The Hartford Treaty with the Narragansetts and the Fenwick Letters," *NEHGR* 46 (1892): 355.

51. John W. De Forest, *History of the Indians of Connecticut from the Earliest Known Period to 1850* (Hartford, 1851), 198; Sylvester, *Indian Wars*, 1:412–413; Trumbull, *Connecticut*, 1:106.

52. Winthrop, *Declaration*, 7; Winthrop, *Journal*, 481.

53. Winthrop, *Declaration*, 7; *RUC*, 1:12; *CR*, 1:94; *NHR*, 1:110.

Chapter 5. To Have Revenge on Uncas

1. John Mason to John Winthrop, 1 December 1643, *WP*, 4:419; Edward Winslow to John Winthrop, 7 January 1644, *WP*, 4:427–428; William Pynchon to John Winthrop, 19 February 1644, *WP*, 4:443–444.

2. Benedict Arnold to John Winthrop, 19 January 1644, *WP*, 4:432–433, and 14 February 1644, *WP*, 4:441.

3. *The Journal of John Winthrop*, ed. Richard S. Dunn, James S. Savage, and Laetitia Yeandle (Cambridge, Mass., 1996) 495; Paul Alden Robinson, "The Struggle Within: The Indian Debate in Seventeenth-Century Narragansett Country" (diss., SUNY–Binghamton, 1990), 148.

4. Pessicus and Canonicus to Commissioners of the United Colonies,

24 May 1644, Massachusetts Archives, Massachusetts State Library, Boston, 30:2; *RUC*, 2:415; *RICR*, 1:134, 137; Winthrop, *Journal*, 509.

5. Winthrop, *Journal*, 509–510.

6. John Browne to John Winthrop, 26 June 1644, *WP*, 4:464–465; Winthrop, *Journal*, 513, 547; *RUC* 1:17, 28–29; Benjamin Trumbull, *A Complete History of Connecticut*, 2 vols. (New London, Conn., 1898), 1:114; William Bradford, *Of Plymouth Plantation*, ed. Samuel Eliot Morison (New York, 1952), 336–337.

7. Frances Manwaring Caulkins, *History of Norwich, Connecticut: From its Possession by the Indians to the Year 1866* (Chester, Conn., 1976), 42; Herbert M. Sylvester, *Indian Wars of New England*, 3 vols. (Cleveland, 1910), 1: 432.

8. Roger Williams to John Winthrop, 23 June 1645, *WP*, 5:31; Thomas Peters to John Winthrop, ca. May 1645, *WP*, 5:19–20.

9. *MBR*, 3:17, 38; Winthrop, *Journal*, 605; Michael Leroy Oberg, *Dominion and Civility: English Imperialism and Native America, 1585–1685* (Ithaca, N.Y., 1999), 130.

10. Bradford, *Plymouth Plantation*, 341.

11. Caulkins, *Norwich*, 40–41.

12. Frank G. Speck, "Native Tribes and Dialects of Connecticut: A Mohegan-Pequot Diary," *Forty-Third Annual Report of the United States Bureau of American Ethnology, 1925–1926* (Washington, D.C., 1928), 258; Patrick M. Malone, *The Skulking Way of War: Technology and Tactics among the New England Indians* (Baltimore, 1991), 85.

13. Caulkins, *Norwich*, 41.

14. *RUC*, 1:33–35; *CR*, 1:128.

15. *RUC*, 1:37–39.

16. *RUC*, 1:43–46. The Narragansetts had to pay the first installment, five hundred fathoms of wampum, within twenty days. Paul Alden Robinson estimates that to produce this sum of wampum would have required an extraordinary commitment of labor—between 3,750 and 5,000 working days. See Robinson, "Struggle," 170.

17. *MBR*, 3:76; Eva L. Butler, "Indian Related Materials," typescript housed in the Connecticut State Library, Hartford, 13, 7; Frances Manwaring Caulkins, *History of New London, Connecticut: From the First Survey of the Coast in 1612, to 1852* (New London, 1852), 51.

18. Kevin A. McBride, "The Legacy of Robin Cassacinamon: Mashantucket Pequot Leadership in the Historic Period," *Northeastern Indian Lives, 1632–1816*, ed. Robert Steven Grumet (Amherst, Mass., 1996), 83–84; John W. De Forest, *History of the Indians of Connecticut from the Earliest Known Period to 1850* (Hartford, 1851), 227.

19. Caulkins, *New London*, 51; Pliny LeRoy Harwood, *History of Eastern Connecticut* (Chicago, 1932), 54.

20. Caulkins, *New London*, 52; Harwood, *Eastern Connecticut*, 54.

21. Petition of the Inhabitants of New London to the Commissioners of the United Colonies, and Memorandum by John Winthrop Jr. to the New London planters, September 1646, *WP*, 5:111–112. See also Thomas Skidmore and others to the Connecticut General Court, in Butler, ed., "Indian Related Materials," 3. For the cutting of hair as a sign of humiliation, see Karen Ordahl Kupperman, *Indians and English: Facing off in Early America* (Ithaca, N.Y. 2000), 56.

22. Eric Spencer Johnson, "'Some by Flatteries and Others by Threatenings': Political Strategies among Native Americans of Seventeenth-Century Southern New England" (diss., University of Massachusetts–Amherst, 1993), 132–134.

23. John Winthrop to Uncas, 20 June 1646, *WP*, 5:82; Thomas Peters to John Winthrop Jr., 29 June 1646, *WP*, 5:85.

24. John Winthrop Jr. to Thomas Peters, 3 September 1646, *WP*, 5:100–101.

25. *RUC*, 1:72.

26. *RUC*, 1:73.

27. *RUC*, 1:73–74.

28. Agreement between Uncas and Robin Cassacinamon, 24 February 1647, *WP*, 5:131.

29. John Winthrop to John Winthrop Jr., 14 May 1647, *WP*, 5:161; Protest of the Inhabitants of New London Against Uncas, ca. 1647, *WP*, 5:124.

30. *CA: Indians*, 1st ser., 1:1.

31. *RUC*, 1:97–99.

32. *RUC*, 1:98.

33. *RUC*, 1:97–101; Johnson, "Some by Flatteries," 183. On Indian marriage, the best statement is Ann Marie Plane, *Colonial Intimacies: Indian Marriage in Early New England* (Ithaca, N.Y., 2000), chap. 1. On the Nipmucks, see Dennis Connole, "Land Occupied by the Nipmuck Indians of Central New England," *Bulletin of the Massachusetts Archaeological Society* 38 (1976): 14–19.

34. *RUC*, 1:98–102; Eric S. Johnson, "Uncas and the Politics of Contact," in *Northastern Indian Lives*, ed. Grumet, 42; McBride, "Robin Cassacinamon," 85.

35. *RUC*, 1:111; *CR*, 1:164.

36. John Mason to John Winthrop Jr., 4 September 1648, *WP*, 5:250; Adam Winthrop to John Winthrop Jr., 14 March 1649, *WP*, 5:319.

37. Edward Hopkins to John Mason, 21 November 1648, *WP*, 5:282; John Mason to John Winthrop Jr., ca. October 1648, *WP*, 5:263.

38. Roger Williams to John Winthrop Jr., 24 January 1649, *RWC*, 1:269; John Mason to Commissioners of the United Colonies, June 1649, *RUC*, 2:417; *RUC*, 1:146; John Winthrop Jr. to the Commissioners of the United Colonies, July 1649, *WP*, 5:354.

39. John Winthrop Jr. to the Commissioners of the United Colonies, July 1649, *WP*, 5:354; Johnson, "Uncas," 42–43.

40. *RUC*, 1:66, 68; Peter A. Thomas, *In the Maelstrom of Change: The Indian Trade and Cultural Process in the Middle Connecticut River Valley, 1635–1665* (New York, 1990), 150.

41. *RUC*, 1:68.

42. Winthrop, *Journal*, 717.

43. *RUC*, 1:75; Winthrop, *Journal*, 691. We know very little about Algonquian mourning rituals in southern New England. Useful discussions can be found in William S. Simmons, *Spirit of the New England Tribes: Indian History and Folklore, 1620–1984* (Hanover, N.H., 1986), 251–256; and Patricia E. Rubertone, *Grave Undertakings: An Archaeology of Roger Williams and the Narragansett Indians* (Washington, D.C., 2001), 166–167.

44. Roger Williams to John Winthrop Jr., 10 October 1648, *RWC*, 1:252; John Winthrop Jr. to Edward Hopkins, 10 February 1647, *WP*, 5:127; Winthrop, *Journal*, 681.

45. *RUC*, 1:85.

46. Winthrop, *Journal*, 717; Roger Williams to John Winthrop Jr., 11 September 1648, *WP*, 5:251; *RUC*, 1:116.

47. *RUC*, 1:116–118; Roger Williams to John Winthrop Jr., 10 October 1648, *RWC*, 1:251–252; Winthrop, *Journal*, 717.

48. Roger Williams to John Winthrop Jr., 10 October 1648, *RWC*, 1:251–252.

49. Roger Williams to John Winthrop Jr., 23 September 1648, *RWC*, 1:248; John Mason to John Winthrop Jr., 9 September 1648, *WP*, 5:250–251; John Winthrop Jr. to John Mason, 19 September 1648, *WP*, 5:255; Timothy J. Sehr, "Ninigret's Tactics of Accommodation: Indian Diplomacy in New England, 1637–1675," *Rhode Island History* 36 (1977), 48.

50. Roger Williams to John Winthrop Jr., ca. April 1649, *WP*, 5:327; De Forest, *Indians*, 236.

51. *RUC*, 2:416–417.

52. Roger Williams to John Winthrop Jr., ca. April 1649, *WP*, 5:326–327.

53. *RUC*, 1:144; De Forest, *Indians*, 236–237.

54. *RUC*, 1:167, 209.

55. *RUC*, 1:206–207.

56. *RUC*, 2:375–377; See also Thomas Minor to John Winthrop Jr., 2 April 1653, in Butler, ed., "Indian Related Materials," 5.

57. *RUC*, 2:4–11. Stuyvesant replaced Kieft, who had been discredited as a result of the warfare that ravaged new Netherland in the 1640s.

58. *CR*, 1:240; *RUC*, 2:4–5.

59. *RUC*, 2:5–10.

60. *RUC*, 2:9, 11, 22–23.

61. *RUC*, 2:23–24, 43–45, 47–49.

62. Peter Stuyvesant to Commissioners of the United Colonies, 26 May 1653, *RUC*, 2:63–64; *RUC*, 2:43, 23–24.

63. De Forest, *Indians*, 244–246; Roger Williams to Massachusetts Bay Colony General Court, 5 October 1654, *RWC*, 2:412; *RUC*, 1:102, 167.

64. *RUC*, 2:94–95.

65. Thomas James to John Winthrop Jr., 4 April 1654, *Trumbull Papers*, Connecticut State Archives, Hartford, part 1, pp. 6–7; Peter A. Thomas, "The Fur Trade, Indian Land, and the Need to Define Adequate Environmental Parameters," *Ethnohistory* 28 (1981): 365.

66. *RUC*, 2:114–115, 125; Trumbull, *Connecticut*, 182.

67. *RUC*, 2:114–115, 131–132, 147–148; Oberg, *Dominion and Civility*, 133–134.

68. *RUC*, 2:116–117; Eric S. Johnson, "Community and Confederation: A Political Geography of Contact Period Southern New England," in *The Archaeological Northeast*, ed. Mary Ann Levine, Kenneth E. Sassaman, and Michael S. Nassaney (Westport, Conn., 1999), 158, 160, 163–164.

Chapter 6. Amongst the English

1. Petition of Pequot Indians, 16 October 1654, Robert C. Winthrop Collection, Connecticut State Library, Hartford, 2:149a–d; *RUC*, 2:142–143; John W. De Forest, *History of the Indians of Connecticut: From the Earliest Known Period to 1850* (Hartford, 1851), 246–248.

2. *RUC*, 2:142–143.

3. *CR*, 1:292–293.

4. *CR*, 1:304.

5. Ibid.

6. *CR*, 1:305.

7. *CR*, 1:305–306.

8. The discussion here is informed by Daniel K. Richter, "War and Culture: The Iroquois Experience," *William and Mary Quarterly* 40 (1983); Gregory Evans Dowd, *A Spirited Resistance: The North American Indian*

Struggle for Unity, 1745–1815 (Baltimore, 1992), chap. 1; and Herbert Milton Sylvester, *Indian Wars of New England*, 3 vols. (Cleveland, 1910), 1:465.

9. De Forest, *Indians*, 251–252.

10. *RUC*, 2:158, 172.

11. John Pynchon to John Winthrop Jr., 16 February 1657, in *Pynchon Papers*, ed. Carl Bridenbaugh, *Publications of the Colonial Society of Massachusetts* 61 (1985), 1:23; *CR*, 1:307n, 345.

12. *MBR*, 3:436–437.

13. *CR*, 1:301–302; De Forest, *Indians*, 353.

14. *CR*, 1:302; *RUC*, 2:178–179.

15. *RUC*, 2:192, 196.

16. John Pynchon to John Winthrop Jr., 16 February 1658, *Pynchon Papers*, 22; John Pynchon to Commissioners of the United Colonies, late 1657, in Eva L. Butler, ed., "Indian Related Materials," typescript housed in the Connecticut State Library, Hartford, 6; John Winthrop Jr. to John Richards, quoted in Peter A. Thomas, *In the Maelstrom of Change: The Indian Trade and Cultural Process in the Middle Connecticut River Valley, 1635–1665* (New York, 1990), 232.

17. John Pynchon to John Winthrop Jr., 22 May 1658, *Pynchon Papers*, 25.

18. *RUC*, 2:211; Connecticut Magistrates, Questions of the Pocumtuck Indians, 26 May 1658, Robert C. Winthrop Collection, Connecticut State Library, Hartford, 2:138a–138b; Eric Spencer Johnson, "'Some by Flatteries and Others by Threatenings': Political Strategies among Native Americans of Seventeenth-Century Southern New England" (diss., University of Massachusetts–Amherst, 1993), 130.

19. *RUC*, 2:200.

20. George Denison and Thomas Stanton, Description of Visit to Uncas, 15 March 1658/9, Massachusetts Archives, Massachusetts State Library, Boston, 30:77.

21. *RUC*, 2:227, 236.

22. *RUC*, 2:214–215.

23. Connecticut Magistrates to the Commissioners of the United Colonies, 9 June 1660, in *CR*, 1:576–577. See *CA: Indians*, 1st ser., 1:4a–4b for slightly different wording on the same document.

24. *RUC*, 2:247; Richard S. Dunn, "John Winthrop, Jr., and the Narragansett Country," *William and Mary Quarterly* 13 (1956): 72–73; Michael Leroy Oberg, *Dominion and Civility: English Imperialism and Native America, 1585–1685* (Ithaca, N.Y., 1999), 134.

25. *MBR*, 4, pt. 2:22.

26. *MBR*, 4, pt. 2:22–23.

27. *RUC*, 2:268–269.

28. *RUC*, 2:269.

29. *CA: Indians*, 1st ser., 1:7. See also ibid., 2d ser., 1:33.

30. *CR*, 1:251.

31. The younger Winthrop's Pequot Plantation took the name of New London on 11 March 1658, *CR*, 1:309–310; New London Land Records quoted in Butler, ed., "Indian Related Materials," 2–4; Henry A. Baker, *History of Montville, Connecticut, Formerly the North Parish of New London, from 1640–1896* (Hartford, 1896), 72; Frances Manwaring Caulkins, *History of New London, Connecticut: From the First Survey of the Coast in 1612, to 1852* (New London, 1852), 425.

32. Haguntas and Allumpps, Deed to Quenebauge, 28 April 1659, in Butler, ed., "Indian Related Materials," 5.

33. Uncas, Owaneco, and Attawanhood, Deed to the Town and Inhabitants of Norwich, 6 June 1659, Norwich Town Records, volume O, *Grants, 1659–1775*, reel 1268, Connecticut State Library, Hartford; Butler, ed., "Indian Related Materials," 7; Lorraine Elise Williams, "Ft. Shantok and Ft. Corchaug: A Comparative Study of Seventeenth-Century Culture Contact in the Long Island Sound Area" (diss., New York University, 1972), 52.

34. *CR*, 1:359; Wendy B. St. Jean, "Inventing Guardianship: The Mohegan Indians and Their 'Protectors'," *New England Quarterly* 72 (1999): 365–370. I am grateful to Dr. St. Jean for providing me with a copy of her essay prior to its publication. See also E. Edwards Beardsley, "The Mohegan Land Controversy," *Papers of the New Haven Colony Historical Society* 3 (1882): 208; and Williams, "Ft. Shantok," 52–53.

35. Uncas, Deed to John Pickett, 14 December 1660, in Butler, ed., "Indian Related Materials," 8; *CR*, 1:359, 366. Laurie Lee Weinstein, in "The Dynamics of Seventeenth-Century Wampanoag Land Relations: The Ethnohistorical Evidence for Locational Change," *Bulletin of the Massachusetts Archaeological Society* 46 (1985): 25, argues that some Wampanoags had adopted an English pattern of land tenure based on ownership of land by the immediate or nuclear family, rather than the community. Such does not appear to have been the case among the Mohegans. Mason has been compared to Josef Stalin, Heinrich Himmler, and other genocidal and racist thugs throughout history by the Pequots and many of their sympathizers. See Edward Mahoney, "History Revised: An Old War, A New Battle," *Hartford Courant*, 26 May 1994. The Uncas-Mason relationship, however, shows that Mason's many detractors have oversimplified the life of a complicated and multifaceted man.

36. St. Jean, "Inventing Guardianship," 367, 376–377.

37. *CR*, 1:366, 393–394, 405, 413; Caulkins, *New London*, 163.

38. Committee Report, 20 October 1666, *CA: Indians*, 1st ser., 1:6.

39. Uncas and Owaneco, Deed to New London, 10 March 1669, in Butler, ed., "Indian Related Materials," 9.

40. William Cronon, *Changes in the Land: Indians, Colonists, and the Ecology of New England* (New York, 1983), 103; Neal Salisbury, "Toward the Covenant Chain: Iroquois and Southern New England Algonquians, 1637–1684," in *Beyond the Covenant Chain: The Iroquois and Their Neighbors, 1600–1800*, ed. Daniel K. Richter and James H. Merrell (Syracuse, N.Y., 1987), 66.

41. John Haynes to John Winthrop Jr., 25 May 1649, *WP*, 5:347; *CR*, 2:165.

42. Cronon, *Changes in the Land*, 103; Williams, "Ft. Shantok," 49–50, 59, 147–152, 203.

43. *CR*, 1:349, 408. Connecticut, of course, was not the only colony to confront the problems that came with Indian drinking. See Peter A. Mancall, *Deadly Medicine: Indians and Alcohol in Early America* (Ithaca, N.Y., 1995).

44. *CR*, 1:254–255, 263, 338, 354, 356; New London County Court Records, Trials, 1661–1667, microfilm, Connecticut State Library, Hartford, 1:93.

45. *CR*, 1:284, 350; 2:61, 117–119.

46. *CR*, 1:355; Caulkins, *New London*, 250. On New England Indians and the law, see James P. Ronda, "Red and White at the Bench: Indians and the Law in Plymouth Colony, 1620–1691," *Essex Institute Historical Collections* 110 (1974): 200–215; Ann Marie Plane, "The Examination of Sarah Ahhaton: The Politics of 'Adultery' in an Indian Town in Seventeenth-Century Massachusetts," in *Algonkians of New England: Past and Present*, ed. Peter Benes, *Dublin Seminar for New England Folklife, Annual Proceedings, 1991* (Boston, 1993), 14–25; Yasuhide Kawashima, *Puritan Justice and the Indian: White Man's Law in Massachusetts, 1630–1763* (Middletown, Conn., 1986).

47. Petition of Robin Cassacinamon, 5 May 1669, in Butler, ed., "Indian Related Materials," 10.

48. *CR*, 2:548–549; John Mulford and Thomas James to John Mason, 1 July 1669, *CA: Indians*, 1st ser., 1:11; Francis Lovelace to Colonial Governors, 5 July 1669, *NYCD*, 14:624–625; John Mason to John Allyn, 8 July 1669, *CA: Indians*, 1st ser., 1:13.

49. John Crandall and Tobias Saunders to Thomas Stanton and Thomas Minor, 18 July 1669, *CA: Indians*, 1st ser., 1:16; *RICR*, 2:59–60, 128.

50. *RICR*, 2:269–273; *CR*, 2:549–550.

51. *RICR*, 2:267, 276–277.

52. *PCR*, 4:25–26.

53. *PCR*, 4:151, 164–166, 5:62; Deposition of Hugh Cole at Plymouth Court, A.D. 1670, 8 March 1671, *MHS Coll*, 1st ser., 6 (1800): 211.

54. Richard Bellingham to John Winthrop Jr., 25 June 1668, *CA: Indians*, 1st ser., 1:8a.

55. D. Hamilton Hurd, *History of New London County, Connecticut, with Biographical Sketches of Many of Its Pioneers and Prominent Men* (Philadelphia, 1882), 20; Town of Norwich, Record of Town Votes, vol. 2, 1669–1723, p. 1, Norwich Town Clerk's Office, Norwich, Conn. The discussion here has been informed by Virginia De John Anderson's fine study, "King Philip's Herds: Indians, Colonists, and the Problem of Livestock in Early New England," *William and Mary Quarterly* 51 (1994): 601–624.

56. New London County Court Records, Trials, vol. 2 (1668–1669), Connecticut State Library, Hartford, 48; Bounds of Uncas's Lands, 9 May 1671, *CA: Indians*, 1st ser., 1:26.

57. Eliot quoted in James Axtell, *The Invasion Within: The Contest of Cultures in Colonial North America* (New York, 1985), 147.

58. *CR*, 1:265; Caulkins, *New London*, 128–129.

59. John Winthrop Jr. to the Corporation for the Propagation of the Gospel, ca. 1661–1663, Trumbull Papers, Connecticut State Library, Hartford, part 1, p. 45; *CR*, 2:111; Axtell, *Invasion Within*, 186.

60. *CR*, 2:157–158; Connecticut Archives, Miscellaneous Papers, Connecticut State Library, Hartford, 1:91; De Forest, *Indians*, 274.

61. St. Jean, "Inventing Guardianship," 379; John T. Fitch, *Puritan in the Wilderness: A Biography of the Reverend James Fitch, 1622–1702* (Camden, Me., 1993), 129–130.

62. Daniel Gookin, *Historical Collections of the Indians in New England* (1674; reprint, New York, 1970), 82–83; Axtell, *Invasion Within*, 146; Harral Ayres, *The Great Trail of New England* (Boston, 1940), 248.

63. Gookin, *Historical Collections*, 82–83.

64. Ibid., 108–110.

65. Ibid., 108–110; Fitch, *Puritan*, 135; Axtell, *Invasion Within*, 146–147; Alden T. Vaughan, *New England Frontier: Puritans and Indians, 1620–1675* (Boston, 1965), 34; Elise M. Brenner, "To Pray or to Be Prey, That Is the Question: Strategies for Cultural Autonomy of Massachusetts Praying Town Indians," *Ethnohistory* 27 (1980): 135–152; Harold Van Lonkhuyzen, "A Reappraisal of the Praying Indians: Acculturation, Conversion, and Identity at Natick, 1646–1730," *New England Quarterly* 63 (1990): 401–402, 407–409.

Chapter 7. Uncas, the Mohegans, and King Philip's War

1. "A Relacion of the Indyan Warre by Mr. Easton of Roade ISLD," in *Narratives of the Indian Wars, 1675–1699*, ed. Charles H. Lincoln (New York, 1941), 7; Francis Jennings, *The Invasion of America: Indians, Colonists, and the Cant of Conquest* (Chapel Hill, N.C., 1975), 294; Douglas Edward Leach, *Flintlock and Tomahawk: New England in King Philip's War* (New York, 1958), 30. On John Sassamon, see Jill Lepore, *The Name of War: King Philip's War and the Origins of American Identity* (New York, 1998), and Yasuhide Kawashima, *Igniting King Philip's War: The John Sassamon Murder Trial* (Lawrence, Kans., 2001).

2. "Easton's Relaycion," in *Narratives*, ed. Lincoln, 9–11; Michael Leroy Oberg, *Dominion and Civility: English Imperialism and Native America, 1585–1685* (Ithaca, N.Y., 1999), 154–155.

3. "Easton's Relaycion," in *Narratives*, ed. Lincoln, 12.

4. Nathaniel Saltonstall, "The Present State of New England," in *Narratives*, ed. Lincoln, 30.

5. William Leete to John Winthrop Jr., 23 September 1675, *MHS Coll*, 4th ser., 7 (1865): 579; Richard R. Johnson, "The Search for a Usable Indian: An Aspect of the Defense of Colonial New England," *Journal of American History* 64 (1977): 639; Harold E. Selesky, *War and Society in Colonial Connecticut* (New Haven, Conn., 1990), 10; Patrick M. Malone, *The Skulking Way of War: Technology and Tactics among the New England Indians* (Baltimore, 1993), 63.

6. Poem quoted in Richard Le Baron Bowen, *Early Rehoboth: Documented Historical Studies of Families and Events in This Plymouth Colony Township* (Rehoboth, Mass., 1945–1950), 3:37.

7. Frances Manwaring Caulkins, *History of New London, Connecticut: From the First Survey of the Coast in 1612, to 1852* (New London, 1852), 181–182; Roger Williams to John Winthrop Jr., 13 June 1675, *RWC*, 2:691; 25 June 1675, *RWC*, 2:693; and 27 June 1675, *RWC*, 2:698.

8. Harral Ayres, *The Great Trail of New England* (Boston, 1940), 252–253; John W. De Forest, *History of the Indians of Connecticut from the Earliest Known Period to 1850* (Hartford, 1851), 279–280; James Fitch to Thomas Allyn, 10 July 1675, *CR*, 2:336.

9. James Fitch to Thomas Allyn, 10 July 1675, *CR*, 2:336; John Mason to John Winthrop Jr., 14 July 1675, "The Wyllys Papers," *Collections of the Connecticut Historical Society* 21 (1924): 213–214.

10. Wait Winthrop to Governor John Winthrop, 8 July 1675, "Wyllys Papers," 210; Fitz-John Winthrop to John Winthrop Jr., "Wyllys Papers," 217; Timothy J. Sehr, "Ninigret's Tactics of Accommodation: Indian Diplomacy in New England, 1637–1675," *Rhode Island History* 36 (1977): 52.

11. *CR*, 2:337. The Council of War, first established during the Anglo-Dutch War in 1672, governed the colony during the conflict. The Connecticut General Court met only once during the war, on July 9, and handed over most of its power to the 18-member Council, which met frequently during the early months of the war. On the Council of War, see Selesky, *War and Society*, 17.

12. Saltonstall, "Present State of New England," in *Narratives*, ed. Lincoln, 34; Increase Mather, *A Brief History of the War with the Indians in New England* (London, 1676), 5; William Hubbard, *History of the Indian Wars in New England*, ed. Samuel G. Drake, 2 vols. (Roxbury, Mass., 1865), 1:91; Frances Manwaring Caulkins, *History of Norwich, Connecticut: From Its Possession by the Indians to the Year 1866* (Chester, Conn., 1976), 106. The captives were sold into slavery in the West Indies. Nipsachuck Swamp is in present-day Smithfield, Rhode Island. For the historic location of various battles in King Philip's War, see Eric B. Schultz and Michael J. Tougias, *King Philip's War: The History and Legacy of America's Forgotten Conflict* (Woodstock, Vt.: 1999).

13. *CR*, 2:345.

14. *CR*, 2:346, 348; Caulkins, *Norwich*, 107.

15. *CR*, 2:351, 353–356.

16. Caulkins, *Norwich*, 107; John Pynchon to John Leverett, 8 September 1675, in *Pynchon Papers*, ed. Carl Bridenbaugh, *Publications of the Colonial Society of Massachusetts* 61 (1985), 152; *CR*, 2:363, 366.

17. Mather, *Brief History*, 12; Hubbard, *History*, 1:113, 115–117.

18. *CR*, 2:371–372.

19. *CR*, 2:374, 267–268, 272; Council of Connecticut to Commissioners of the United Colonies, 7 October 1675, "Wyllys Papers," 227–228.

20. Oberg, *Dominion and Civility*, 158–159.

21. William Hubbard, *The Happiness of a People in the Wisdome of their Rulers* (Boston, 1676), 54; Nathaniel Saltonstall, "A New and Further Narrative of the State of New England," in *Narratives*, ed. Lincoln, 78.

22. Mather, *Brief History*, 48; Malone, *Skulking Way of War*, 109.

23. *CR*, 2:379, 381, 385, 387.

24. *RUC*, 2:357; *CR*, 2:387; De Forest, *Indians*, 282; Selesky, *War and Society*, 21–22.

25. George Madison Bodge, *Soldiers in King Philip's War* (Baltimore, 1967), 185–198; Nathaniel Saltonstall, "A Continuation of the State of New England," in *Narratives*, ed. Lincoln, 58–59; Hubbard, *History*, 1:146–147; Douglas Edward Leach, ed., *A Rhode Islander Reports on King Philip's War: The Second William Harris Letter of August, 1676* (Providence, 1963), 36.

26. Schultz and Tougias, *King Philip's War*, 266–267.

27. *CR*, 2:400, 403.

28. *CR*, 2:402, 406; Caulkins, *New London*, 185.

29. *CR*, 2:407; Caulkins, *Norwich*, 110; Ayres, *Great Trail*, 263.

30. *CR*, 2:411–412, 417; Saltonstall, "New and Further Narrative," in *Narratives*, ed. Lincoln, 67–68, 89; Jennings, *Invasion*, 312.

31. *CR*, 2:421–422, 418.

32. *CR*, 2:423–424; Schultz and Tougias, *King Philip's War*, 57, 274–283.

33. De Forest, *Indians*, 282–283; Saltonstall, "New and Further Narrative," in *Narratives*, ed. Lincoln, 90–91.

34. Hubbard, *History*, 2:62–64.

35. Will of Joshua, Sachem, Son of Uncas, living nigh Eight Mile Island on the River of Connecticut and within the bounds of Lyme, 25 February 1675/6, *CA: Indians*, 1st ser., 1:30; *CR*, 2:448.

36. On Andros, see Stephen Saunders Webb, *1676: The End of American Independence* (New York, 1984), 303–404; Francis Jennings, *The Ambiguous Iroquois Empire: The Covenant Chain Confederation of Indian Tribes with English Colonies from Its Beginning to the Lancaster Treaty of 1744* (New York, 1984), 148–171; and Oberg, *Dominion and Civility*, 160–165.

37. Rev. James Fitch to John Allyn, 14 July 1676, "Wyllys Papers," 246; Caulkins, *New London*, 186; Schultz and Tougias, *King Philip's War*, 232–233.

38. John Mason Jr. to John Allyn, 27 March 1676, "Wyllys Papers," 240.

39. *CR*, 2:390, 408–409. John Winthrop Jr. recognized that many of Philip's followers wanted to settle in Mohegan villages. If the Council of War directed Uncas to "draw of from the enemy all that will come ine and live quietly" under him, it would be, Winthrop believed, "an expedient towards peace." See John Winthrop Jr. to William Leete, 24 February, 1676, *MHS Coll*, 5th ser., 8 (1882): 177.

40. On the aftermath of the war and the fate of the defeated Indians, see Oberg, *Dominion and Civility*, 170–173. See also T. H. Breen, "Creative Adaptions: Peoples and Cultures," in *Colonial British America; Essays in the New History of the Early Modern Era*, eds. Jack P. Greene and J.R. Pole (Baltimore, 1984).

41. Mather, *Brief History*, 45.

42. Ibid.; Hubbard, *History*, 1:289–290.

43. Hubbard, *History*, 1:289–290.

44. James Fitch to John Allyn, 5 May 1678, *CA: Indians*, 1st ser., 1:33. On Connecticut's call for moral regeneration, see *CR*, 2:280–283. On New England's attempt to make intellectual sense of King Philip's War, see

Lepore, *The Name of War,* and Michael J. Puglisi, *Puritans Besieged: The Legacies of King Philip's War in the Massachusetts Bay Colony* (Lanham, Md., 1991).

45. James Fitch to John Allyn, 5 May 1678, *CA: Indians,* 1st ser., 1:33; *CR,* 2:434–435, 472–475. That colonists in Connecticut were buying and selling Indians is evident in John Talcott's account book, quoted in Samuel Orcutt, *The Indians of the Housatonic and Naugatuck Valleys* (Hartford, 1972), 38.

46. James Fitch, Suggestions Concerning Uncas, Late 1676, "Wyllys Papers," 257–259; Nowwaquaw to the Connecticut General Court, 7 October 1676, "Wyllys Papers," 253; Roger Williams to Governor John Leverett, 16 October 1676, *MHS Coll,* 3d ser., 1 (1825): 70–71.

47. *CR,* 2:297–298, 481–482.

48. *CR,* 2:487–488; Pawpeqwenock's Engagement, 16 August 1677, "Wyllys Papers," 265–267.

49. James Fitch to Connecticut General Court, 4 May 1678, *CR,* 2:591; James Fitch to John Allyn, 5 May 1678, *CR,* 2:592–593.

50. James Fitch to John Allyn, 5 May 1678, *CR,* 2:593.

51. *CR,* 2:297–298, 487–488; Pawpeqwenock's Engagement, 16 August 1677, "Wyllys Papers," 265–267; Council Minutes, 30 May 1676, *NYCD,* 13:496–497; Webb, *1676,* 359; Oberg, *Dominion and Civility,* 160–165.

52. Webb, *1676,* 357–358; Oberg, *Dominion and Civility,* 165.

53. James Fitch to John Allyn, 5 May, 1678, *CR,* 2:592–593.

54. Andros refused to allow Connecticut's forces to pursue fleeing Indians into his jurisdiction. See Connecticut Council to Andros, 19 August 1676, *CR,* 2:470–471, and 24 September 1677, "Wyllys Papers," 267–268. Andros also refused to allow the forces of the Massachusetts Bay Colony to enter his colony. See Council Minutes, 8 September 1676, *NYCD,* 13:501.

55. Pawpeqwenock's Engagement, 16 August 1677, "Wyllys Papers," 265–267.

56. Uncas to the Governor and Council in Connecticut, May 1678, *CA: Indians,* 1st ser., 1:37.

57. Ibid.; *CR,* 2:499; Council Minute, 11 June 1677, *NYCD,* 13:508; Webb, *1676,* 386–387.

58. Uncas to the Governor and Council in Connecticut, May 1678, *CA: Indians,* 1st ser., 1:37.

59. Uncas and Owaneco, Pledge to be Friendly to the Colony of Connecticut, 14 May 1678, *CA: Indians,* 1st ser., 1:34; *CR,* 2:314–315.

60. On racism toward Indians after King Philip's War, see Oberg, *Dominion and Civility,* 158–159, 171–173.

61. *CA: Indians,* 1st ser., 1:35a; *CR,* 3:42–43.

62. *CR*, 3:29, 43.

63. *CR*, 3:55.

64. *CR*, 3:56–57.

65. *CR*, 3:81–83. Similar contests over land were occurring elsewhere in New England after King Philip's War. See Jean M. O'Brien, *Dispossession by Degrees: Indian Land and Identity in Natick, Massachusetts, 1650–1790* (Cambridge, England 1997), 72–78.

66. Agreement between William Leete and Uncas, 18 May 1681, Robert C. Winthrop Collection, Connecticut State Library, Hartford, vol. 2, 127a.

67. Ibid.

68. Uncas and Owaneco, Deeds to Samuel Rogers, 4 October 1676 and 10 March 1677, in Eva L. Butler, ed., "Indian Related Materials," typescript housed at the Connecticut State Library, Hartford, 11, 13.

69. Owaneco, Deed to Charles Hill, 22 February 1679, in Butler, ed., "Indian Related Materials," 15; Deed to Samuel Rogers, 6 April 1679, ibid., 16; Deed to Samuel Buell, 8 June 1680, Norwich Town Records, vol. O, *Grants, 1659–1774*, 118, Connecticut State Library, Hartford; Owaneco to Stephen Merick, in Butler, ed., "Indian Related Materials," 18–19; Deed to Samuel Foresdick, 8 January 1682, ibid., 21; Grant to Thomas Tracy and Jonathan Tracy, 26 May 1682, Norwich Town Records, vol. O, *Grants, 1659–1774*, 8–9.

70. Owaneco, Deed to James Fitch, 22 December 1680, in Butler, ed., "Indian Related Materials," 20; Norwich Town Records, 1:3–6, Norwich Town Clerk's Office; Wendy St. Jean, "Inventing Guardianship: The Mohegan Indians and Their Protectors," *New England Quarterly* 72 (1999): 382–383.

71. Caulkins, *New London*, 426.

72. Sachems of Mohegan to Samuel Chester, 13 June 1683, in Butler, ed., "Indian Related Materials," 24; Uncas, Owaneco, and Josiah, Deed to Ralph Parker, 13 June 1683, ibid., 25.

73. Owaneco, Land Grant, 6 March 1683/4, *CA: Indians*, 1st ser., 1:40; Caulkins, *Norwich*, 426.

74. On mortuary practices among the southern New England Algonquians, see Kathleen J. Bragdon, *Native People of Southern New England, 1500–1650* (Norman, Okla., 1996), 233–241, and Patricia E. Rubertone, *Grave Undertakings: An Archaeology of Roger Williams and the Narragansett Indians* (Washington, D.C., 2001), 117–188.

Conclusion

1. "An Account of the Mohegan Sachems Native Boundaries and Royalties (1684)" Robert C. Winthrop Collection, Connecticut State Library, Hartford, 119b–119c; Robert Treat, on Ascertaining Mohegan Bounds, 28

May 1703, Robert C. Winthrop Collection, 1:122; The report is reprinted in *CR*, 3:148–150.

2. Connecticut Colony, *The Moheagan Indians Against the Governor and Company of Connecticut, and Others, Further Appendix to the Case of the Respondents the Landholders* (1767), reprinted in *CA: Indians*, 1st ser., 2:234a, p. 6.

3. Confirmation by Owaneco to Grant Made by Uncas to John Mason, 12 February 1684, Henry E. Huntington Library, San Marino, Calif., MSS. No. HM573; Owaneco, Land Grant, 6 March 1684, *CA: Indians*, 1st ser., 1:40; Governor and Company of Connecticut, and Mohegan Indians, by their Guardians, *Certified Copy of Book of Proceedings Before Commissioners of Review, 1743* (London, 1749).

4. *CR*, 4:86. Samuel Mason was the son of Major John Mason.

5. Owaneco, Deed of land to John Plumb and Joseph Hill, 30 September 1704, *CA: Indians*, 1st ser., 1:53; John W. De Forest, *History of the Indians of Connecticut from the Earliest Known Period to 1850* (Hartford, 1851), 313–314. The grantor index to the New London Town land records lists 55 grants from Owaneco to English grantees.

6. David W. Conroy, "The Defense of Indian Land Rights: William Bollan and the Mohegan Case in 1743," *Proceedings of the American Antiquarian Society* 103 part 2 (1993): 402.

7. Owaneco, Ben, and Mahomet to Connecticut General Court, 13 October 1703, *CA: Indians*, 1st ser., 1:52; *CR*, 4:415; Conroy, "Defense," 402–403.

8. Hearings before the Commissioners, 24 August 1705, *Certified Copy of Book of Proceedings*, 65. On the "disappearance" of Indians from New England, see Ruth Wallis Herndon and Ella Wilcox Sekatau, "The Right to a Name: The Narragansett People and Rhode Island Officials in the Revolutionary Era," *Ethnohistory* 44 (fall 1997): 433–462; Paul R. Campbell and Glenn W. La Fantasie, "Scattered to the Winds of Heaven: Narragansett Indians, 1676–1880," *Rhode Island History* 37 (1978): 67–83; and Jean M. O'Brien, *Dispossession by Degrees: Indian Land and Identity in Natick, Massachusetts, 1650–1790* (Cambridge, England, 1999).

9. Conroy, "Defense," 403. On the legal history of the Mohegan case, see Mark D. Walters, "*Mohegan Indians v. Connecticut* (1705–1773) and the Legal Status of Aboriginal Customary Laws and Government in British North America," *Osgood Hall Law Journal* 33 (1995): 785–829. A number of imperial officials felt that Connecticut's Restoration-era charter, which allowed for local election of the colonial governor, and which had survived intact the Dominion of New England, ought to be replaced with an instrument allowing for more effective imperial control. See the brief but

helpful discussion in Robert Taylor, *Colonial Connecticut: A History* (Millwood, N.Y., 1979), 194–195.

10. *Certified Copy of Book of Proceedings*, 28; De Forest, *Indians*, 311.

11. Protestation of Connecticut Commissioners to Governor Dudley, 24 August 1705, in *Certified Copy of Book of Proceedings*, 32–33; *Further Appendix*, 9.

12. *Certified Copy of Book of Proceedings*, 58.

13. Testimony of Nicholas Hallam, 24 August 1705, in *Certified Copy of Book of Proceedings*, 55. Owaneco complained in October 1702 that the governor of Connecticut "did in a time of snow last winter turne our women and children out of our planting fields claiming it was for his own and the people of N. London did take a way greate part of our planting land." Owaneco, Ben Uncas, and Mahomet to Connecticut General Court, 13 October 1703, *CA: Indians*, 1st ser., 1:52.

14. *Further Appendix*, 11.

15. Poem in De Forest, *Indians*, 314; *Further Appendix*, 11; Conroy, "Defense," 404–405. For the effects of alcohol on the Mohegan Indians, see Petition of Ben Uncas to the Connecticut General Court, 1 October 1733, *CA: Indians*, 1st ser., 1:161.

16. Laura Murray, ed., *To Do Good to My Indian Brethren: The Writings of Joseph Johnson, 1751–1776* (Amherst, Mass., 1998), 36; De Forest, *Indians*, 318.

17. Mohegan Petition to George II, May 1736, Henry E. Huntington Library, MSS. no. FAC788.

18. Conroy, "Defense," 406; *Minutes of the Court of Commissioners Appointed to Examine the Controversy Between Connecticut and the Mohegan Indians*, 1743 (New York State Archives, Albany, MSS. no. A1889).

19. Conroy, "Defense," 409; *Certified Copy of Book of Proceedings*, 77, 113.

20. Conroy, "Defense," 412–413; *Further Appendix*, 22.

21. *Further Appendix*, 23–24.

22. *Minutes of the Court of Commissioners*; Commissioners' Judgment, 16 August 1743, *Certified Copy of Book of Proceedings*, 143.

23. Conroy, "Defense," 420.

24. Stephen Saunders Webb, *1676: The End of American Independence* (New York, 1984), is the best study of this crisis year in American history.

Index

Lin[...]
Pom-pro[...]

Pud-hun-sk

Pond ◦ Ah-Yoh-Sup Suck

Masha-poquot-tuck-sunkapog
Or Cold Spring

Pond ◦ Mah-man Suck

Stonehouse ◦ Sneek-Suck

Preston

Norwich

Pond ◦ Yosk-convvong-ga-nuck

Pine Hill ◦ Chau-bæn-nungkue

Neck of land
by Parchaug ◦ Shaw-wog-mug

Lebanon

◦ May-o-man-suck

Falls

Eg[...]ake Sank-a-poug

Major Fitch's
house

Tracy

Canterbury

Plainfield

Windham

Spring ◦ Pat-tug-wad-
-chaug

S

W

E

Queribaug River

Mansfield

N

Oc qui-unk

Nemos
Fort

Appa quag

On-wae-nu[...]
gan-nu[...]

Whetstone
Country

A flaggy Meadow
The Wabbequasset Country called the
Mohegan Conquered Country

Man-hum-Squeeg

Road from